DISCARDED

How to Prepare a Standout College Application

Expert Advice That Takes You from LMO* to Admit

(*Like Many Others)

Alison Cooper Chisolm and Anna Ivey

JB JOSSEY-BASS™

A Wiley Brand

Cover design: JPuda
Cover images: dandelion © Andy Roberts/Getty; sky © Thinkstock/Getty

Copyright © 2013 by Alison Cooper Chisolm and Anna Ivey. All rights reserved.

Published by Jossey-Bass
A Wiley Brand
One Montgomery Street, Suite 1200, San Francisco, CA 94104-4594—www.josseybass.com

No part of this publication may be reproduced, stored in a retrieval system, or transmitted in any form
or by any means, electronic, mechanical, photocopying, recording, scanning, or otherwise, except as
permitted under Section 107 or 108 of the 1976 United States Copyright Act, without either the prior
written permission of the publisher, or authorization through payment of the appropriate per-copy fee
to the Copyright Clearance Center, Inc., 222 Rosewood Drive, Danvers, MA 01923, 978-750-8400,
fax 978-646-8600, or on the Web at www.copyright.com. Requests to the publisher for permission
should be addressed to the Permissions Department, John Wiley & Sons, Inc., 111 River Street, Hoboken,
NJ 07030, 201-748-6011, fax 201-748-6008, or online at www.wiley.com/go/permissions.

Limit of Liability/Disclaimer of Warranty: While the publisher and author have used their best efforts
in preparing this book, they make no representations or warranties with respect to the accuracy or
completeness of the contents of this book and specifically disclaim any implied warranties of merchantability
or fitness for a particular purpose. No warranty may be created or extended by sales representatives or
written sales materials. The advice and strategies contained herein may not be suitable for your situation.
You should consult with a professional where appropriate. Neither the publisher nor author shall be liable
for any loss of profit or any other commercial damages, including but not limited to special, incidental,
consequential, or other damages. Readers should be aware that Internet Web sites offered as citations and/or
sources for further information may have changed or disappeared between the time this was written and
when it is read.

Jossey-Bass books and products are available through most bookstores. To contact Jossey-Bass directly
call our Customer Care Department within the U.S. at 800-956-7739, outside the U.S. at 317-572-3986,
or fax 317-572-4002.

Wiley publishes in a variety of print and electronic formats and by print-on-demand. Some material included
with standard print versions of this book may not be included in e-books or in print-on-demand. If this
book refers to media such as a CD or DVD that is not included in the version you purchased, you may
download this material at http://booksupport.wiley.com. For more information about Wiley products, visit
www.wiley.com.

Library of Congress Cataloging-in-Publication Data
Chisolm, Alison Cooper.
  How to prepare a standout college application : expert advice that takes you from LMO* (*like many others)
to admit / Alison Cooper Chisolm and Anna Ivey. – First edition.
       pages cm
  Includes index.
    ISBN 978-1-118-41440-8 (pbk.); ISBN 978-1-118-70206-2 (ebk.); ISBN 978-1-118-70207-9 (ebk.)
  1. College applications–United States.   I. Ivey, Anna, author.   II. Title.
  LB2351.52.U6C45 2013
  378.1'616–dc23

                         2013017889

Printed in the United States of America

FIRST EDITION

PB Printing   10 9 8 7 6 5 4 3 2 1

CONTENTS

Preface   v

PART 1 Getting Started   1

1   Big Decisions   3
2   Your Plan   13
3   Your Story   22
4   Your Résumé   35

PART 2 Completing the Application   61

5   The Application as a Whole   63
6   Factual Questions about You and Your Family   72
7   Education and Academic Questions   85
8   Activities Lists   91
9   Really Short Answer Questions   117
10 Short Answer Questions   127
11 Essay Questions   133
12 "Why College X?" Questions   167
13 Disciplinary and Criminal Background Questions   179
14 Miscellaneous Other Questions   188
15 Additional Information Questions   197
16 Supplementary Materials   201
17 Test Score Reports   212
18 School Reports   229
19 Recommendations   250
20 Interviews   271
21 The Application as a Whole Redux   290

PART 3 Crossing the Finish Line 295

22   The Logistics of Submitting and Following Up   297
23   Application Updates (Including Deferrals, Wait Lists,
       and Correcting Mistakes)   310

Closing: You're Done, Now What?   327
About the Authors   331
Index   333

At soccer matches and in Starbucks lines around the country, students and their parents are talking about that "great kid" from their local high school—the one with the "great grades" and the "great scores" and the "great extracurriculars"—who got denied by all of the elite colleges. No one can believe it. It's D-Day, also known as Decision Day, and the news has everyone baffled and a bit panicked.

They can't imagine how this could have happened. It's especially confusing for the students who are just a year or two behind that senior because they have been knocking themselves out trying to acquire the same kinds of stellar credentials as the great kid who got rejected. Now they want to know exactly what it takes to get into the best colleges. Their parents don't know what to say because left without a better explanation, the parents themselves ruefully conclude that getting into the top colleges must require making a seven-figure donation, having some kind of magic hook, or turning into Tiger Mom.

But they are wrong. It's not about pull or having a hook, and it's certainly not about having better qualifications. The superstar *was* in fact qualified, and he had all the right credentials. So what went wrong?

The application itself.

When read as a whole, the application failed to make that particular "great kid" stand out from all the other "great kids" in the applicant pool. Admissions officers have shorthand to describe these kinds of applicants, the ones with the right credentials who don't submit standout applications. They're called *LMOs*, short for *like many others*.

Stellar credentials are great, but without a standout application, they are not enough. It really is as simple as that. So when people ask us, "What's the secret?" our answer is always the same: *The application is the secret.*

EVERYONE IS LMO (LIKE MANY OTHERS)

There is a single, brutally hard reality that drives everything about admission to a top US college: there are more than enough qualified applicants to go around. Whether you compare the number of available seats to the number of applicants with the best grades, the highest test scores, or another best something, the math doesn't budge. There are many, many applicants just like them. Consider these sobering statistics regarding academic credentials alone:

- Are you ranked number one in your high school class? So are more than forty-two thousand others.

- Have you been recognized as a National Merit Scholar? So have about fifty thousand others.

- Did you score in the top 5 percent on the SAT or the ACT? So did more than eighty-two thousand others.

No matter what your credentials, your demographic characteristics, or your connections, you will start off as an LMO.

YOU *CAN* GO FROM LMO TO ADMIT

So you're an LMO. Does that discourage you? It shouldn't. If you're an LMO, you already have solid credentials and noteworthy accomplishments or you wouldn't even be considering applying to a top US college. Your LMO status provides the foundation you need in order to go from LMO to Admit. That's great news.

Remember: What's the one thing that makes the difference for LMOs? Not better credentials, which you already have (or are well on your way to having), but a *well-prepared and compelling application.*

You already have what it takes; now you need to *present* it in the right way. You need to produce a standout application, and that's why we wrote this book.

YOU *CAN* PRODUCE A STANDOUT APPLICATION

A standout application showcases your excellent credentials. It conveys a coherent and compelling story about who you are and why you should be admitted. It brings you to life for the admissions officer. You're no longer just a piece of paper or like many others.

Not surprisingly, a standout application is not something you produce in an afternoon or bang out in a couple of hours at the computer. It requires time and effort. But if you are willing to put in that time and effort, we are certain that you can produce a standout application.

Why are we so confident that you can? Because we are seasoned admissions experts and we know how to coach you through the process step by step, from just getting started to crossing the finish line. We will give you practical advice for how to complete *every component* of your standout application.

It all starts with a brief overview of our seven proven strategies and a few tips for how to use this book. Then it's time to get to work.

OUR SEVEN PROVEN STRATEGIES

Working with all different kinds of applicants over the years, we have developed seven strategies that are the keys to producing a standout application. These strategies have been tested and proven to work for applicants just like you. Throughout this book, we will introduce you to each of the strategies and show you exactly how to use them in the context of the various parts of your application. By the time you are ready to hit "submit," you will have mastered all seven of them.

Ivey Strategy #1: Work Smarter, Not Harder

You do not have time to waste. You need to work efficiently and effectively when it comes to your college applications. Ivey Strategy #1 shows you how to do that.

Ivey Strategy #2: Think Like an Admissions Officer

The purpose to your application is to influence the decision maker. In this case, that's the admissions officer. In order to influence a decision maker, you have to understand how the decision maker thinks so that you can frame your presentation in the way that will be most persuasive. That's what Ivey Strategy #2 helps you do.

Ivey Strategy #3: Tell Your Story

A standout application conveys your story. Read as a whole, your application presents a coherent and compelling story about who you are and what you will bring to the college. But you can't convey your story if you do not know what your story is. Ivey Strategy #3 teaches you how to discover and convey your story.

Ivey Strategy #4: Focus on the Core Four—Passion, Talent, Initiative, and Impact

In order to present yourself in a way that stands out, you must focus on the characteristics and attributes that all admissions officers want to see—passion, talent, initiative, and impact. Ivey Strategy #4 gives you the answer to the most common applicant question: what are admissions officers actually looking for in an applicant?

Ivey Strategy #5: Sweat the Details

Every single thing on your application contributes to the impression you make on the admissions officer, whether for good or bad. Too many applicants concentrate on one or two aspects of the application and neglect the others. Ivey Strategy #5 shows you how to attend to every detail of your application because they all matter.

Ivey Strategy #6: Make the Form Work for You

Your application is a set of forms. Figuring out how to make each form work best for you is essential if you are going to convey your story. As improbable as it may seem to you now, figuring how to say what you want to say *within the very limiting confines of the form* is often one of the biggest hurdles you will encounter in the application process. Ivey Strategy #6 gives you everything you need to know to conquer any application form.

Ivey Strategy #7: Show, Don't Tell

A standout application is a memorable application, and an application that *shows* rather than *tells* is the one that the admissions officer will remember. Ivey Strategy #7 will teach you how to show instead of tell and how to make a memorable impression.

HOW TO USE THIS BOOK

We wrote this book primarily for applicants, but also for their parents because we know that applying to college is a family enterprise.

For Applicants

This book is your do-it-yourself (DIY) guide to producing standout applications. We have crammed it full of everything a DIYer could want: practical advice, tips and tricks, and dos and don'ts, beginning with these tips for how to use this book.

Applicant Tip #1: Follow the Path We Have Mapped Out for You from Start to Finish

If you skip over the "Getting Started" part because you are impatient to dive right in, you will have to double back because choosing a topic for your essay depends on having discovered your story first. If you skip the "Crossing the Finish Line" part, you may discover that all your hard work on your standout application has come to nothing because your application wasn't completed by the deadline. We've sequenced the advice throughout the book to be useful (and used!) in the order in which you'll need it, so stick with that order as you move forward. That's part of working smarter instead of harder (Ivey Strategy #1)!

Applicant Tip #2: Keep This Book Close at Hand and Consult It as You Go

In our experience as coaches, we have learned that a book like this is most helpful if it is kept close at hand and consulted as you go rather than read from cover to cover and then parked on a shelf. (Or even better: read it cover to cover to get the lay of the land, and then consult it again as you work your way through the applications. Just don't stick it on the shelf when it's game time!) That's why we have organized the book into sections that map out your path from beginning to end, and we've devoted each chapter to one of the big tasks you have to tackle as you are preparing your applications. We encourage you to delve into the parts of the book that are relevant to whatever you are working on at the time. For example, the tips for choosing an essay topic will make a lot more sense and be much more helpful to you if you read them as you are working on your essays.

Applicant Tip #3: If You Are an International Student or a Homeschooled Student, Look for the Information Tagged "Just for International Applicants" or "Just for Homeschooled Applicants"

We know that international students and homeschooled students comprise a significant percentage of today's applicants. We also know that you face particular and unique issues throughout the admissions process. Most of our advice in the book will be generally applicable, but we have broken out special tips for those instances in which our advice to you differs.

For Parents

Things have changed *a lot* since you applied to college, and this book is intended to provide you with up-to-date knowledge about the application phase of the college admissions process. We also give you some pointers for helping and supporting your child throughout the process. Please do read the book as a whole, but pay special attention to the Parent Tip sections. Here's our first one.

Parent Tip: Consult the Recommended Timeline First

Parents are usually the planners for the whole family, and the college admissions process has important implications for the family calendar. So we always suggest that parents consult the recommended application timeline before they make big family plans. You will find our recommended timeline in chapter 2.

ABOUT THE STORIES AND EXAMPLES IN THIS BOOK

All of the stories and examples in this book have been inspired by our experiences with real-life applicants and families. We are grateful that they have given us their permission to reproduce some of their materials from their applications in order to help all of you. However, because of the personal nature of the stories and examples, we have altered identifying details in order to preserve the privacy and confidentiality of the applicants and their families.

WHY WE WROTE THIS BOOK

We are seasoned admissions experts with more than twenty years of collective experience in the trenches. We have seen how admissions works from every vantage point, and we know what it takes to get in.

We both started our careers on the admissions side, where we decided the fates of thousands of applicants. We both worked in admissions at the University of

Chicago (where we met), and Alison also worked in admissions at Southern Methodist University and Dartmouth College. We know how an application is read and evaluated. We know how every kind of application is handled and what separates the LMOs from the Admits. Top-of-the-class students, bottom-of-the-class students, international students, homeschoolers, students with disabilities, students of color, students with disciplinary or criminal records, students with pull and clout, recruited athletes, performing arts students, celebrity students—we have seen them all, and we know how their applications are handled.

Alison complemented her admissions experience with a stint in senior leadership at an innovative public school in Chicago called the Young Women's Leadership Charter School. There she got to see admissions through the eyes of the school counselors whose recommendations are such an important component of the college application. She learned how the best school counselors work and how applicants can collaborate with their school counselors to make their applications even stronger.

While Alison was working at the charter school, and later at Dartmouth, Anna was busy founding Ivey Consulting, an admissions consulting firm that provides one-on-one admissions coaching to applicants and their families. Anna built Ivey Consulting into one of the premier admissions consulting practices in the nation, so when she asked Alison to join as head of the college admissions practice, Alison said, "yes!"

Through our one-on-one coaching, we have been able to offer our guidance to applicants and their families from all over the United States and across the globe. Although our firsthand admissions experience has been invaluable, our one-on-one coaching has helped us focus on the practical advice that is most helpful to applicants (and their families)—the information and guidance they actually need and want. Not surprisingly, merely *telling* applicants that it takes a "standout application" is not very helpful to them, so we also offer them the tools and methods to produce one. (See? We take our own medicine; we show and don't just tell [Ivey Strategy #7]!)

Inspired by the success of the many applicants we have coached (and Anna's previous book, *The Ivey Guide to Law School Admissions*), we wanted to make our college expertise more broadly available. This book is the result. It distills our best advice about producing a standout application into a guide available to every applicant. We hope that you find it useful and that it helps you navigate this part of the process with less stress and more success!

PART 1

Getting Started

CHAPTER 1   Big Decisions

CHAPTER 2   Your Plan

CHAPTER 3   Your Story

CHAPTER 4   Your Résumé

Big Decisions

Before you start working on your applications, there are two big decisions you should make in advance: (1) *where* you'll be applying and (2) where, if anywhere, you'll be applying *early*. We call them the big decisions because they are decisions that can have a big effect on your admissions outcomes.

These big decisions can also require some trade-offs, and that's why many people procrastinate in making them. (Nobody likes trade-offs!) But those trade-offs don't go away if you procrastinate; by putting them off, you just end up forcing yourself to make them when you're rushed and trying to get applications out the door, and by then you may have missed some very beneficial opportunities along the way. You'll maximize your options down the road—and your admissions success—if you make those big decisions before you start working on your applications rather than trying to muddle through and make them as you go along.

BIG DECISION #1: WHERE TO APPLY

A sensible list of colleges is often a work in progress, and that's entirely appropriate. It will morph over time as you get more information about *yourself* (new grades, new test scores, new classes you're excited about), about your *goals* (what kinds of majors you might be interested in, what kinds of careers you imagine for yourself), and about your *college options* (selectivity, academic and nonacademic offerings, location, your reactions after visiting, and so on).

At some point, though, you need to treat your list as final so that you can commit with your whole heart (and your whole brain) to the task of producing standout applications for the colleges on your list. In the next chapter we'll go into much more detail about your ideal timeline, but for now, the most important thing to realize about timing is that you should have a final list of schools in front of you in the *July before you apply*.

Parent Tip: Helping with the Final List

You can make it easier or harder for your child to finalize his or her college list. Obviously, we encourage you to make it easier (and we assume that's what you want, too!), so here are our tips for how to do that:

- Do your best to call on your rational self when you have conversations with your child about the college list. Your rational self knows that your child's college choices should reflect your child's preferences, not yours, so your rational self would never insist that your child keep a particular college on the list when it really isn't the right fit for your child just because you fell in love with it on the tour and would have loved to go to college there yourself. And your rational self would allow your child to apply to colleges out of state, even though you hoped that your child would attend college within driving distance from home.
- Recognize that everything you say about any college, even in an offhand or joking manner, reverberates for your child as a personal commentary on your child or his or her choices. Your child is exquisitely tuned to all things college right now and has no capacity for objective distance. Imagine you are all at a family reunion and you teasingly say, "Hey, why is College X a reach on your list? It should be a safety because if Uncle Jerry could get in there, it can't be very selective." What do you think your child hears? Your child hears that you don't think much of College X or your child's credentials.

- Educate yourself about the colleges that your child is considering before offering an opinion about whether they should be on the list or not. Just because you have never heard of a college doesn't mean it wouldn't be an excellent choice for your child. Just because the college had a reputation for being a party school when you were in college doesn't mean it is a party school now. Just because you've heard from several people that a particular college is great doesn't mean it would be great for your child. You owe it to your child to educate yourself before you speak up.
- Engage with your child in researching the likelihood for admission to the colleges on the list. Set aside a couple of hours on a Saturday afternoon and work on it together. You both need to be realistic about your child's chances for admission, and the best way to form a realistic opinion is to look at the data. The numbers don't lie. An additional benefit of tackling this task together is that it makes you and your child allies in the enterprise rather than pitting you against each other. For example, rather than having a painful and tortured conversation in which you try to extract information from your child about why a particular college is not a realistic safety, you discover the information together, and the information speaks for itself. Tortured conversation averted!
- Have a full and frank discussion with your child about the affordability of the various colleges on the list. You'll have to do some preparatory work for this conversation including determining what financial support you can provide to your child during college and what the financial aid options are. Financial aid is a complicated subject, and it will take you some time and effort to research the options on each college's website, but it is important you do it now. You don't want your child to apply to colleges that he or she couldn't attend, even if admitted, because they simply aren't affordable.

How many schools should make it onto your final list? There are more than two thousand four-year colleges in the United States, and even though it is easier than ever to apply to multiple colleges, you aren't going to want to spend your time applying to every college out there. You want to limit yourself to a reasonable number of colleges; in our experience, that means your final list should have *no more than fifteen colleges* on it.

If you have more than fifteen colleges on your list, you need to revisit it and make some hard decisions about which colleges to cut, because your list is too long. Otherwise, you'll learn the hard way that *nothing wastes more of your time, energy, and money* than applying to too many colleges, especially if some of the colleges on your list aren't even really right for you.

How you go about selecting the right colleges for yourself is the subject for a whole book unto itself, but in a nutshell, a sensible college list is a list of eight to fifteen colleges that offer a range in terms of your likelihood of admission:

- Two to three colleges should be ones where you have a high likelihood of admission (usually called *safeties*)
- Four to eight should be colleges where you have a good likelihood of admission (usually called *targets*)
- Two to four colleges should be ones where you have a low likelihood of admission (usually called *reaches*)

There are a few classic mistakes to avoid when compiling your college list. First, be realistic when you assess your chances for admission and distinguish between low-likelihood and no-likelihood colleges. When it comes to getting a basic handle on your chances for admission, it is all about your *academic credentials*. Even if you have other standout credentials and a standout application, you have to have competitive academic credentials if you are going to have a chance. A *low-likelihood* college is a college where your academic credentials fall into the bottom 25 percent of those admitted, and a *no-likelihood* college is one where no one with your academic credentials was admitted. Take all no-likelihood schools off your list. (Okay, if you really *have* to apply to Stanford because you've always dreamed of going there, then leave that one no-likelihood college on your list, but let go of Caltech and Princeton.)

GPA AND TEST SCORE STATISTICS FOR SPECIFIC COLLEGES

You can look up statistics about the test scores and grades of applicants who have been previously admitted to a particular college. They are available on a variety of websites and in multiple books. However, you'll know you're getting the most current information if you go to each college's website and search for a link or tab called something like "profile of the incoming class." You can also find this kind of information on the College Board's website (www.collegeboard.org) or the Department of Education's College Navigator website (www.nces.ed.gov/collegenavigator). These two sources are completely reliable, but the data you find there may not be as current due to a time lag between when the college reports it and when it is posted.

You will find different formats for reporting the information, but the most common format reports it in terms of percentages. So, for example, you will find that test scores are generally reported in terms of the "mid-50." The mid-50 range shows the scores distributed by quartiles, and those scores in the mid-50 range are those that range from the 25th to 75th percentiles. From that mid-50 you can easily deduce how you stack up: are you in the mid-50 or in the bottom 25 (below the lower score of the mid-50) or in the top 25 (above the top score of the mid-50)?

For grades, the format is less standardized, with colleges reporting percentages in terms of class rank and GPA. For example, you might find that the college reports what percentage of admitted students were ranked in the top 10 percent, the top quarter, or the top half of their classes. Or you might find that the college reports what percentage of students had GPAs of 3.75 or better, 3.5–3.74, 3.25–3.49, and so on. (Note these GPAs are unweighted, and you can learn more about weighted versus unweighted GPAs in chapter 18. The College Board has a tool on its website that allows you to calculate your unweighted GPA on a 4.0 scale.) Once you know the percentages regarding grades, you can easily deduce how you stack up.

It is pretty easy to figure out whether your academic credentials are competitive. All you have to do is compare your grades and test scores to those of applicants that the college has admitted in recent years. You can find that information on many websites or directories, but the best place to get the most current and accurate information is on the colleges' own websites. Usually the college makes it easy to find by collecting it into a set of "fast facts" or a "profile of the incoming class."

Also, understand that you will not increase your chances of admission to a particular college simply by applying to more colleges. College admissions isn't a lottery. Your chances of admission to a particular college have nothing to do with the number of applications you submit overall. You are far better off using your time and energy to submit twelve *standout* applications than you are firing off twenty so-so applications.

BIG DECISION #2: WHERE (IF ANYWHERE) TO APPLY EARLY

One of the major changes in college admissions in the last twenty-five years is the proliferation of early admissions options. As of the writing of this book, the vast majority of top colleges in the United States offer one or more of these options (including Harvard and Princeton, who both reinstated the option in 2011 after doing away with it for a while). Because applying early will impose certain restrictions on you (when you must submit your application and where else you may apply), it is important that you decide where, if anywhere, you are going to apply early *before* you start working on your applications.

Should you apply early? There is no one right answer that applies to everyone, so we'll give you some pointers to make the best decision for yourself.

First, figure out what early options are available to you by looking them up on your colleges' websites. Early options are called a variety of things by the colleges, but all of them have *early* somewhere in the title, and they all fall into one of three categories: *Early Decision, Early Action*, or *Restrictive Early Action* (sometimes called *Single-Choice Early Action*). Don't be surprised if you discover that a college offers more than one early option.

EARLY DECISION VERSUS EARLY ACTION VERSUS RESTRICTIVE (SINGLE-CHOICE) EARLY ACTION

Early Decision (ED) options are binding—an applicant who applies ED is *bound* to accept that offer if admitted. At most colleges, an ED applicant may not apply early to any other college. However, some do allow their ED applicants to apply EA to other colleges or to apply early to public (state) colleges.

Early Action (EA) options are nonbinding—an applicant who applies EA and is admitted is *not bound* to accept that offer of admission. An applicant may typically apply EA to more than one college.

Restrictive Early Action (REA) options are *nonbinding*, but an REA applicant may not apply early (ED or EA) to any other college.

Now that you know your early options at each of the colleges on your list, you need to weigh the *benefits* offered by those early options against the *restrictions* that they impose. This, too, will require you to do a bit of digging into the fine print of each college's early options.

There are generally two primary benefits to applying early. First, if you apply early, you might also receive a final decision from the college earlier. Check the notification deadlines for each early option to learn exactly when you will receive a decision, and also check to see whether the college can choose to defer the decision to a later round of decision making.

Second, applying early can increase your odds for admission. How much it increases your odds of admission largely depends on the option itself. Early Decision increases your odds the most; Early Action increases your odds the least; and Restrictive Early Action falls in the middle. Why the difference? Without getting into too much unnecessary detail, colleges use these early options to increase their yield (the percentage of admitted applicants who accept their offers of admission) because a higher yield benefits the colleges. The more a particular option increases a college's yield, the more it will increase your odds for admission. Early Decision increases a college's yield the most because it *commits* you to accept an offer of admission (if you receive one); in other words, the Early Decision yield is 100 percent.

To give you some sense of how much your odds of admission change if you apply early, consider these statistics for Harvard and Williams. For the class of 2016 (admitted in 2011–2012), Harvard admitted only 5.9 percent of its applicants overall. But if you break out the acceptance rates by early versus regular, you'll notice a dramatic difference: Harvard admitted only 3.8 percent of those who applied Regular Decision but admitted 18.2 percent of those who applied under its Single-Choice Early Action option. (Even better: Harvard deferred nearly two-thirds of the early applicants, so those 2,838 applicants got a second shot at admission in the regular round of decisions, with the benefit of an extra semester's worth of grades and accomplishments.) Similarly, Williams admitted 16.7 percent of its applicants overall but admitted 42.2 percent of those who applied Early Decision. That's quite a difference!

Given how much applying early can benefit you, you are probably inclined to apply early *somewhere*. But—and this is a big caveat—before you commit yourself to applying early, you must consider the restrictions. Typically, you will find that the restrictions concern *when* you must apply, *how many* colleges you may apply to early, and whether you must *commit* to attending the college if accepted (a so-called binding early option). You'll have to consult the policies for each college carefully because the restrictions can be a bit complicated, and there are often important details buried in the fine print. For example, many REA options (including Harvard's) actually allow you to apply early to other colleges but only if those colleges are public colleges. Also, now that many colleges have two ED options, you will discover that only the first ED round has an earlier deadline for submission of your application. So make sure to spend some time getting a handle on the details and understanding what the trade-offs are for the different early options.

Once you know the benefits and restrictions for each college on your list, you must balance them against each other. Not surprisingly, the early options that offer the biggest boost to your chances are also the ones that impose the most restrictions, so you have to weigh your choices carefully. Whatever you do, don't lose sight of your own true preferences as you make your decision.

There will be trade-offs no matter what you decide. Sometimes limiting your options can actually improve your odds, and there can be a penalty for leaving all your options open. Welcome to the world of grown-up decision making!

Because weighing the benefits against the restrictions can be quite difficult given all of the various combinations and permutations possible, we've developed two basic rules to help you as you are making your decision. Of course, like all rules, there are exceptions, and we have noted the most common exceptions along with the rules themselves.

Early Rule #1: If You Have a Top-Choice College and It Has an Early Option, Then Apply Early There

- *Exception:* You cannot fulfill the application requirements by the early deadline. For example, you will not have taken the required tests by then.

- *Exception:* You cannot live with the restrictions imposed. For example, this is your top-choice college, but you are not so in love with it that you are willing to commit yourself to accepting their offer of admission without knowing what your other choices are, or perhaps you want to compete for a merit scholarship at another college on your list, and you won't be able to do that if you apply early at your top-choice college.

- *Exception:* The early option is binding, and you are unsure whether you can afford to attend the college if accepted. Unfortunately, you will likely not have a firm commitment from the college about your financial aid package until mid-March (well after you have learned you are accepted and must withdraw other applications). However, you can often get a basic sense of what your financial aid package will be if you ask the college. So, before you back away from the early option, ask!

- *Exception:* Your top-choice college is a no-likelihood rather than low-likelihood college. Applying early is not a magic trick: it improves your odds of admission only if you are a competitive applicant in the first place. If you have a second or third choice that is a low-likelihood college, you might be better advised to use your early application chip on it, especially if you can apply early to only one college.

Early Rule #2: If You Are Not Applying Early to Your Top-Choice College or Your Top-Choice College Does Not Restrict Your Ability to Apply Early Elsewhere, Then Apply Early to Any College on Your List That Has an Early Action Option

An EA option is one that does not limit the number of colleges where you can apply early, and it does not bind you to accepting an offer of admission before the universal deposit date of May 1.

- *Exception:* You cannot prepare a standout application by the early deadline. As we said earlier, applying early is not a magic trick. Early application only helps if it is a "cherry on top of the sundae," and the sundae is a standout application from a competitive applicant.

If neither of these rules fit your situation exactly, then you should consider the early options available to you in the spirit of these rules. Apply early when it boosts your chances at a college that is at or near the top of your list and you can live with the restrictions (early rule #1), or apply early when the restrictions are minimal and you have nothing to lose (early rule #2). If you don't identify early options that meet one of these rules, then applying early probably isn't in your best interests. It isn't for everyone, and you shouldn't apply early just because everyone says you should or the statistics suggest it. You should decide based on your own true preferences and best interests.

Whatever your final decisions are about where to apply and whether to apply somewhere early, the most important thing is that you make those big decisions *before* you get to work on your applications. We promise it's worth it because once you make these big decisions, you are ready to move on to the next step—making your plan.

CHAPTER 2

Your Plan

Todd prided himself on being a sane, balanced guy who got everything done with a minimum of drama. He was expecting to manage all his college applications with his usual combination of organization, planning, and hard work. And he was already off to a good start. He had made his big decisions: he was applying to ten colleges total, and he was applying Early Action to his top-choice college, MIT.

Like many applicants, Todd was already pretty savvy when it came to college applications. He knew that they were more than just a fill-in-the-blank forms, and he had already been warned about the essays (as a science-math type, Todd was dreading those). He also knew that he needed teacher recommendations and that his school counselor had to send in some forms along with his grades. Todd had even heard of the Common Application, and he knew that although nine of the colleges on his list accepted it, MIT did not.

Todd came up with what he thought was a pretty solid plan for completing his applications. He would get his applications under way as soon as school started in the fall. He would allot most of his time to completing his MIT application (because it was his first choice and did not use the Common Application), and then he would knock out the applications to the Common Application colleges in one intense weekend. He did not anticipate having any trouble getting his MIT application in by the early admissions deadline of November 1, and he knew he could get his other applications in by the end of November, no sweat.

But when Todd talked to us, we explained that his plan was not going to work, despite his good intentions. There were two big problems.

First, he had dramatically underestimated the time he would need to devote to his college applications. He was not going to be able to knock out nine of his applications in one weekend, even if all of those nine colleges used the Common Application, because he, like many applicants, fundamentally misunderstood how the Common Application works. And even though he knew that there were parts of his application that he had to request from other people (like his teacher recommendations) and that it was going to take some time for him to finalize and submit the applications, he hadn't allotted any time for getting those additional tasks done.

Second, Todd was starting work on his applications too late. In order to get his applications done with minimal drama, Todd needed to start working on them in the summer *before* his senior year rather than waiting until school started.

Todd is not particularly unusual. Many, many applicants fall victim to poor planning (or its evil cousin: no planning). But you don't have to be one of them. Even though applying to college is a big and complicated undertaking, you *can* apply to college without driving yourself or your family crazy, and you *can* do it all in a way that will maximize your admissions results. It requires some more work up-front, but it will save you so much stress and time in the longer term. That's the philosophy behind our first strategy:

Ivey Strategy #1: Work smarter, not harder.

In order to work smarter, not harder, you first need a good plan. That's what you'll have by the end of this chapter.

SOME PLANNING REALITIES

Much of the reason Todd came up with a bad plan was that he didn't really understand the planning realities of applying to college. We don't want you to be in the same position; we want you to have a firm grasp on these realities, so you can avoid magical thinking and make a good plan.

Planning Reality #1: Each College Has Its Own Application

What every applicant needs to understand from the outset is that every college has its own application. If you are applying to ten colleges, you will have to complete ten applications. Todd didn't understand this. He assumed that the nine colleges on his list that accepted the Common Application all used the same application. It is an understandable mistake (the application is called *common*, after all), but that's not the way it works.

The Common Application is *not* a common application. It's true that the Common Application (also called the *Common App* for short) and other similar cooperative ventures (such as the Universal College Application or ApplyTexas) were created to standardize forms and minimize the amount of time you have to spend completing your applications. But the standardized components form only the *core* of each application, not the *whole* application for each college. Every college can (and usually does) customize these applications. For example, on the Common App, colleges routinely use one or more of these customizations:

- They add their own questions to the Common App itself or to a separate writing supplement. More than three-fourths of the Common App colleges add college-specific questions.

- They request that certain information from the Common Application be "suppressed" or "undisclosed." For example, many colleges choose not to receive the information you share about your religion in the Demographic section of your application. So although you might enter that information on the Common Application, some schools might see it and others won't.

- They can require different kinds of additional materials and also refuse to consider certain additional materials. For example, each college has its own particular requirements for teacher recommendations, and each college can decide whether or not to accept arts supplements.

So although the Common App and other similar "common" applications are definitely time-savers, they are not miracle shortcuts through the application process.

We know that this can be a particularly hard concept to grasp, especially if you come from another country that does use a truly common application, such as the UCAS application in the United Kingdom. But in the United States, admissions policies and requirements are *not* standardized across colleges, and US college applications are *not* the same, even among schools that use the Common Application.

So if your copy of this book gets washed away by a flood and you retain nothing else, remember this: *If you have ten colleges on your list, you have ten applications to complete, even if all of ten colleges on your list accept the Common App.*

Planning Reality #2: Applying to College Takes a Lot of Time

Applying to college takes a lot of time for three reasons. First, as we have just explained, every college has its own application, so you have to allot a certain amount of time for every application you have to complete. Because most of you will have ten or so applications to complete, there is simply no way to avoid spending a fair amount of time on your applications.

Second, college applications consist of more than just the forms that *you* have to complete. As we explain in the next section of the book, your "application" is actually a set of materials that include supporting materials that you must request from others. You must budget time for requesting those additional materials.

Finally, applying to college involves a lot of administrative tasks, including entering information into online forms and following up on different parts of the application. Those tasks are not particularly hard, but they do take time.

You should assume that you will devote about *one hundred hours total* to complete eight to twelve applications. We know that sounds crazy, and you're thinking that it couldn't possibly take that much time. But trust us, it will. If you budget one hundred hours, what's the worst that can happen? You find yourself in the happy situation of having more free time than expected. Compare that to what happens if you fail to budget enough time for your college applications. You'll have to scramble to make time when you are under serious pressure, and it won't be pretty.

How do you make room for one hundred hours of application work? The hard truth is that you may have to let go of some activities in order to make time for your college applications. That's just the way it is. There are no shortcuts, and living on three hours of sleep each night is not a good solution. You can't perform well if you are relying on Red Bull, coffee, and sugar to get you through the application season. Lack of sleep is the number one contributor to seismic senior year meltdowns, so make room for those one hundred hours, and sacrifice activities if need be so that you can still get enough sleep.

Parent Tip: Adjust the Family Schedule

Your child needs time to apply to college, and unfortunately the time that's needed often falls during the time that's usually set aside for family vacations and holidays. You can be a huge help to your child if you adjust the family schedule to give your child the time he or she needs to focus properly on the college application process. Consider taking the family vacation earlier or later than usual. Plan to be at home from August 1 to December 31 (or, if traveling, make sure your child has access to the Internet and quiet time to work). Avoid scheduling big events at or near the submission deadlines or notification deadlines. In other words, make your family schedule fit the college admissions timeline rather than trying to make the college admissions timeline fit your family schedule.

Planning Reality #3: Colleges Dictate the Timeline

The timeline for applying to college is driven by two things: the application submission deadlines and the application release dates. Both are set by the colleges.

Most top US colleges have application submission deadlines between November 1 and November 15 for the first round of early admissions and deadlines between January 1 and January 15 for both the second round of early admissions as well as regular admissions. When it comes to the application submission deadlines, the colleges do not negotiate them with individual applicants, and they are not soft deadlines. There are no extensions or incompletes. (This comes as a surprise to some non-US-based applicants, who might be used to softer application deadlines in their home countries.) The deadlines are not suggestions. They are firm. That means that at many colleges, if you fail to submit your application by the deadline, your chances of acceptance are reduced to *zero* because the application will not be considered, no matter how much you beg and plead (or worse, have your mom call up to beg and plead).

Most top US colleges also release their applications between mid-July and mid-August. The Common Application releases a preview in March, along with the essay topics for the year, but does not go live until August 1. Although applications often remain much the same from year to year, colleges can and do change them, and it is generally unwise to begin working on college applications before they have been released.

So there is no way around a timeline that has a crunch time from August 1 to December 31 of the year before you start college. That is just the way it is. Make sure to plan for it and clear your schedule accordingly.

YOUR PLAN

Your plan should be a plan that is based on the essential realities. It should be a plan that plots all of your major activities and gives you an overview of what you will be doing when. Over the years, we've developed a sample master plan that we use as the starting point with all the applicants we work with, and that's what we have provided to you in the following section. You will need to adjust the plan to suit your particular situation, and we'll give you some tips on how to do that right after the plan.

Sample Master Plan

Start: June 1 before senior year (fifteen months before start of college)

End: July 31 after senior year (one month before start of college)

June

- Shift gears: Stop building credentials and start presenting them.
- Make big decisions about where to apply and where to apply early. (chapter 1)

July

- Make your plan. (this chapter)
- Write your story. (chapter 3)
- Create your résumé. (chapter 4)

August

- Complete your applications for two colleges on your list. (chapters 5–15 and chapter 21)
- Get started on supplementary materials. (chapter 16)

September

- Complete your applications for three colleges on your list. (chapters 5–15 and chapter 21)
- Arrange for supporting materials. (chapters 17–20)
- Continue preparing your supplementary materials. (chapter 16)

October

- Complete your applications for two colleges on your list. (chapters 5–15 and chapter 21)
- Finish your supplementary materials. (chapter 16)
- Submit any applications with deadlines in early November. (chapter 22)

November

- Complete your applications for three colleges on your list. (chapters 5–15 and chapter 21)
- Do the necessary follow-up on submitted applications. (chapter 22)

December

- Receive any decisions from early admissions applications and follow up if necessary. (chapters 22–23)
- Submit all applications that have not been previously submitted if continuing in process. (chapter 22)

January

- Follow up on applications submitted in December. (chapter 22)

February

- Submit required supporting materials. (chapter 18)

March–April

- Receive decisions from colleges.

- Choose which college to attend.

- If accepting a place on a wait list, follow wait-list procedures. (chapter 23)

May–June

- Follow up on wait lists.

July

- Shift gears: End the process of *getting into college* and begin the process of *going to college*!

Planning Tip #1: If June 1 before Your Senior Year Has Already Passed, Compress Your Timeline

The most important thing is to follow the basic path we have laid out; if you try to skip steps, you will only have to circle back around. If you are really late to the party, we suggest that you focus on producing standout applications to your *top three* colleges. Do everything we suggest, in the order we suggest, for those applications *only*, and then do as much of it as you can with the others.

Planning Tip #2: Add or Subtract Colleges from Your Master Plan

This master plan assumes that you are applying to ten colleges. If you are applying to more than ten or fewer than ten, then you need to add or subtract them from the sample master plan.

Planning Tip #3: Add Any Activities Related to Standardized Tests

This master plan does not include any activities related to standardized tests because it is focused solely on the applications themselves. Many of you will be preparing for and taking standardized tests during the same time period. To ensure that you allow yourself sufficient time for those, we suggest you add all those test-related activities to your master plan as well.

Planning Tip #4: Add Any Activities Related to Financial Aid, Including Scholarships

Applying for financial aid is its own process with its own timeline, and it will overlap with the application process. To ensure that you do not lose track of the financial aid process, add all of those activities to your master plan.

Planning Tip #5: Add Your Deadlines and Notification Dates and Tweak if Necessary

This master plan does not show any application submission deadlines or notification dates, because they will depend on where you are applying to college and where, if anywhere, you are applying early. But in order to sequence all your activities, the master plan incorporates some assumptions. It assumes that the early admissions deadline is November 1 and that the early notification date is early December. It also assumes that the regular deadline is January 1 and that the regular notification date is April 1. The master plan has you submit your applications at least two weeks before each deadline. But in order to save you time and expense, it does not have you submit your regular applications until you have received news about your early applications. The dates set for follow-up in response to decisions are aligned to the assumed notification dates. Once you add your own deadlines and notification dates, you may need or want to tweak the plan. As you make adjustments, we suggest that you follow the structure we've described. For example, if your deadlines are later than the assumed deadlines, then you can shift your submission dates, but we encourage you to stick with the plan's structure that has you submit at least two weeks before the deadline.

At this point, you have made your plan. That's a huge step. The only thing left to do is to work the plan you've created. Good plans only lead to smarter work and better results *if you actually follow them*, and that's what the rest of this book is about.

CHAPTER 3

Your Story

Lucy was feeling confident as she was hitting "submit." Her SAT score was in the top quarter for applicants accepted last year. Her GPA was above the median. She was a four-year varsity gymnast on a team that had won the state championship last year. And she'd attended a summer program at her first-choice college. Then she got her ding letter. What happened?

If you looked inside Lucy's file, you would find this summary from the admissions officer who read her application and denied her:

> Lucy has great test scores but not similarly great grades. That puts her in the "mushy middle." Outside of school, Lucy devotes herself to gymnastics. She is team captain and was part of a state championship team last year. In the summers, she has worked in her father's office. She used her essays to talk about these experiences, but she didn't offer anything more than what I could get from her activities list. I'm left with no real impression of who Lucy is, or what she would bring to our community, or why she is so interested in us, especially since we don't have a women's gymnastics program. There's nothing here that compels me to admit.

It turns out that test scores and athletic trophies aren't enough to warrant admission, and so Lucy had been relegated to the realm of the LMO ("like many others"). As you already understand (but she didn't), her credentials weren't enough. She needed to consider her application *as a whole* and use it to tell a coherent and compelling story about herself, but she didn't. Here's the rub: Lucy did in fact have a good story to tell, and if she had told it, she probably would have been admitted.

YOUR APPLICATION SHOULD TELL YOUR STORY

Why didn't Lucy tell a coherent and compelling story in her application? Because she didn't know she was supposed to. It's not as if the standard college application says, "Please tell us your story." No, the standard college application looks like a collection of to-do items—lists, essays, transcripts, and recommendations prominent among them. As an applicant, Lucy took the checklist approach, working her way through the various components of the application one by one. She filled out the activities and honors lists. She had her transcript and test scores submitted. She wrote an essay that had been proofread by her English teacher and her mom. They both told her that it was well written (and it was). In other words, she did everything that was *explicitly* required, but she didn't understand that she was also supposed to do what is *implicitly* required, namely, to tell a coherent and compelling story about herself.

If that is what college admissions officers want, why don't they just say so? Most colleges believe they do. They point to their repeated statements (in their presentations, in their materials, and on their websites) that they take a "holistic approach" to the admissions process. And they are right. That is exactly what those colleges say and do. Unfortunately, unless you've been an admissions officer yourself or are getting advice from someone who has been, you probably have no idea what these statements really mean. You think that the "holistic approach" means that activities and essays matter and not just the numbers. That is indeed true, but it never dawns on you that by saying they take a holistic approach, they are directing you to *tell a coherent and compelling story about yourself.*

And that brings us to two more Ivey Strategies:

Ivey Strategy #2: Think like an admissions officer.

and

Ivey Strategy #3: Tell your story.

Why the focus on how admissions officers think? Because at the top US colleges, admissions officers, not faculty (or a computer formula), make the decisions: they are the people who decide your fate. Whether the admissions officers act independently or through a committee, they have the power. Obviously, then, you want to understand how admissions officers think. If you actually use Ivey Strategy #2 and develop an ability to think like an admissions officer, you have a competitive edge. (We are using *admissions officers* as a generic term here to refer to all the people in the admissions office who have decision-making authority, even if they have different titles such as *admissions director* or *enrollment manager*.)

How do admissions officers think when it comes to evaluating an application? At top colleges in the United States, admissions officers are evaluating your application (and you) on three dimensions: (1) academic achievements, (2) extracurricular accomplishments (also known as *activities*), and (3) personal qualities and character. This 3-D evaluation can vary a bit in how it is implemented from college to college, but all three dimensions are always considered in a holistic review, and each relates to an essential aspect of your qualifications and your potential for contribution to the college. The academic rating is an assessment of your academic (and intellectual) abilities and potential. It is a prediction of how you will fare in the classroom and what you will contribute to the academic life at that college. The extracurricular rating is an assessment of what you would accomplish and contribute to the college community beyond the classroom. The personal rating is an assessment of your personal qualities and character. That's obviously highly subjective, but you'd be surprised how often admissions officers see eye-to-eye across various applicants even on the personal dimension. Admissions officers believe that strong personal characteristics are intangible but significant attributes that will contribute to your ultimate success at college.

DISCOVERING YOUR STORY

What we're calling *your story* distills what you want the admissions officer to know about you in relation to each of these dimensions. It isn't a classic biography or a résumé in prose form; instead, it is a structured and succinct statement of who you are that will persuade an admissions officer to admit you. It highlights your best credentials and characteristics in terms of what matters to the admissions officer. Are you intimidated by the idea of trying to write your story? Don't be. We're going to give you a template for your story that is only five sentences long.

The story you come up with using the template will not actually be included word for word in your application; it is not a personal statement or an essay or a piece that you will be submitting as part of the application. Rather, it is a tool that you will use to guide you as you complete all of the application components going forward. It will help you decide what information to include, what to leave out, how to order the items on your lists, what to write about in your essays, whom to choose as recommenders, how to present your activities, how to guide your recommenders, and how to present yourself in your interviews. Whew! Your five-sentence story is going to do some heavy lifting.

Here's the template:

My Story

1. A few important things to know about me before you read my application are _____, _____, and _____.
2. As a student, I _____.
3. Outside the classroom, I _____.
4. Close friends and family describe me as _____, _____, and _____.
5. Right now, I imagine that I will pursue a career in or as ___ _____.

That's it. By writing your five-sentence story, you're taking the first step toward an application that presents you in your best light. Discover and tell your story, and you're on your way to an application that will make you stand out; skip this exercise and you'll be another Lucy—denied when you could have been admitted, another LMO wondering why she didn't get in.

Here are five examples of applicant stories.

THE STORY THAT COULD HAVE CHANGED EVERYTHING AND OTHER STORY SAMPLES

Lucy

A few important things to know about me before you read my application are that I am the only child of Chinese immigrants, and I grew up speaking Chinese at home. As a student, I love math, biology, and other life sciences. Outside the classroom, I have devoted myself to gymnastics and I have achieved a lot in the sport, but because of a recurring strain in my right ankle, I am retiring from the sport, and I am ready to pursue my photography and martial arts with the same devotion I gave to gymnastics. Close friends and family describe me as persistent, kind, and inquisitive. Right now, I imagine I will pursue a career in sports medicine.

Matthew

A few important things to know about me before you read my application are that I live in rural Vermont and that I am homeschooled. As a student, I'm most interested in subjects that have practical applications (like history, because you learn from the past), and I like hands-on learning. Outside the classroom, I'm either working at my part-time job or doing something sports related. Close friends and family describe me as upbeat, encouraging, and fanatical about my "teams." Right now, I imagine I will own and operate my own business, probably a restaurant.

Rania

A few important things to know about me before you read my application are that I am a citizen of Jordan, an observant Muslim, and from a family that is prominent in the Middle East and noted for our civic and political involvement. As a student, I am a voracious reader of literature (in three languages) and I love debating all things political; I love any assignment that includes writing (even my extended essay for the IB program). Outside the classroom, I'm into a little bit of everything because my parents are big believers in cultivating your body, mind, and soul—my favorite activities are playing the piano, tennis, yoga, working in my mother's recently opened boutique, and doing community service in the nearby farming village. Close friends and family describe me as cosmopolitan, energetic, and determined. Right now, I imagine that I will work in business, journalism, or politics with the aim to restore relations between the Middle East and the West.

Tom

A few important things to know about me before you read my application are that I'm the oldest child in a very close-knit family and that I would be the first person in my family to leave the state to go to college. As a student, I'm into science, and inspired by physicist Richard Feynman; I've even done summer courses in astrophysics just for fun. Outside the classroom, I play drums in a garage band and water polo. Close friends and family describe me as curious, smart, responsible, and funny (once you get my brand of humor). Right now, I imagine myself as a physicist who makes some miraculous scientific breakthrough.

Nancy

A few important things to know about me before you read my application are that I am a city girl, having been raised in Manhattan, and that I'm named for Nancy Drew, of teenage girl detective fame. As a student, I've always done well because I'm the kind of person who just loves learning but I didn't speak that much in class because I was a bit shy—that is until 10th grade when I got furious when a group of loud mouth boys were dominating the discussion and then I found my voice! Outside the classroom, I read contemporary fiction, write short stories and poetry (two of my stories and one of my pieces of poetry have been published in anthologies by a major publishing house), and participate in drama club and school plays. Close friends and family describe me as thoughtful, creative, and passionate about words. Right now, I imagine that I will be a writer (and hopefully make enough money that I won't have to live with my parents).

As you work on your own five-sentence story, here are some tips to help along the way.

Story Tip #1: In the First Sentence of Your Story, Think Demographics

When completing the first sentence ("A few important things to know about me before you read my application are . . ."), think about your demographic characteristics. These include things such as age, sex, race, nationality, religion, class, family, neighborhood, and community. Why make demographic facts front and center? Simple. These are some of the facts that admissions officers consider when evaluating other aspects of your application. They are the facts that help put all the other information in context.

This is a good time to remind you that you shouldn't treat all facts about yourself as equally important to your application. It's your job to single out and highlight the facts you want to emphasize about yourself—the details that you want the admissions officer to remember about you. And, just as important, you're also deciding which facts to *leave out* because they just don't rise to the same level of importance. So when you write the first sentence of your story, include only those facts that you consider essential for a total stranger, in this case an admissions officer, to understand who you are.

Some of you may object to disclosing these kinds of demographic facts because you think that they should not matter in the college's evaluation of you. You're thinking that you want to be evaluated on what you've done, not on who you are. But to be blunt: your opinion about what admissions officers should or shouldn't consider in their evaluation is irrelevant. The colleges make the rules about what they evaluate and reward in the admissions process, not you. Admissions officers *do* consider these demographic facts, and that's why every application has information sections that ask about them, and they often show up right on the first page of the application. You can, of course, refuse to disclose. That is your right. But be aware that you may be putting yourself at a disadvantage in the process and, at worst, failure to disclose certain required demographic information (such as citizenship) will result in your application being rejected as incomplete.

Story Tip #2: In the Second Sentence, Use Words Not Numbers

In the second sentence of your story ("As a student, I . . .") you want to describe yourself in a way that will distinguish you from other similarly well-credentialed students. Words can do that; numbers (GPA, class rank, test scores) cannot. Words can make each of the more than forty thousand valedictorians who apply to college every year come alive as distinct individuals with particular talents and passions. Numbers turn them all into number one in their class and make them completely interchangeable as applicants. So push beyond the numbers to the words when you write this second sentence. For those of you whose numbers are one of your best selling points, feel free to include them, but don't stop there. Get to the words, too.

Give the admissions officer a peek into your mind and your intellectual self. Share what subjects you love, your intellectual qualities, how you learn, or what you contribute to a classroom. If you're a bit unsure of who your intellectual self is, think about your answers to the following questions:

- Are you more of a humanities–language arts type, a math-science type, or a history–social sciences type? Which class that you've taken would you rate as the most interesting ever? If we asked you to educate us about a topic from a past class, what topic immediately comes to mind? What subject is on your mind outside of class?

- Are you curious? Are you creative? Are you unconventional in your thinking? Do you seek out challenges? Are you good at making connections between different ideas or different subjects? Are you eager to learn?

- What's your favorite way to receive information—in words, pictures, sounds, or some other way? How do you lock something into your brain? What do you do when you don't understand something?

- Are you the first to contribute in class? Do you work best in teams or alone? Would you prefer to take a final, write a paper, or make a presentation? Do classmates ask you for help? Can you explain what you know to others?

Your answers to these questions should give you plenty of material for describing yourself as a student.

Story Tip #3: In the Third Sentence, Think Impact

When choosing which of your many activities to list when completing the third sentence ("Outside the classroom, I . . ."), think about those that show you've made an impact. What's impact? Impact is the mark left by what you've done; it is the positive effect you have had on you, your family, your school, your local community, your state, or the world. Admissions officers care about your past impact because they use it as an indicator of what you will contribute to the college community.

Those students who are the perfect tens when it comes to impact are those who in their short seventeen or eighteen years have managed to have a worldwide impact—the Olympic gold medalist, the author published in multiple languages, the self-made entrepreneur who developed a killer app, the major film-TV-theater star, the founder of a nonprofit organization that built a school in Africa. If you have had this kind of impact, it should be ridiculously easy for you to complete the sentence about what you do outside the classroom.

What should you focus on if you're one of the 99.9 percent of teenagers who are great but at least a few years away from worldwide impact? You highlight the responsibilities you've had at home, the tangible and meaningful things you've been able to accomplish at your school, the leadership roles you've had, your selection as an all-star or all-state athlete, the hours you committed to meaningful community service, or the body of artistic work you've produced and had published, displayed, or performed.

Story Tip #4: Have Proof for Everything You Say about Yourself but Especially for the Fourth Sentence

In the fourth sentence of your story ("Close friends and family describe me as . . ."), we ask you to describe yourself. You must be able to back up what you list there. A fundamental attribute of the best college applications (or any other application for that matter) is that they show rather than tell (Ivey Strategy #7). Showing is only possible if you have evidence in the form of anecdotes, examples, and experiences. For any adjective you list in your story, make sure you can elaborate on them in a longer format when it comes time to work on your application. For example, don't bother to describe yourself as *curious* if you can't back that up with stories of how you've gone to great lengths to learn about things that piqued your interest. You have no claim that you are *perseverant* if you can't give an example of how you persisted when others gave up. If you truly are a *committed volunteer,* you need to be able to discuss important volunteer experiences you've had (sorry, required community service doesn't count). In other words, anything you list in your story must be something you can back up when the time comes.

Story Tip #5: In the Fifth Sentence, Be Bold

Don't be shy when it comes to imagining your future in the fifth sentence ("Right now, I imagine that I will pursue a career in or as . . ."). Admissions officers are not just picking future students, they are also picking future alumni. They take that responsibility seriously because they know that the colleges expect them to admit women and men who will go on to lead exemplary lives.

So be bold when stating your career and life ambitions. Go big. Anything you can say with a straight face and have some hope of achieving is fine. Really! It's okay to say that you want to become president of the United States (as long as you meet the Constitutional requirements) or that you are going to run the largest private equity firm in the world by the age of forty (if in fact you know what private equity is) or that you want to cure cancer (provided you know your way around a research lab and are okay with animal testing). Your goals have to make sense, though, given what else you've told us about yourself in your story. So if you haven't said you're a science type, then the cancer-curing goal might seem silly rather than bold.

Story Tip #6: Claim Your Strengths Honestly

Your story is an important way to demonstrate what you have to offer a college, so it is important that you claim your strengths in your story and in your application. You want the admissions officer to know what your most important strengths are, but it can sometimes be hard to strike the right tone. Promoting yourself can be awkward for anyone, but it is particularly awkward for those of you who are modest by nature or for those of you who come from cultures in which humility is highly valued. Most people err on one side on the other. You'll discover that you either tend to *exaggerate* or *understate* your strengths. The cure for either is the half-step approach. If you tend to exaggerate your strengths, then you need to take a half-step back. If you tend to understate your strengths, then you need to take a half-step forward. You'll know you've moved enough when you are slightly uncomfortable and are having one of these thoughts:

Exaggerator: "Hmmm. I don't think I've really emphasized enough how great I am at . . ."
Understater: "Wow. I think I may be showing off just a little too much."

Story Tip #7: Be Specific, Not Generic

Generic is boring; specific is compelling. So be specific! As you write, reflect on your personal quirks, review the anecdotes that are always told about you, and use precise vocabulary. Avoid descriptors that apply to 90 percent of those applying to selective colleges—*intelligent*, *hard-working*, and *well-rounded* are top offenders. You aren't a *good student*; you are "an ambitious learner who commutes forty-five minutes each way, so you can go to the best school in your district." You don't *love reading*; you "devour nineteenth-century English fiction." You aren't just a *helpful volunteer*; you are "the one student worker who helps after every community supper to clean all the dishes." See the distinction?

When you've finished the first draft of your story, use this test to see if you've been specific enough: reread your story substituting the name of someone you know who has similar interests and credentials for your name. If the story describes that person as well as it describes you, then you haven't been specific enough. Go back to the drawing board and refine, refine, refine until your story is about you and only you. If you don't, you'll be another LMO.

Story Tip #8: Make Any Adversity the Subplot Rather Than the Whole Story

Many students applying to college have had pretty good lives in their seventeen or eighteen years on the planet. Food, shelter, and clothing have been provided for them; they have good health and loving families; and they don't have any history of academic probation, school disciplinary problems, or a criminal record to explain. If that describes you, be grateful. But if you are someone who has confronted and overcome adverse circumstances, be thoughtful about how you address that adversity in your application.

First, consider whether your story of overcoming adversity is really a core part of your identity. You may not feel that it is, and you may be right. If you wouldn't even know how to answer the question, "How has overcoming these adverse circumstances shaped you into who you are today?" then you shouldn't make it a part of your story.

Second, remember that although your story of overcoming adversity may be a core part of your identity, it is not your magic ticket into a selective college. No matter how admirable it is that you overcame adversity *x*, that experience alone doesn't make you qualified for a selective college. You still need to demonstrate that you have the knowledge and skills to excel at high-level academic work and that you will make a positive contribution to community life at the college.

The way to incorporate adversity without making it the whole story is to weave it in as a subplot. Reference it but go beyond it in other parts of your story.

Story Tip #9: Tweak Your Story for Each College

Every good storyteller tweaks the story to appeal to the audience: the essentials remain the same, but details that have special meaning for a particular audience are highlighted or brought out. You are a storyteller and, broadly speaking, admissions officers are your audience. Your story is designed to appeal to that audience. But if you tailor your story to each college, you become an even better storyteller. Consider the colleges on your list and identify any details of your story that might have particular appeal to specific colleges.

Think first about any connections or relationships that you might have to each college. For example, are you a legacy applicant (a member of your family graduated from the college or is currently attending the college)? Have your parents ever worked for the college? Has anyone in your family made a noteworthy gift or been a significant donor to the college? These are all connections and relationships that you'll want to bring out, so add them to your story for that college.

Then think about how your story aligns with each college's specific programs, culture, and goals. If a college makes a big deal of its study abroad programs and you are dying to study abroad, then incorporate that into your story for that college. It is an easy tweak to the sentence about you as a student. Or if a college advertises itself as all about creative expression, then you want to highlight your artistic endeavors. That's an easy tweak to your description of things you do outside the classroom. If you've chosen the schools on your list thoughtfully, it is usually easy enough to tweak your story to emphasize that perfect fit. (In Lucy's case, it would simply have been a matter of changing the topic of her essay and adding an explanatory note that she wasn't seeking to continue with gymnastics and would be devoting that energy to x and y activities offered at that college.)

A cautionary note: If you find yourself completely distorting your story for a school rather than just tweaking it, the problem isn't your story, it's your college list. In that case, the fit just isn't there, and you should take the problem college off your list.

Story Tip #10: If You Are Really Stumped, Get Help

This "your story" exercise is going to stump some of you. That's okay as long as you don't just give up on it or skip it. If you want to maximize your chances for admission, you need to write your story, but you don't have to do it on your own. You can get help.

Family members, friends, trusted teachers, coaches, and mentors are all great resources to enlist in this effort. They will be flattered and eager to help. Take fifteen or twenty minutes each with two or three people and brainstorm together. Use what they tell you as a catalyst for your own thinking. Draft a first version and then circulate it to those two or three people you talked with as well as two or three more. Ask them to tell you if they think your story accurately captures the best and most important things about you. If it doesn't, what should be added, subtracted, or modified? Then revise your story based on the feedback you get. Let it sit for a few days and then go back and reread it yourself. Do you recognize the person described as you? If your answer is "yes," you're done. If your answer is "no," work on the parts that seem off until they ring true to you.

Parent Tip: Be a Conversation Partner, Not a Coauthor

Be a conversation partner, not a coauthor, as your child develops his or her story for the college application. No one knows your child better and your contributions can be quite valuable. As a conversation partner, you can help your child identify and claim a positive and realistic story about who he or she is. If you stay in the role of conversation partner, your child is likely to welcome your insight and appreciate your help. But if you slip into the role of coauthor (which is oh so easy to do) and try to dictate what your child should include in his or her story, then your child is likely to reject any suggestions you make (even the really good ones). This response is a healthy assertion of your child's ownership of his or her own story (and it is indeed your child's story, not yours) but not particularly pleasant for either of you. It is a fight that you don't need to have, so why go there?

CHAPTER 4

Your Résumé

Very few college applications require that you submit a résumé. So why do we have you create one? Simple: because it is another way for you to work smarter, not harder (Ivey Strategy #1). Putting together your résumé will help you gather, organize, and prioritize the many details about your life that all applications require. Once you've created your résumé, you'll be able to use it for every single application in multiple ways:

- You'll be able to consult it as a source of information for filling in your activities list. (chapter 8)

- You'll give it to your recommenders as a way of helping them write better recommendations for you. (chapter 19)

- You'll give it to your interviewers and impress them before the interview even begins. (chapter 20)

- You'll submit it as supplemental information with your application, if possible. (Some applications will not permit you to.) (chapter 16)

WHAT A RÉSUMÉ IS . . . AND ISN'T

A résumé presents certain factual information about you in a particular and universally recognized format. In the college application process, you'll hear people refer to your *résumé*, your *brag sheet*, and perhaps your *CV* as if they are interchangeable. However, they really are different things, and we're going to have you create a *résumé*.

Why a Résumé and Not a Brag Sheet?

We know that many college counselors suggest that students create a brag sheet—a document that details their activities and honors—rather than a résumé. But we give different advice because a brag sheet just isn't as helpful to you as a résumé in the grand scheme of things. A brag sheet doesn't help with as many sections of the application, because it doesn't collect as much information. It doesn't help recommenders and interviewers as much because it elaborates on only certain parts of your story. Furthermore, many recommenders and interviewers don't even know what a brag sheet is because that term is something used only in the context of college admissions, so they aren't even sure what to make of it. And, of course, for that reason, you'll never use a brag sheet beyond your college applications, but you can use a résumé for the rest of your life. Given how much more useful and versatile a résumé is, we recommend you produce a résumé rather than a brag sheet, especially because a résumé takes hardly any more time to produce than a brag sheet.

Why a Résumé and Not a Curriculum Vitae?

In many countries, *résumé* and *curriculum vitae* (or CV for short) are interchangeable terms. But in the United States, that is not the case. Here, résumés and CVs differ in content and format, and they are used for different purposes. In the United States, CVs are used exclusively by academic professionals seeking professor positions at universities and by people applying for certain research grants. A college applicant is neither, so you want a résumé, not a CV.

Telling Your Story through Your Résumé

The résumé you're going to create follows the universally recognized format, but it will be tailored to the college application process. It will tell your story, so as you start working on your résumé, you should have a copy of your story close at hand because you will be consulting it frequently. Creating your résumé will also require you to continue to think like an admissions officer as you decide what you do and don't include in your résumé and what language you use in each entry on the résumé. Admissions officers are examining your credentials, experiences, and accomplishments in hopes of discovering evidence of four things. We call these the *core four*, and that brings us to Ivey Strategy #4:

Ivey Strategy #4: Focus on the core four—passion, talent, initiative, and impact.

Passion

What are you passionate about? People generally express their passions by devoting their thoughts, time, and energy to them. Admissions officers are looking for your passions both *inside* and *outside* the classroom.

Talent

What do you do well? Your accomplishments generally announce your talents, but you want to go beyond just announcing your talents and describe how you have *developed* your talents. Admissions officers want to see that you are more than just a gifted slacker. They want to see that you challenge yourself, that you have a work ethic, and that you are striving to be the best you can be.

Initiative

Initiative is not as easily understood or demonstrated as passion or talent. When admissions officers talk about students with initiative, they are talking about students who *make things happen* or who *lead others*. They are talking about students who start clubs or lead teams, think up and do projects on their own, seek out challenges, and generally use their efforts to create opportunities for themselves and others. You get no points for initiative when all you do is join, enroll, show up, or meet the requirements.

Impact

Impact in this context is tricky because it is an example of an admissions code word that you can't possibly understand unless an admissions insider decodes it for you. You've already learned a bit about it in chapter 3. But we want to give you more information about what impact means because it is so important. In the context of college admissions, impact is the answer to the question, *"So what?"* If you want to talk about the impact of your experiences, think about your experiences in these terms:

- How have you been changed by your experiences?
- How have others benefitted from what you have done?
- What have you added to your classroom, your school, your community, or the world?

Admissions officers want to see that what you have done *mattered*. That's what *impact* means in this context.

Here's an example. Say you love science (*passion*), have a special gift for organizing groups (*talent*), and started the Project Sunshine Club at your school (*initiative*). Don't stop there! You must also answer the implicit follow-up question, "so what?" (*impact*). To answer the "so what?" part, you would talk about how you got the school excited about alternative energy, how you figured out that the school could acquire solar panels for free by encouraging people in the community to sign up for a special program offered by the local electric company, and how you organized that effort. And you would explain that as a result, solar panels are now installed at your school and providing 5 percent of the school's energy needs. That's impact. Impact is about *results*, so make sure you expressly mention them.

YOUR FIRST DRAFT

For your first draft, you will be thinking about which information you need and putting it down on paper. Here is information you *must* include in your first draft:

- Name and contact information
- Educational credentials
- Extracurricular activities, hobbies, and work experience
- Honors, awards, and other recognitions
- Any other information that is relevant to your story

Name and Contact Information

Your résumé will begin with your name and some information about how to reach you. Include your snail-mail address, your mobile telephone number, and your e-mail address.

Put your official name on your résumé. If you typically go by a nickname that's different from your official name, you can include your nickname (if that's what you prefer people call you) by putting it in quotation marks or parentheses. Examples:

- Patricia "Tricia" Lawton
- Michael Christopher (Chris) Chandler

Make sure to use an e-mail address that is worthy of a serious candidate for admission to a top US college. If you don't have an appropriate e-mail address, create one. No more cute, clever, or political e-mail addresses. Choose a plain vanilla e-mail address that is some version of your name. Examples:

- No: FunnyBunny87@wahoo.com, AbercrombieFan@wahoo.com
- Yes: Tricia.Lawton@wahoo.com, ChrisChandler26@wahoo.com

Educational Credentials

Start with the basic information about your high school experience. That means listing any schools you've attended since ninth grade, their location(s), and when you attended and expect to receive your diploma. For those of you in nontraditional situations (such as homeschoolers), you can use a minor variant on this format and give a brief description of your schooling. Examples:

- Plano East Senior High School. Plano, TX.
  Graduation Expected, May 2014.

- Southbank International School. London, England.
  IB Diploma Expected, July 2016.

- McCoy Academy (Homeschool)
  High School Diploma Expected, June 2017.
  I am homeschooled using a college-preparatory program designed by my mother and approved by the State of California.

If you have attended more than one school since ninth grade, give a brief explanation in a bullet point. Example:

- Transferred to Southbank when my family moved from India to England.

Include any summer study or academic enrichment programs you completed since ninth grade in your Educational Credentials section. Example:

- Computer Programming in Java and Python
- Educational Program for Gifted and Talented Youth, Stanford University, Summer 2013
- Online Courses in Philosophy offered by Duke University through Coursera, Fall 2013.

Beyond these formal educational credentials, include any additional information that is important to conveying some part of your story. Consider your numbers as well as what you've included in your story. What information can you include here in your résumé that relates to your academic or intellectual abilities? Here are some ideas:

- Class rank
- GPA
- Test scores
- Favorite subjects
- Special programs
- Honors or AP classes
- Academic honors or awards
- Topics of major academic papers or projects
- Research
- Stories, poetry, or papers that have been published somewhere (in your student newspaper, an online poetry journal, and so on)

Use your judgment, though, and be just as mindful about leaving things out as you are about adding things in. Résumés are not tell-alls, so you don't have to share everything. Don't list every honor or every AP class you've ever taken—that's nothing more than duplicating your transcript. Instead, on your résumé, list only the honors and AP classes you've taken in subjects that relate to your core interests. For example, if you show that you have taken all the advanced classes offered in the sciences, you jump off the page as the girl who is "crazy about science." Likewise, if your standardized test scores aren't great, then leave them off the résumé, and instead note that you've been named to honor roll every semester.

Extracurricular Activities, Hobbies, and Work Experience

After you've listed your educational credentials, you have an opportunity to share what you do when you aren't doing schoolwork. You are expected to include what you've done since you entered secondary school (from ninth grade forward). Examples:

- Clubs
- Student government
- Peer mentoring or counseling
- Sports
- Drama and theater
- Speech and debate
- Mock Trial, Model UN, or other simulated competitive experiences
- Music study or performance, bands, choirs
- Film or photography
- Scouting or other outdoor experiences
- Camps
- Faith and religious activities
- Hobbies

- Internships
- Part-time jobs
- Volunteer work
- Travel

For each activity, hobby, or work experience, list your role or position, the organization, club, or team (if relevant), and the grades or years in which you participated. Examples:

- CEO. Cool Things. Junior Achievement Business Competition. (12–13)
- Pianist. (3–12)
- Goalie. JV and Varsity Ice Hockey Teams. Cherry Creek High School. (9–12)

Honors, Awards, and Other Recognitions

List your honors, awards, and other recognitions and give a short explanation of how you were chosen or why the award was significant. For example, you can't assume that the people reading your résumé will know what it means to be nominated and selected for the governor's honors program in biology, so you'll have to tell them. Example:

- Participant. Governor's Honors Program in Biology. (Summer 2013)
  The governor's honor program is a six-week summer program for intellectually gifted students in particular subjects. Teachers may nominate one student annually; final selection is made after a weekend-long evaluation that includes testing, presentation of a paper, and an interview with faculty. Only one in twenty nominees are ultimately chosen.

If you don't remember all the details for your honors and awards, you can often find great descriptions on the websites of the organizations that granted them. Are you stumped about what it takes to be on honor roll at your school or why you were named scholar-athlete in track by a local sports association? Check out their websites and you'll probably find an answer worth including on your résumé.

Any Other Information That Is Relevant to Your Story

You may discover that you need or want to include some information that doesn't fall neatly under educational credentials or activities, interests, and work experience. For example, where would you note that you speak three languages fluently and have dual citizenship, that you have been a contestant on a game show, or that you have read all of the Great Books just for fun?

The all-purpose Personal section is the answer. In this section, you can add two to three additional pieces of information, but *only if the information is necessary or adds to your story*. Examples:

- Fluent in Chinese and English (for the applicant whose story is all about his desire to pursue a career in international business)
- Cast as extra on sitcoms from ages of three to seven (for the applicant whose story includes a desire to be an actor, and who experienced a major interruption in her path to fame and fortune when her parents divorced and she moved from Los Angeles, California, to Ames, Iowa)

Resist the temptation to include unique, witty, and cool tidbits that are unrelated to your story. Many students think (mistakenly) that admissions officers are on a quest to find unique, witty, and cool kids, and so they spend endless hours trying to coming up with unique, witty, and cool things for the Personal section. But by now, we hope you are starting to think like an admissions officer (Ivey Strategy #2) and know that admissions officers are not swayed by the random tidbit. Admissions officers admit students who present coherent and compelling stories. So if part of your story is that you are an accomplished musician, then by all means include the tidbit about traveling to Timbuktu and learning how to play *Twinkle, Twinkle Little Star* on a native instrument. But if your story is about your passion for world affairs, leave out the music lesson and focus on the time you got to meet an ambassador.

You now have the basic information you need for your résumé. That means you are done with the first draft and ready for draft two.

YOUR SECOND DRAFT

In your second draft, you are going to refine the information you've included and organize it so that your résumé tells your story and highlights your core four—your passion, talent, initiative, and impact. This revision will transform your first draft into a full-blown résumé.

Add the Meaningful Details

Your goal in adding information is to make you come alive as a distinctive individual with your own combination of credentials, experiences, and accomplishments. In order to do that, you need to include *meaningful* details, not just add more for the sake of bulking up your résumé.

This exercise is important because details distinguish you from other applicants who may have similar but never identical stories to tell. Look carefully at every item currently on your résumé. What information could you add that would reveal more of your story, illustrate your passions and talents, or show more initiative or impact? That's the kind of detail you want to add. For example:

- To elaborate on your interest in playing the piano: "Trained as a classical pianist for 8 years but now mastering jazz. Most recent piece: *Take Five* by Dave Brubeck."

- To elaborate on your term as president of Key Club: "Reinvigorated the Key Club at my school by finding a new sponsor, organizing quarterly weekend projects, and actively recruiting new members at the fall club fair."

- To elaborate on your service as a tutor: "Tutored middle school student in math and helped her raise her grade from a C to an A."

If you have nothing to add to a particular entry on your résumé, then that may be a sign that this entry is not worth including. *Fluff adds nothing to your résumé.* If all you can say about being a member of the French Club is that you went to meetings every so often and brought some croissants to share at your school's International Food Festival in ninth grade, then French Club doesn't belong on your résumé.

Parent Tip: Collaborate on the Résumé

The résumé is another opportunity for you to be a conversation partner with your child. There are so many parts of the application for which you should be pretty hands-off, but the résumé is a great and completely appropriate opportunity for hands-on collaboration. You can be a major help with your child's résumé. You are an easily accessible and reliable repository of all the data your child could want—you know when he began playing soccer and how many games the team won last season, you know which Girl Scout badges she earned, and you even remember the most obscure blue ribbons. All of this information is a great resource for your child in both the first draft and second draft stages. You can also be a great proofreader. But you need to remember that you may be just a little bit biased and think that every single thing your child has ever done is worth putting on the résumé. Your rational self knows you're biased, but your parental self keeps insisting that your child list every perfect attendance award or Zumba certification. Kids have a good instinct about what is and isn't parental hyperbole. Accept your child's judgment about what to include and what to cut.

Use Effective Language

Continue reworking the information to make sure you've packed a punch with every word because *every word counts on a résumé*. Use words that convey the core four wherever possible. Here are some examples of words that, when used properly and in context, convey each of the core four. (It's fine for verb tenses to vary in your résumé, depending on whether the activity is still ongoing or has already concluded.)

- Passion: favorite, interest, like, pursue, dedicate, devote, committed, seek
- Talent: skill, ability, aptitude, expertise, forte, knack, facility, capacity, mastery
- Initiative: started, founded, lead, direct, organize, manage, persuaded, identified, explored, discovered
- Impact: help, assist, benefit, changed, transform, learn, taught, enhanced, improve, better

But what if the things you did don't actually sound all that impressive? Most seventeen-year-olds don't have internships or work experience that would be considered "high impact," but that doesn't mean you have nothing to say. Did you get a promotion or earn some recognition? Include that as evidence of your hard work, your dedication to doing a good job, and your all-around ability to wow people. The summer you spent scooping ice cream starts to sound more impressive when you note that the owner promoted you to shift manager, that you oversaw two employees, and that you were voted "friendliest scooper" by customers.

Even if you weren't promoted or recognized in some official way, you should have some interesting things to share. But here's the trick: instead of reporting, for example, what you *did* as an employee at a retail store ("helped customers, counted inventory, rang up sales," and so on), report what you *learned* about the retail business ("learned that average mark-up on a clothing garment is *x*%; learned that the best hours for sales are from 12 to 2 pm on Tuesdays for *xyz* reasons; learned that Buyer is the best job in retail but that it's not a good fit for me long-term"). The impact you're describing is how this experience expanded your knowledge and clarified your own career ambitions. That's the answer to the implicit "so what?" question in this example.

Organize the Information

Now that your content of your résumé is in good shape, it's time to figure out the right way to organize it so that the big themes of your story leap off the page. Think about how to cluster the information, how to title the sections of your résumé, and how to sequence the sections. Look back to your story to create an organization that reflects *your* big themes and no one else's.

You have a lot of flexibility here, but however you choose to present the different parts of your résumé, you *must* start your résumé with the information related to your educational credentials, and you *must* title that section *Education*. That's ultimately the most important part of your application résumé, so you want to lead with it.

Beyond that, the organization is up to you. If you look at the samples we've included at the end of the chapter, you'll see that each one has different clusters of information after the Education section and that the titles go beyond a simple label and also offer a preview of the content. That's the general approach you should emulate. Just glancing at the résumés, you'll have no trouble spotting right away that one résumé is for a student whose singular passion is musical theater and another is for a student who is a school leader and serious athlete. You should also be able to guess the one-line description of each applicant for the other sample résumés we've provided. That's because each of their résumés is organized to convey a particular story, and the chosen format makes it easy for the reader to spot the big themes very quickly.

And a word about where to put honors and awards: you might choose to list your honors and awards in their own, separate section of your résumé, but we generally recommend that you embed them within the other sections, attached directly to the activity or experience that generated them. Honors and awards are, by definition, evidence of your impact. If you separate the honors and awards from the underlying activity or experience, you put too much visual distance between the activity and the answer to the "so what?" question. Don't deprive yourself of the chance to closely connect the activity with its impact.

WELL-ROUNDED OR LOPSIDED, IT'S ALL ABOUT THE CORE FOUR

Long, long ago and far, far away—back when your parents were applying to college in the late twentieth century—the perfect college applicant was described as *well-rounded*. The well-rounded college applicant had played at least one sport, was involved in several different clubs at school, did some community service, and was a walking advertisement for the "kid who's done a little of everything."

Then college admissions went through a period where the lopsided kid was in. The lopsided applicant goes deep with a few passions rather than going broad with super-ficial involvement in a bunch of things; this applicant is a walking advertisement for the "kid who's all about *x*."

Today, college admissions has moved beyond the well-rounded or lopsided applicant. Today's perfect applicant can be either, just as long as there is a track record of passion, talent, initiative, and impact. As a practical matter, that usually means that you can't do a little bit of everything, but you can often do several different things, as long as you do them well and can demonstrate the core four.

YOUR THIRD (AND FINAL) DRAFT

You are now ready for the third and final draft of your résumé. All that is left is to prettify and professionalize it using conventional formatting standards. When it comes to formatting, you *want* to be conventional. The goal of good formatting is to make your résumé easy to scan and understand. For that reason, your résumé formatting is not where you want to demonstrate your creative flair or your quirky sensibilities. Leave that to your art portfolio and instead stick with these time-honored standards for résumés:

- Use a traditional font and stick with it. Don't mix and match fonts. Cambria, Century Schoolbook, Georgia, or Times New Roman are all good options.

- Use 10-point, 11-point, or 12-point for the font size and only black for the color.

- Use capitalization, indentation, line spacing, bold, italics, and underlining *consistently* and in ways that help rather than distract the reader. For example, make every section title all caps and bold. If in doubt, keep it simple.

- Use parallel structures for the various sections, subsections, and entries to help the reader move more quickly through the résumé and find the information she wants. For example, put the dates you participated in an activity in the same place and in the same format for every activity you list.

- Make use of white space. Use standard margins (at least one inch on all four sides) and be generous about skipping lines. Here's a good test: look at your résumé through squinted eyes. You'll know you have the right amount of white space if it looks like several smaller blocks of text instead of one solid, mooshed-together page of text.

This formatting advice applies only to hard copy applications that permit hard copy attachments or to a PDF version of your résumé that you can upload as an attachment to your online applications; note that some applications will not permit you to upload attachments.

THE FINAL CHECK

There are three things you must do before you submit the final version of your résumé: check for truthfulness, proofread, and convert to PDF (for those online applications that permit you to upload an attachment).

Check for Truthfulness

Your résumé is the first document you've produced that you will include with your college application, so now is the right time for us to remind you that you *must* be scrupulously honest in the entire application process, and that includes your résumé.

Although you can and should report your credentials and experiences in the way that is most favorable to you, that does not mean that you can invent things, lie, or stretch the truth. We assume that you know what a lie is, but we know that students often have trouble knowing when they've crossed the line from positive spin to falsehood. (Plenty of adults have trouble with that, too!)

For example, it is fine to say that you "earned As in every English class" rather than list your 2.7 overall GPA; rounding that overall GPA up to 3.0 is not. It is fine to say that you had a small pet portrait business and that you gave 10 percent of profits to charity (because you did in fact do portraits of five pets for your neighbors and friends, sell them for $50 each and have $100 in profits, and you did give $10 to charity); that does not make you "founder of a wildly successful entrepreneurial venture and major philanthropist," which is stretching the truth too far. So before you submit your résumé, review all the information you've included and make sure that you've been honest.

Proofread

We hope it goes without saying why you need to proofread your résumé carefully. No mistakes are acceptable. It's best to recruit someone else to proofread for you. Your eyes can play tricks on you when you've stared at the same content for too long. A fresh pair of eyes is more likely to catch errors you've either stopped seeing or didn't know were errors in the first place. Parents often make great proofreaders!

Convert to PDF

As much as we love the convenience of electronic submissions in the college application process, some glitches can arise. These glitches might be small (your font changes mysteriously) or big (hidden editing notes are revealed, formatting is lost, content is lost). You can avoid many glitches altogether through the magic of PDF. Once your résumé is in final form, save it (along with any other documents you're attaching to your application) as a PDF and upload it as an attachment if your online application permits you to. Microsoft Word typically lets you select that format as a drop-down option in the "Print" menu. Make sure you also keep a final copy for yourself in a format (such as MS Word) that you can edit again if necessary.

PREPARE TO BE CONTACTED

Once you begin circulating your résumé, be aware that admissions officers or others related to the college admissions process might actually contact you! Here are some good habits that will serve you well throughout the process (and beyond).

Answer every call from an unidentified caller using your professional-level telephone manners. That means answering pleasantly and formally and having a message on your voicemail that is G-rated and appropriate for anyone to hear. You'll have to ditch your voicemail greeting that says, "Hey, what's up, leave me your deets." A professional greeting sounds more like this: "Hi, you've reached Andrea; please leave me a message and I'll call you back."

Check your snail-mail, your voicemail, and your e-mail regularly! And then respond. If you tell people they can contact you through one of these methods, then you are making an implied commitment that if someone contacts you, you will respond. *Promptly.* It's best to reply within twenty-four hours, so that means checking and responding daily.

Use the following sample résumés to guide you as you are working on your own résumé. Pay particular attention to how they have each highlighted their passions, talents, initiative, and impact.

GABRIELLA DELGADO
1321 West Culverson, Chicago, IL 60699
999.555.1122 (cell)
gabidelgado@wahoo.com

EDUCATION
Lane Technical College Preparatory High School. Chicago, IL.
Graduation from Honors Alpha Program expected June 2014.
Currently Ranked 47/1100.
ACT: 32.
APs: AP Physics, AP Environmental Science, AP Chemistry, and AP Biology.

SCIENTIFIC PUBLICATIONS AND PRESENTATIONS
*"The Viability of Microbial Fuel Cells as both Mechanisms for Cleaning the
Chicago River and as Clean Energy Source for Chicago."* by G. Delgado (2013)

- Paper and Exhibit produced for the Chicago Science Fair and Symposium competition.
  Advanced to the citywide level and presentation at Symposium ranked in top 50.
- Selected for presentation at Illinois Junior Academy of Science Fair, where I
  received a superior rating (given to top 10%).
- Invited by Mayor of Chicago to present findings to his senior cabinet and other leaders.

*"An Evaluation of the Measuratron's Ability to Measure Fine Particular Air
Pollution on Heavily Trafficked Roadways."* by G. Delgado (2012)
- Paper and Exhibit produced for the Chicago Science Fair and Symposium competition.
  Advanced to the citywide level and presentation at Symposium ranked in top 50.
- Selected for presentation at Illinois Junior Academy of Science Fair.

"The Efficacy of Home-Made Green House Cleaning Products." by G. Delgado (2011)
- Paper and Exhibit produced for the Chicago Science Fair and Symposium
  competition. Advanced to the citywide level.

SCIENCE RELATED ACTIVITIES
Volunteer. TEENS Program. Peggy Notebaert Nature Museum. Chicago, IL.
Summer 2012 and 2013.

- Volunteered 35 hours per week during summers.
- Completed several outdoor restoration projects in and around the Chicago area.
  Most ambitious project was clean-up of the northern fork of the Chicago River.
- Helped build collections on trips; caught multiple fish and a wolf spider, which
  are now living in the Mysteries of the Marsh exhibit.
- Helped install the Bikes! Go Green Transportation exhibit.

SCIENCE RELATED ACTIVITIES, continued
Intern. Chicago Center for Green Technology. Chicago IL.
Summer 2011.

- Worked full-time (40 hours per week) during summer.
- Developed "Green Cleaning 101" Program that is offered monthly. Program shows participants how to make their own natural and effective cleaning products and incorporates my research. As of now, more than 500 people have completed the program.

Founder and Chair. Project Sunshine. Lane Technical College Preparatory High School. 2011–present.

- Founded a club at Lane Tech to bring solar energy to school.
- Identified opportunity to get solar panels for free though a special ComEd program if we could enroll a certain number of Chicago residents in a ComEd clean energy plan.
- Organized teams of students to set up booths at malls and other public locations where we could enroll Chicago residents in the ComEd plan.
- Enrolled enough residents in the ComEd plan that school got free solar panels and now provides 5% of school's energy needs.

MUSICAL ACTIVITIES
Pianist.
Age 6–present.
- Began studying piano in first grade and continue to play for enjoyment.
- Current favorite piece to play is Debussy's *La Cathédrale Engloutie*.

Alto II. Lane Technical College Preparatory High School Choir.
Fall 2010–present.
- Perform in three concerts per year.
- Chosen for solo at Spring 2012 Concert.

Alto II. Youth Choir. Old St. Pat's Church.
Fall 2007–present.
- Perform monthly in Sunday worship services.

PERSONAL
- Youngest of 5 children and first generation American.
- Fluent in English and Spanish.

Andrew Smithson

5 Old Farm Road, Westport, CT 06555 | 1-999-555-1133 | asmithson@wahoo.com

Education
Deerfield Academy. Deerfield, MA
Graduation Anticipated, June 2013

- Current GPA: 90.7 (Honors)
- SAT: 1990 (660 CR, 690 MA, 640 WR)

Leadership
Proctor, Johnson-Doubleday Dorm (12)
- Provide day-to-day mentoring and help to underclassmen in dorm.
- Chosen by faculty.

Student Council (9–12)
- Elected as class representative for all four years.
- Serve on Academics Committee: created summer research fellowship program for students.
- Serve on Public Relations Committee: developed Deerfield's "Event Tweet" Twitter stream to promote events and keep both day and boarding students better informed.

Tour Guide (10–12)
- Lead 50-minute campus tours for prospective students, alumni, dignitaries, and university representatives.

Sports
Lacrosse (9–12)
Play midfielder on school team.
- Captain (12)
- Varsity (9–12)
- All Conference (11); Academic All American (11); Top Rookie (9)
- Invited to train at The Elite 150 Camps. (Summers 2010–2011)

Ice Hockey (9–12)
Play center on school team.
- Captain (12)
- Varsity (11–12), JV (9–10)
- All Conference (11); Sportsmanship Award (10–11)

Personal
- Third generation baseball card collector; attend collector conventions with father and grandfather.

BETHANY MACLEOD

2 Rose Lane | Memphis, TN 13576 | 999-555-1144 | bethanymacleod@wahoo.com

EDUCATION

Gateway Christian School. Memphis, TN.
Anticipated Graduation from Total Home Education Department: June 2012
<u>Honors</u>: Inducted into the Eta Society, an honors society for home-schooled students in Memphis.

WRITING

Blogger. www.BethanysBlog.com (7th–12th Grades)
- Started a blog about home-schooling from the kid's perspective.
- More than 250 posts to date and had 1,217 visitors to my blog as of my 250th post.

Novelist. (9th–12th Grades)
- Have written a novel every year during National Novel Writing Month (NaNoWriMo) since 9th grade.
- Published short story in online literary magazine, *TeenWriters* (www.teenwriters.org).

COMMUNITY SERVICE

Reading Tutor. Haven House. (10th–12th Grades)
- Meet weekly with adult with autism (Laura) and work through a set of flashcards and other exercises designed to improve her reading and vocabulary.

Volunteer. St. Jude Children's Hospital. (9th–12th Grades)
- Worked as a full-time "in-hospital" Volunteer for summer following 11th grade. Selected for one of 30 spots. Assigned to work with patients receiving stem cell and bone marrow transplant treatments; gathered information for clinical studies; learned about careers in research and clinical medicine.
- Work 5 hours per week as "at-home" volunteer producing various items requested by hospital. Projects have included craft kits to make hand puppets and sewing fleece mask straps for patients who must wear masks (improves their comfort).

Mission Worker. Good Things Orphanage. Zomba, Malawi. (9th–12th Grades)
- Volunteer at orphanage "adopted" by my church for two three-week sessions every year.
- Help girls ages 6–12 with schoolwork.
- Maintain pen pal relationship with two girls that are being sponsored by our family.

RELIGIOUS ACTIVITIES

Member. Bellevue Baptist Church. Cordova, TN (lifelong)
- Attend worship weekly with my family.
- Chosen for Girls Council by youth ministry team and senior pastor. Help plan and lead special events for girls including the annual "Girls Lock In" and "Girls Night Out." Act as "Big Sister" to assigned 7th grade girls to help them feel welcomed into the Youth Ministry.

Member. K-Life Klub. Memphis, TN (9th–12th Grades)
- Attend a weekly worship, bible study, and fellowship organized as part of the K-Life ministries in Memphis. K-Life is a community-wide, non-denominational Christian ministry that operates in multiple cities and states.

PERSONAL
Attended Kanakuk Kamps for ten summers; served as CIT and camp officer in final summer.

RODNEY YANG

1017 South Carmelita Avenue

Los Angeles, CA 90549

+1.999.555.1515 (cell)

rodneyyang@wahoo.com

EDUCATION

Crossroads School. Santa Monica, CA.

Anticipated graduation: June 2013

- Selected for the Drama Conservatory Program (11–12). Selection is by audition, technical theater evaluation and interview; must be re-selected each year. Allows for intensive immersion into Drama, while simultaneously pursuing a traditional college preparatory program.
- Theater Classes: Theater 1 and 2, Technical Theater 1 and 2, Directing, Acting, Improvisational Acting, Movement, Playwriting, Viewpoints, Lighting Design, Musical Theater.

Musical Theater Program. Northwestern High School Institute Theatre Arts Cherub Program. Northwestern University. Evanston, IL. Summer 2012

- 7-week by-invitation-only intensive program, culminating in production of my one-man original musical theatre production, *Fallen Cherub*.
- Training in performance theory, text analysis, voice and movement, acting, directing, costuming, theatre for social change, musical theatre acting, dance (jazz, tap, and musical theatre styles), and musical theatre history.

Private Coaching and Classes. Los Angeles, CA. (2007–present)

- Work with private acting coach, Ima Star, for two hours weekly.
- Work with renowned voice coach, Yoo Sing, for four hours weekly.
- Take four hours of dance class weekly at Fame Studios. (Ballet, Hip Hop, Tap, and Jazz)

PERFORMING ARTS EXPERIENCE

Musical Theater

- *Fallen Cherub.* One Man Musical. 2012. Produced at Northwestern High School Institute.
- *Little Shop of Horrors.* Role: Seymour. 2012. Produced by Crossroads School.
- *Jekyll & Hyde.* Role: Newsboy/Soloist. 2012. Produced by Crossroads School.
- *The Who's Tommy.* Role: Lead Dancer. 2010. Produced by Crossroads School.
- *Smokey Joe's Café.* Role: Singer. 2010. Produced by Crossroads School.
- *The Secret Garden.* Role: Colin. 2010. Produced by Local Company X.

Operas

- *AIDA.* Role: Radames. 2011. Produced by Crossroads School.
- *Her Lightness.* Role: Repertory. 2011. Produced by Local Company X.

Stage Management and Set Design

- *Once on This Island.* Set Designer. 2012. Produced by Crossroads School.
- *Beauty and the Beast.* Lighting Crew. 2011. Produced by Crossroads School.
- *The Wiz.* Stage Manager and Set Designer. 2010. Produced by Crossroads School.

JACQUELINE MAGAUD

54 rue de Genéve

14489 Geneva

Switzerland

jmaguad@wahoo.com

+41.99.7632145

EDUCATION

International School of Geneva. Geneva, Switzerland.

- Anticipated graduation from IB Program, June 2013.
- Predictors: 38/42. Higher Levels: Geography, Economics, History.
- Topic for extended essay: The Role of "Transit Countries" in Human Trafficking.

SPEECH AND DEBATE ACTIVITIES

Model United Nations. (Grades 9–13)

- Selected as MUN team captain (13).
- Awarded best speaker at MUN Conference in Hungary (12).
- Attended 9 MUN conferences, where I have represented Austria, Belize, Bolivia, Egypt, Greece, Iran, Macedonia, Morocco, and South Korea.
- Proposed global resolutions addressing human trafficking and absence of human rights for children in certain countries.

Debate Team. (Grades 10–13)

- Compete in Parliamentary style debate at tournaments affiliated with the World Schools Debating Society.
- Competed at World Schools Debating Society Championships as member of Swiss national team in South Africa (12) and Scotland (11).
- Ranked as one of top 100 speakers at the World Schools Debating Society Championships in South Africa (12).

BUSINESS INTERNSHIPS

Marketing Intern. Get Help Now Hotline. Geneva, Switzerland.
(Summer 2012)

- Worked in communications department for a hotline that serves as a resource for victims of human trafficking.
- Learned that Switzerland is both a destination and a transit country for women trafficked mainly from Eastern Europe, Brazil, the Dominican Republic, and Africa.
- Designed a social media campaign to raise awareness of the presence of the Hotline and its services for victims.

Banking Intern. Mirabaud & Cie. Geneva, Switzerland. (Summer 2011)

- Chosen as one of 5 interns at one of the oldest family-owned banks in Switzerland.
- Rotated through 3 areas of the bank and learned core functions for each through assigned projects.
- Favorite Rotation: private wealth management where I put together a proposed portfolio that was actually used by a banker for a client.

PERSONAL

- Fluent in English, French, and German.
- US and French citizenship.

PART 2

Completing the Application

CHAPTER 5 The Application as a Whole

CHAPTER 6 Factual Questions about You and Your Family

CHAPTER 7 Education and Academic Questions

CHAPTER 8 Activities Lists

CHAPTER 9   Really Short Answer Questions

CHAPTER 10   Short Answer Questions

CHAPTER 11   Essay Questions

CHAPTER 12   "Why College X?" Questions

CHAPTER 13   Disciplinary and Criminal Background Questions

CHAPTER 14   Miscellaneous Other Questions

CHAPTER 15   Additional Information Questions

CHAPTER 16   Supplementary Materials

CHAPTER 17   Test Score Reports

CHAPTER 18   School Reports

CHAPTER 19   Recommendations

CHAPTER 20   Interviews

CHAPTER 21   The Application as a Whole Redux

CHAPTER 5

The Application as a Whole

If you are working your plan (and you are working your plan, right?), you know that you are finally ready to begin working on your applications. You also know that you are going to tackle them application by application, and you have picked your first application to complete. Now what?

Most applicants dive right in to one particular part of the application or one particular question. But you can probably guess that this is a mistake because you have already begun thinking like an admissions officer (Ivey Strategy #2). You know that admissions officers read and evaluate the application as a whole. You know that your goal is to tell a coherent and compelling story about yourself (Ivey Strategy #3). So you are not surprised to hear that the first thing you should do is to approach the application as a whole.

THE APPLICATION

What makes up a college application? Most applicants think first (and sometimes only) about the application form that they must prepare themselves. They are usually fixated on the essay questions on that form, because those essays scare them. Then, usually belatedly, they think about the other parts of the college application—the recommendations and such.

But that's not how an admissions officer thinks about the application at all. The admissions officer thinks about the application as the entire set of application materials that come together in your *application file*. In fact, admissions officers use the terms *application* and *application file* almost interchangeably, and you'll commonly hear admissions officers talking about all the *files* they have to read on a given day. So if you are thinking like an admissions officer, you too think about your application as the entire set of materials that go into your application file.

That means step one in approaching your application as a whole is to identify what the college's requirements are for a complete application file, and then gather up all of the forms that must be submitted by you or others. You can find both the application requirements and the forms on the college's website. Most colleges are making use of technology and moving away from paper forms to online applications. For example, Common App 4.0 no longer has a paper version of the application available for download and completion. You must complete the application online. However, some applications and forms are still available in a paper version. Regardless of the format of the forms, you want to review all of the forms together and as a whole before you fill in a single word on any part of your application.

While you are doing this work, it is also a good idea to gather up all the application instructions that the college provides. What you will discover is that the typical application file will have the following items in it once it is complete.

Your Application

Your application consists of the required materials you produce and submit yourself. It might consist of one form or multiple forms. For example, your application to a Common Application college could consist of the Common Application alone or the Common Application plus a college-specific writing supplement.

Regardless of the number of forms that make up your application and regardless of whether or not you use the Common Application or an application that a school produces itself, you will need to know how to answer the following types of questions:

- Factual questions about you and your family (chapter 6)

- Education and academic questions (chapter 7)

- Activities lists (chapter 8)

- Really short answer questions (chapter 9)

- Short answer questions (chapter 10)

- Essay questions (chapter 11)

- "Why College X?" questions (chapter 12)

- Disciplinary and criminal records questions (chapter 13)

- Miscellaneous other questions (chapter 14)

- Additional Information questions (chapter 15)

Supplementary materials (chapter 16)

Supplementary materials are any materials that usually are *not required*. You are choosing to submit them because they will enhance your application file in some important way. They could be materials that you produce and submit yourself or materials that others produce and submit on your behalf. Examples of common supplementary materials include the following:

- Abstracts of scientific research

- Art portfolios

- Athletic statistics and clip reels

- Performing arts portfolios (theater, dance, music)

- Additional recommendations

- Samples of academic work

- Your résumé

Supporting Materials

Supporting materials are the required materials that *others produce and submit on your behalf*. You will have to request these materials from your school, your counselor, your teachers, and others. They include the following:

- Test score reports (chapter 17)

- School reports (chapter 18)

- Recommendations (chapter 19)

- An interview report, if the college uses evaluative interviews in the admissions process (chapter 20)

Other Materials

These are all of the other materials that might end up in your application file. Some, but not all of them, will be required. Examples of these kinds of materials include the following:

- Proof that you have paid your application fee or received a fee waiver

- A signed ED agreement

- Various forms related to securing a student visa

- Correspondence between you and the admissions office

That looks like a daunting list, doesn't it? But you can manage it. As you can see from the chapter references, we are going to walk you through each of these components in detail. For now, it is simply important to get the big-picture sense of what makes up your whole application to the college.

THE APPLICATION THROUGH THE EYES OF AN ADMISSIONS OFFICER

Now that you have a handle on the application from your perspective, it is important to shift your perspective and see the application through the eyes of an admissions officer. Seeing it that way allows you to employ Ivey Strategy #2 and think like an admissions officer as you work on each of the various components.

An important first thing to understand is that an admissions officer never even sees your application until your application file is complete. At that point, the admissions officer sits down with your file and reads it in its entirety. As the admissions officer reads, he or she evaluates and decides your fate. That is why you sometimes hear admissions officers say, "I don't admit applicants; I admit applications."

So what will compel an admissions officer to admit your application (that is, you)? Remember that the admissions officer is evaluating your application (you) on three dimensions—academic achievement, extracurricular accomplishments, and personal qualities and character (see chapter 3). In addition, the admissions officer will also consider some other factors (more about that toward the end of this chapter). To give you a better sense of what the admissions officer considers when evaluating you on these three dimensions, let's take a look at the contents of your application file organized in a different way than we organized it in the previous section. This organization shows what parts of the application are considered for each factor being evaluated.

Academic Achievement Dimension (Academic Rating)

The academic rating is an assessment of your academic (and intellectual) abilities and potential. It is a prediction of how you will fare in the classroom and what you will contribute to the classroom at that college. The parts of your application that the admissions officer will consider when evaluating you on the academic dimension include the following:

- *Your application:* Education and academic questions, activities list (for any academically oriented activities, such as math club), really short answers, short answers, essays, and "Why College X?" questions to the extent they pertain to or reference academics or intellectual qualities

- *Your supplementary materials:* Anything academically related, such as research abstracts, samples of academic work, and so on

- *Your supporting materials:* Your test score reports, your school reports, your recommendations, your interview report

Extracurricular Accomplishments Dimension (Extracurricular Rating)

The extracurricular rating is an assessment of what you would accomplish and contribute to the college community beyond the classroom. The parts of your application that the admissions officer will consider when evaluating you on the extracurricular dimension include

- *Your application:* Activities list, really short answers, short answers, essays, and "Why College X?" questions to the extent they pertain to or reference extracurricular activities or accomplishments

- *Your supplementary materials:* Anything talent related, such as arts or athletic supplements or your résumé

- *Your supporting materials:* Your recommendations and your interview report

Personal Qualities and Character Dimension (Personal Rating)

The personal rating is an assessment of your personal qualities and character. The parts of your application that the admissions officer will consider when evaluating you on the personal dimension include the following:

- *Your application:* Activities list, really short answers, short answers, essays, and "Why College X?" questions to the extent they pertain to or reference your personal qualities or character

- *Your supplementary materials:* Anything that reflects your personal qualities or character

- *Your supporting materials:* Your recommendations and your interview report

Other Factors That May Be Considered

As the admissions officer reads and evaluates your application (you), he or she may also consider other factors beyond these three dimensions when making his or her decision. These other factors are usually not determinative in and of themselves but can tilt the balance for many applicants. Although these factors vary considerably from college to college, there are some that are common enough that you should be aware of them and consider whether any of them could weigh in your favor.

Demographics

All colleges set goals regarding the demographic composition of the incoming class. The top colleges in the United States value diversity in their classes and work hard to achieve it. Their ideal incoming class is gender balanced (unless it's a single-sex college), has students from all of the various recognized racial and ethnic categories, has students from every socioeconomic background, and has students from all over the United States and the world. How demographics come into play in the admissions decision itself is constantly shifting because it has been the subject of ongoing legal battles since the 1980s. So there is no general rule, except that colleges do what they can to achieve their ideal class.

If the admissions officer considers demographics in the evaluation, then the parts of your application that the admissions officer will consider include the following:

- *Your application:* Factual information about you and your family, really short answers, short answers, or essays should you choose to disclose or discuss demographics in those

Demonstrated Interest

Demonstrated interest is a relatively new buzz phrase in college admissions. It basically refers to the things an applicant has done to demonstrate interest in that college. Methods of demonstrating interest include applying early, writing a great response to the "Why College X?" question, visiting the college, meeting with an admissions representative at a college fair, and the like. Top US colleges are split on what level of demonstrated interest is desired and whether it should be factored at all into the initial decision, but at a minimum, it is likely to be a factor in a wait-list decision. You can usually find out on the college's website whether it is considered.

If the admissions officer considers demonstrated interest in the evaluation, then the parts of your application that the admissions officer will consider include the following:

- *Your application:* Miscellaneous other questions that ask about these topics, "Why College X?" questions
- *Supporting materials:* Recommendations (a counselor or teacher may mention this topic), your interview report

Ability to Pay

Ability to pay is not a new buzz phrase in college admissions, but it is always said in a whisper because the colleges that consider it do not want to broadcast that fact. Ability to pay refers to the applicant's ability to pay the tuition from family resources. If you pay for college without any need-based financial aid, then you have the ability to pay. Colleges that consider your ability to pay when making decisions are called *need-aware* colleges; colleges that do not consider your ability to pay are called *need-blind* colleges. Top colleges can be either need aware or need blind. Determining whether ability to pay is factored in is a bit tricky because colleges are so reluctant to broadcast it. If you want to be on the safe side, assume that the college is need aware *unless* the college specifically states that it is need blind.

If the admissions officer considers ability to pay in the evaluation, then the parts of your application that the admissions officer will consider include the following:

- *Your application:* Miscellaneous other questions about your intent to apply for need-based financial aid

- *Other materials:* Your financial aid applications and status

Flags on Your File

In admissions speak, a *flag* on an application file signals to the admissions officer that there is something extra to consider about this particular applicant. It usually signifies that the applicant has some pull operating in his or her favor. The most common flags on application files are these:

- *Legacy:* One or more of the applicant's close relatives is a graduate of the college.

- *Faculty or staff:* The applicant is the son or daughter of a faculty or staff person at the college.

- *Development (aka fundraising):* One of the college's major donors has an interest in the applicant.

- *Special talent recruit:* The applicant has a special talent and is being recruited by a coach, a faculty member, or other program director because of that special talent.

- *VIP interest:* Someone of significance to the college has an interest in the applicant.

If you have flags on your file, then the admissions officer will consider whatever parts of the application pertain to the particular flag. Generally the parts of your application that the admissions officer will consider include the following:

- *Your application:* Miscellaneous other questions about whether members of your family have graduated from the college or work for the college (legacy, faculty, staff)
- *Supplementary materials:* Arts or athletic supplements (special talent flag)
- *Supporting materials:* Recommendations from donors or VIPs (development, VIP)
- *Other materials:* Correspondence from high-level college officials, donors, or VIPs expressing special interest (development, VIP)

Seeing the application through the eyes of an admissions officer puts a completely different spin on the various components of the application, doesn't it? It gives you insight into what matters to the admissions officer, not just overall but for each and every part of your application. Because your goal is to persuade the admissions officer to admit you, you want to focus your application on *what matters to the admissions officer*, and now you have an even better idea of what that is and where it goes on your application.

Ready to delve into the nitty-gritty of completing the application? Each of the chapters that follow focuses on one application component or on one type of application question. We begin with the factual questions about you and your family that you will encounter first on any application, and then move through the other types of questions before going to the supplementary and supporting materials. This sequence aligns with how most applicants go about completing an application. However, we encourage you to consult the chapters in the order that works for you, and we remind you that your master plan calls for you to handle supplementary and supporting materials early, so you should consult those chapters when it is time.

CHAPTER 6

Factual Questions about You and Your Family

Oh, the stories we can tell, none of them pretty. All of them begin, "I was devastated when I realized I had messed up . . ." and go on to recount how the applicant made some mistake on the easiest part of the application—the basic facts such as name, address, and phone number.

Here's the good news: There is absolutely no reason why you should make a mistake on this part of the application. In fact, as long as you follow this next Ivey Strategy, you will sail right through this part of your application.

Ivey Strategy #5: Sweat the details.

Yes, even the smallest details matter on your application, and in this chapter we'll show you why they matter so much and how to get them just right.

There's even better news: these questions look so basic—"What's your name? What's your citizenship? What's your race?" and so on—that you might not realize that they are also valuable opportunities to tell important parts of your story. They are deceptive that way! But you can indeed use these questions to your advantage by using another important Ivey Strategy:

Ivey Strategy #6: Make the form work for you.

Your application forms might ask for this factual information in an order different from how we've laid it out here, but the principles remain the same.

Let's start with the most basic of the identifying information.

NAME, BIRTH DATE, SOCIAL SECURITY NUMBER

Believe it or not, there are actually a few ways you can go wrong with something as basic as your name! We want to save you that embarrassment as well as the endless complications you will face as a result of getting your identifying information wrong. Here are our tips to avoid blowing it with the easiest of all questions.

Identification Tip #1: Use Your Legal Name on All College Application Documents

Your legal name is the name that appears on all your official documents, such as social security card, passport, and school record. Colleges are sticklers about this for lots of good reasons, and you should be, too. Do not misspell your name (really, it does happen!).

And make sure the *same* name appears on all the supporting documents that will be part of your college application, such as your high school transcript and your recommendations. If there are different names on these supporting documents, you run the risk that someone creates a filing or data-entry mix-up in the admissions office, and the documents might never make it to your application file. These kinds of name and identification problems are a hassle to fix once you have submitted your applications, and it's an even bigger problem if you never even know that there's been a mix-up. It's best to prevent these problems altogether by getting it all right before you submit.

Identification Tip #2: Be Thoughtful about Nicknames

If you go by a nickname in your day-to-day life that's different from your legal name, most forms will allow you to indicate your preferred name in addition to your legal name. For example, if you use a shortened version of your given name (like Sam instead of Samuel) or use your middle name instead of your first name, then this is the section where you indicate that.

But before you enter your nickname "Bootsie," which is what everyone has called you since you were little, consider whether you should disclose your nickname or not. Remember that you always need to be thinking like an admissions officer (Ivey Strategy #2). What impression does your nickname convey about you to a stranger? Lots of nicknames, like Bootsie, have a childish connotation that might be funny and cute within your family but that probably doesn't serve you well in the context of your applications. Other kinds of nicknames might set you up for being cast as the "stereotypical *x*," whether you like it or not. For example, someone with the nickname Susie-Belle might be assumed to be the Southern debutante type, and someone who goes by Shaq might be assumed to be the basketball jock. Maybe those assumptions would be correct but maybe not. Decide whether you want to include your nickname based on the impression it will make on the admissions officer. Some nicknames are perfectly neutral and fine to include; others might best be left off your application.

Identification Tip #3: Follow Rules of Capitalization for Proper Names When Typing Your Name

Students often ignore capitalization when filling out online application forms. In a world of text messaging and online forms that don't distinguish between lowercase letters and uppercase letters, that's no surprise. But capitalization does matter on your online college applications, and failing to capitalize your name properly will make a poor impression. Admissions officers are scrutinizing every word of your college application, and they expect you to use formal rules of grammar and spelling, which includes capitalizing proper names (including your own).

Identification Tip #4: Put Your Birthdate in the Format Used in the United States: Month, Day, Year

If your birthday is April 7, 1996, then enter it like this: 04/07/1996. Note that the *month comes first*, not the day. Most countries do not use this format, so international applicants should check their date entries especially carefully.

Identification Tip #5: Social Security Numbers Are Optional

You do not have to include your social security number, unless you are a US citizen or permanent resident and plan to apply for financial aid. We also recommend that you do use your social security number if you have a name that is shared by other people (John Brown or Elizabeth Smith). In that case, the social security number helps prevent your application materials from getting mixed up with the other Johns or Elizabeths. But if you don't have a social security number (international student) or if you don't want to use it, that's fine. Just be extra vigilant about including some other piece of identifying information (such as birth date) on all your materials in addition to your name.

Identification Tip #6: Proofread Your Name, Birthdate, and Social Security Number on Every Document

Check every document, including the school forms and so on before submission. The earlier you catch typos or mistakes, the better. For example, if you misspell your name when registering for the Common Application and you don't catch the typo until you've started filling out the applications, then the typo will probably have been reproduced automatically in the various subpages of the applications, and you will have to manually correct each instance of the misspelling. That's a big hassle.

CONTACT INFORMATION

Giving the college the right contact information to reach you is critical—how else will you get the news that you've been admitted? You've already listed your contact information on your résumé, so you can probably just transfer it to your Information section on the application, although we discuss a few exceptions here.

Contact Tip #1: Use a Reliable Snail-Mail Address

Although this practice might change in the future, currently your formal offer of admission, along with other essential documents (such as financial aid awards), will be sent to you via snail-mail. So if you are not living at your permanent home address during your application year, look for the places on the forms that allow you to list a separate current mailing address for correspondence from the admissions office.

However, if you are off doing a gap year in the remotest jungle where snail-mail delivery to your current address would be slow or unreliable, stick with your permanent address, and make sure someone is keeping an eye out for your mail. We heard about one applicant who was studying abroad and whose dad came home to find a thin envelope from a school. Dad assumed it was a rejection and didn't bother to tell her about the letter or even open it, figuring she could find out the disappointing news after she returned home. In fact, the letter was offering her a spot on the wait list, and after she failed to claim her spot by the given deadline, she was automatically rejected. She was not too pleased when she figured out what had happened. So make sure your mail deputies back home notify you in real time about every snail-mail communication from a school. Turnaround time can mean the difference between acceptance and rejection.

Contact Tip #2: Translate International Telephone Numbers into US Format

Most US college applications are formatted for US telephone numbers, which are composed of a three-digit area code followed by a seven-digit telephone number. If you have an international telephone number, read the instructions to find out how to enter your telephone number. Generally, you are instructed to enter the country code in the Area Code section and enter the city code and telephone number in the Telephone Number section. If you aren't sure of the country code for your telephone number, go online and search for "calling [your country] from US" and you'll find the information you need.

Contact Tip #3: Proofread, Proofread, Proofread

You are probably getting used to this mantra by now, but we cannot say it frequently enough: typos are not acceptable. If a school isn't able to reach you because you entered your contact information incorrectly, you might actually lose out on an offer!

DEMOGRAPHIC QUESTIONS

The demographic questions on college applications are all those that ask you about characteristics that you share with a subset of the human population. There are eight demographic questions that are typically asked on college applications:

- Age and birth date
- Gender
- State of residence

- Citizenship and national identity

- Language proficiency

- Ethnicity

- Race

- Veteran status

Forms might also ask other demographic questions, such as marital status and religion. The demographic questions do vary and change, so don't be surprised if the list looks a bit different by the time you apply. For example, as we write this book, there is an ongoing conversation among admissions officers about whether to add a demographic question about sexual orientation, and there have been a few rumblings about a question about disabled status. Here we'll limit ourselves to tips about how to approach the existing demographic questions, but if you follow the advice we give, you'll know how to handle any demographic question.

Start by recalling Ivey Strategy#2 and thinking like an admissions officer. As you already know from chapter 5, all colleges set goals regarding the demographic composition of the incoming class, and therefore your demographic characteristics may be a factor in admission. For example, your chances for admission to a public state college will vary depending on your state of residence.

Now consider the story you created using Ivey Strategy #3. Look back to the first sentence where you noted "a few important things to know about me." Did you include any demographic characteristics? Many times these are an important part of your story. For example, you may have noted that your racial or ethnic identity has shaped who you are. Because demographic characteristics matter to admissions officers and may be a central element to your story, take your time to work through the demographic questions and take the opportunities they offer.

Demographic Tip #1: Answer All the Demographic Questions, Even the Optional Ones

Some of you may be reluctant to answer some of the optional demographic questions. And you don't have to answer them—that is what makes them optional. But here's why we think you should: they won't hurt you and they might even help you. For example, if you are a veteran of the US Armed Services, sharing that information will not jeopardize your admission in any way, and it could help because it is quite common for colleges to give preferential treatment to veterans at various points in the college admission process. But they can only do that if you answer the question and alert the admissions officer to the fact that you are indeed a veteran. Why not put yourself in a position to benefit? Make it easier for them to admit you.

Demographic Tip #2: Use the Additional Information Question When Some Extra Demographic Information Would Help Tell Your Story

The demographic characteristics that you want to highlight as part of your story may or may not be offered as options among the factual questions. If they are not, then consider including those demographic characteristics as a response to the Additional Information question (see chapter 15 for more about this opportunity).

Demographic Tip #3: List All of Your Citizenships

First, listing all your citizenships is the most accurate answer. Second, it reveals something inherently interesting and perhaps distinctive about you. For example, the student who is a US, Brazilian, and Italian citizen immediately stands apart from the student who is a citizen of only one of these countries. Third, it gives you the opportunity to be considered in multiple subpools of applicants, thus increasing your chances for admission. For example, when the admissions office is reviewing the composition of the admitted class and discovers that they have admitted only very few South Americans, you could be reconsidered for admission because you can be counted as a South American, even if you listed your US and Italian citizenships as well.

Some students (and their parents) who have dual or triple US citizenship with other countries worry that disclosing anything but the US citizenship may create problems for enrollment or financial aid. That is not the case. If you have valid US citizenship, you will not have to obtain a visa to enroll in a US college, and you will be eligible for all financial aid on the same basis as other US citizens, so just make sure you include your US citizenship among your others.

Demographic Tip #4: List English among Your Languages

Even though these questions aren't going to be used to evaluate your English language abilities, you do want to state for the record that you are in fact proficient in English, assuming that's the case. If your first language wasn't English, don't hesitate to list your native language as well. Some non-native speakers are tempted to list only English so that admissions officers won't worry about their English skills, but multiple languages actually look impressive, and it is not a liability that you acquired English as a second or third or fourth language.

Demographic Tip #5: Describe Your Proficiency with Each Language as Accurately as the Form Allows and Don't Exaggerate

You aren't *proficient* in Spanish if you know a few phrases from your spring break trip to Mexico. Don't suggest that you speak Arabic if you can only read it. You never know when you'll find your language skills being tested in the admissions process (for example, in an interview), so don't exaggerate.

Demographic Tip #6: It's Fine to List Multiple First Languages, if the Form Permits

A *first language* is the language you spoke when you first began speaking. It is entirely possible and plausible that you had multiple first languages. Maybe your father spoke to you in Russian, your mother spoke to you in English, and your grandparents, who lived with your family during your childhood, spoke to you in Polish. In that case, your first words were probably some of each. Similarly, if a question asks about your language spoken at home, list the language or languages you use regularly and fluently when speaking with your immediate family.

Demographic Tip #7: If the Form Limits the Number of Languages You Can Include, Prioritize

Let's say you are proficient in four languages—Arabic, English, French, and Spanish—but the form allows you to list only three. Following demographic tip #4, you list English. So what are the other two you should choose?

Let's say part of your story is that you have both a European and Middle Eastern identity. To support that part of your story, it makes sense to list Arabic as the second language. For the third (and last) language in the permitted list, do you choose French or Spanish? Both are European, so both support the European part of your story. In that case, prioritize by relative proficiency. For example, say you live in Geneva, Switzerland, and use French daily. You have studied Spanish for four years and recently did a community service immersion program where you spoke nothing but Spanish for four weeks. In this case, you would choose French over Spanish because you have more fluency. You can always include Spanish in the Additional Information section (see chapter 15).

Demographic Tip #8: Understand the Definitions for the Ethnic and Racial Categories Offered

Each ethnic or racial category listed on the application form gives a specific definition of different races and ethnicities that are determined by the United States Department of Education. You may or may not agree with the categories or the definitions, but we recommend you make your peace with them and work with them rather than against them. You can always say more about your ethnic or racial identity elsewhere in the application if you have strong feelings on the subject. Here are the current definitions from the US Department of Education (you can do an online search to confirm them at the time you apply, and the application forms themselves might have their own definitions):

- *Hispanic or Latino:* A person of Cuban, Mexican, Puerto Rican, South or Central American, or other Spanish culture or origin, regardless of race

- *American Indian or Alaska Native:* A person having origins in any of the original peoples of North and South America (including Central America) who maintains cultural identification through tribal affiliation or community attachment

- *Asian:* A person having origins in any of the original peoples of the Far East, Southeast Asia, or the Indian subcontinent, including, for example, Cambodia, China, India, Japan, Korea, Malaysia, Pakistan, the Philippine Islands, Thailand, and Vietnam

- *Black or African American:* A person having origins in any of the black racial groups of Africa

- *Native Hawaiian or Other Pacific Islander:* A person having origins in any of the original peoples of Hawaii, Guam, Samoa, or other Pacific Islands

- *White:* A person having origins in any of the original peoples of Europe, the Middle East, or North Africa

Demographic Tip #9: Check as Many Ethnic and Racial Categories as Apply

Many students fly right by the instructions that invite them to check more than one category. The instructions are often not terribly clear, but now you know you can, so take advantage of that option if it applies to you.

Demographic Tip #10: Don't Stretch the Truth

Identify yourself as a member of a particular ethnic or racial category only if you can legitimately claim that identity. Only you know the truth about that. If you disagree with the way the form categorizes you (for example, if you object to being labeled *White* rather than *African* when your family is from Algeria), check the box as the form instructs, but feel free to clarify your background in a way that you consider more accurate in the Additional Information section (see chapter 15).

FAMILY INFORMATION

Families of the twenty-first century are quite diverse in their makeup, but you wouldn't actually know that by looking at a typical college application form. Although the new Common Application has made strides forward in this regard, many of the questions on college applications still conjure images of the TV family of the 1950s and 1960s: a mother, a father, and two children all living together in a lovely home. Needless to say, answering questions that assume the 1950s TV family can be a bit tricky for a twenty-first-century applicant. But you can still make the form work for you, as long as you remember that it is your job to use the questions and sections of the application to tell your story fully and accurately. Along the way, you might also discover that there are good opportunities for you to highlight something about your family life that makes you stand out.

Family Tip #1: Your Household

You are typically asked a few questions that are designed to give the admissions officer a snapshot of who lives with you in your household and what their relationship is to you and each other. All of the questions assume that you are a typical teenager and live with at least one adult who heads the household and has legal responsibility for you. But the questions also allow for the possibility that you are not typical and give you an "other" option. If you fall into the "other" category, you are sufficiently atypical in the selective college admissions applicant pool that you should offer some explanation of your situation in the Additional Information section (see chapter 15) or make this the topic of one of your essays.

Family Tip #2: Your Parents, Stepparents, or Other Legal Guardians

You are asked to give information about two parents, and you may be asked about stepparents as well. If you come from a family with a different configuration than the form contemplates, here are some guidelines about how to make the form work for you (Ivey Strategy #6):

- If you have only one known parent: Give all the information about your one known parent and then check the "Unknown" box for parent 2, instead of checking "Mother" or "Father" for parent 2.

- If you are being raised by a single parent or your parents are divorced: Give information about both of your parents, even if you no longer have much contact with one of them. If you don't have full information about one parent, give as much information as you have.

- If you have one or more stepparents and there are no questions about them: Give the information about your biological parents in the Family Information section and give information about your stepparents in the Additional Information section (see chapter 15).

- If you have a deceased parent: Give information about both of your parents, but show that one parent is deceased by checking "no" for the question asking whether that parent is still living and give the date that your parent died.

- If you are adopted: Give information about your adopted parents because they are deemed to be your parents by law. (Don't be confused by the language in the instructions that asks for information about a parent who "no longer has legal responsibilities to you.")

- If your parents are the same sex: Give information about both parents and designate both as "Mother" or both as "Father."

- If you are a legally emancipated minor: Give information about your parents, but include a brief explanatory statement about your status in the Additional Information section (see chapter 15).

- If you have a legal guardian other than one or both of your parents: Give information about your parents *and* give information about your legal guardian in the separate section labeled for legal guardians other than your parents. Include a brief statement that explains the situation in the Additional Information section (see chapter 15).

- If you have a family that doesn't meet any of these descriptions: List the information you have, and then include a brief statement that accurately describes your family situation in the Additional Information section (see chapter 15).

Family Tip #3: Your Siblings

You are asked to give some basic information about your siblings. Here are a few special circumstances that will require you to make the form work for you (Ivey Strategy #6):

- If you are a multiple (twin, triplet, and so on) and more than one of you is applying to the same college in the same year, you should report that in the Additional Information section (see chapter 15) because colleges do take note of that, and it can influence their decisions.

- If you have more siblings than there are spaces allotted, then you should include that information in the Additional Information section (see chapter 15), and you might also consider making "coming from a big family" a topic for an essay.

- If you have half-siblings or step-siblings or are being raised with other kids who function as your siblings, we encourage you to list them. The information can't hurt you and will give a truer picture of your family situation.

Parent Tip: Investigate the Family Tree

Help your child claim any legacy status to which he or she may be entitled by investigating your family tree and determining if any relatives have graduated from the college. Although the fact that great-uncle Henry graduated from the college in 1927 might not be a huge boost to your child's application, it can't hurt, either.

Family Tip #4: Think Legacy

Colleges give preferential treatment to legacy applicants. Basically, if you have a relative who graduated from that college, you could be considered a legacy applicant. Each college sets its own policies regarding who will be treated as a legacy applicant and what preferential treatment is given. But don't worry about figuring all the policies out; just fill out the family information with legacy in mind by doing the following:

- List the colleges and graduate schools for your parents or legal guardian and siblings

- List every single family member (grandparents, stepparents, aunts, uncles, cousins, and so on) who attended or received any sort of degree from the college by full name, degree pursued or obtained, and dates of attendance

- List any siblings who are currently studying at that college and any siblings who are applying at the same time (typically a twin)

If you aren't offered an opportunity to provide legacy information in response to a question on the application, then give this information in the Additional Information section (see chapter 15), but don't use the word *legacy*, which is too obvious; you're just listing the family members affiliated with that college. The college will know what to do with that information, if anything.

CHAPTER 7

Education and Academic Questions

These questions require you to list information about your high school (also called secondary school) and provide an opportunity for you to list your academic honors. If you've attended more than one high school, or you've gone to school outside the United States, or you've taken classes at the college level, or you've ever had to take a leave of absence from school for any reason, you should consider the Your Schools section carefully. For everyone else, you can probably just skim the Your Schools section, but make sure to read the rest of the chapter carefully.

YOUR SCHOOLS

Every application will ask you to provide basic information about your education. For example, where have you gone to school and when do you expect to graduate from high school?

School Tip #1: Figure Out Which Secondary Schools You Must List

For those of you who live in the United States and have attended the same school for grades 9 through 12, this section of the application is not hard. But for those of you who live outside the United States and are in another national school system, you will have to investigate what the equivalent of US grades 9 through 12 are. Start by seeing if your school counselor knows. If you do not have a school counselor or the school counselor does not know, contact the college and ask for advice. If you are based in the United States but attended more than one school during grades 9 through 12, you have to include the other schools, too. Even that can be a bit tricky. For example, if you attended an online school through your high school, you may not need to list it. Again, your best bet is to ask your school counselor and then follow up with the college to confirm.

School Tip #2: Highlight Whenever You Have Gone above and beyond in Your Education

Have you done college work during the school year through a dual enrollment program? Maybe you took math courses at a local college, which is a nice piece of evidence to support your passion for math. Or maybe you've done a summer program in architecture that greatly inspired you and changed everything for you academically. If so, you absolutely should list those schools in the Education and Academic sections of your applications (and not, for example, in the Extracurricular Activities section), even if you did not receive credit and even if it took place over the summer.

School Tip #3: If Your Education Was Interrupted, Explain

If you had to sit out a term for any reason, then you have what admissions officers call an *interruption* in your education, and you should explain it. Most often you will be required to provide a brief narrative explanation in response to a follow-on question, but if not, then you should offer the explanation in the Additional Information section (see chapter 15). The most common reasons are illness or family situations, and often there are some pretty personal details that you may prefer to keep private. That is absolutely okay. You do not have to disclose all the details in order to explain what's behind the interruption, but you do need to offer sufficient information so that the admissions officer understands the basic reasons for the interruption and is reassured that whatever the circumstances, the situation has resolved itself and should not prevent your graduation from high school or keep you from enrolling in college next fall. Here are some examples:

Insufficient: "I was not in school for the year between 9th and 10th grade for personal reasons. I returned and have had no interruptions since."

Sufficient: "I was not in school for the year between 9th and 10th grade because I was being treated for and recovering from a serious illness. My doctor released me as fully recovered after eight months, and I was able to return to school. I have been healthy ever since."

If you feel comfortable with your school counselor, you can also ask that he or she address the situation in the counselor's recommendation (see chapter 19). An additional explanation and endorsement from your counselor goes a long way to alleviating any concerns the admissions officer might have.

GRADES AND TEST SCORES

Most college applications (including the Common Application) allow you to self-report certain information about your grades and test scores. Take your time as you work through these questions, because they are often a bit trickier than they seem. Furthermore, it is essential that you employ Ivey Strategy #5 and sweat the details when it comes to reporting grades and test scores. Any difference between what you self-report and what shows up on the supporting materials will make a negative impression on the admissions officer and might even be considered fraud.

Parent Tip: Set the Highest Standard for Ethical Behavior

Because you exert a huge influence over how much integrity your child exhibits in the college admissions process, you want to model the highest standard of ethical behavior. None of your actions will go unnoticed, so be hyperaware of how you handle every interaction with your child about the college application. For example, if your child asks you how he or she should report grades or test scores, make sure you communicate that your child should report only what is completely accurate and can be documented. If you casually say that you can't imagine why it would be a problem for your child to round up his GPA, he might register that as license to tweak the facts. That's not a good outcome.

Self-Reporting Tip #1: Check That Your Grades and Scores Are Supported and Confirmed by Official Documentation

Do not calculate your GPA on your own; use only the GPA that shows on your transcript. If your school does not rank its students, then do not guess your class rank. Do not report test scores that cannot be documented by a test score report from the testing agency. Special note to those of you who get IB predictors: these are not valid or official IB scores to report on your part of the application, but your counselor may report them on the school report (see chapter 18).

Self-Reporting Tip #2: Self-Report Your GPA, Class Rank, or Test Scores on the Common Application Only if They Put You at the Top of the Applicant Pool at Every College Where You Are Applying

Yes, colleges can and will get this information from your supporting materials, but there is no reason to put it front and center on your application unless it serves you well. It belongs there only if your numbers are not just awesome but awesome by the standards of the toughest schools that will be receiving your Common Application.

Self-Reporting Tip #3: If You Are Asked to Self-Report Your Entire Transcript, Make It Error Free by Copying from Your Actual Transcript

A significant and growing number of colleges are asking students to self-report their transcripts on the application and asking for the school to send a final and official transcript *only if* the student is admitted and intends to enroll at the college. This saves the college and the high school a huge amount of time, but a self-reported transcript is a real hazard for the student. If the student's self-reported transcript and final transcript do not match, then an offer of admission can be revoked. Many students make careless errors on their self-reported transcript, so the best way to make your self-reported transcript error free is to request a transcript from your school—the one that the school would have submitted on your behalf—and *copy* the information there onto your application. You may find that easier or harder to do, depending on how the college has structured its form for self-reporting the transcript.

Whenever you encounter a question that does not permit you to simply copy the information, then you need to stop and read the instructions provided by the college very carefully and thoroughly. For example, if your school uses a 0–100 grading scale but the college asks for A–F letter grades, then you need to find out what you are supposed to do. Look at the college's instructions to find out how to convert your numerical grades to letter grades and follow their instructions exactly. If you cannot find an answer to your question in the college's instructions, then e-mail the college with your question and wait for their reply before completing this section of the application. (And keep a copy of the e-mail, so you have it as documentation.) Take no chances here.

ACADEMIC HONORS

Every college application gives you a chance to list academic honors you have received. An academic honor is any recognition or award that you have received based on your performance in the classroom or on a competitive examination. Common academic honors include the following:

- National Honor Society and other honor societies
- National Merit Award (multiple levels)
- National Examination Awards (such as the National Latin Examination Awards)
- Book Awards
- Honor Roll or other school-based recognition

Honors Tip #1

If the question asks for academic honors (as the question on the Common Application does), make sure you are listing only your *academic* honors. It makes you look like a less than outstanding student if your answer lists "best stand-up comic, Midwest Youth Comics Association, 11th grade, regional" as an academic honor. True, it is an honor, but it is not an academic honor. Likewise, an award for outstanding community service is absolutely an honor but not an academic one. Demonstrate that you have a basic skill of all good students—answering the question that was asked.

Honors Tip #2

If you have a lot of academic honors, be selective about those you list, and list only the most significant. Go for quality, not quantity. Mixing them all up regardless of importance will dilute the impact of the important ones. If you bury the fact that you're an Intel Scholar (an honor bestowed on only about forty high school students per year from the entire United States) in a list with fifteen other honors, like that high honor roll award given every semester to almost one hundred people at your school, you're not showcasing your most important honor effectively. Cut the fat, so that the muscle stands out.

Honors Tip #3

If the honor you have received is not self-explanatory, provide a brief explanation in the Additional Information section (see chapter 15) and direct the admissions officer there, or if the college permits you to upload your résumé, direct the admissions officer there for further detail. The explanation you provide in the Additional Information section or on your résumé should describe the honor in sufficient detail that the admissions officer understands its significance.

CHAPTER 8

Activities Lists

What do you do with your time when you aren't at school, doing school-work, or attending to the basics of life such as sleeping and eating? Admissions officers, who are evaluating you on the extracurricular dimension (see chapters 3 and 5) hope you do something that gives them evidence that you have the core four—passion, talent, initiative, and impact. You probably remember them from chapter 4 on your résumé. If not, take a minute and go back and reacquaint yourself with the core four and Ivey Strategy #4.

The first place on your application where you get to present your extracurricular activities is in a detailed list. That format, although efficient and helpful to admissions officers, trips up many applicants who just start filling it in without giving much thought about how to use the list to tell their own stories. Those applicants don't use any of the six Ivey Strategies that we've already introduced and that you've already learned. That's bad for them but good for you because you won't be tripped up! You will capitalize on the activities list in a way that makes you stand out.

The activities list on the Common Application is usually introduced with instructions like these:

Please list your **principal** extracurricular, volunteer, and work activities **in their order of importance to you**. Feel free to group your activities and paid work experience separately if you prefer. Use the space available to provide details of your activities and accomplishments (specific events, varsity letter, musical instrument, employer, etc.). (Common Application 2012–13)

A typical application would allow you to list a certain number of activities and specify a format for the bits of information that you can provide about each activity. In Common App 4.0, list up to ten and provide the following information for each:

- Activity (one- to three-word description chosen from a drop-down menu)
- Grades in which you participated
- When during the year you participated
- Time devoted (hours per week and weeks per year)
- Whether you intend to participate in college
- Positions held, honors won, letters earned, or employer (up to fifty characters)
- Details and accomplishments (up to 150 characters)

Yes, the list format is quite constraining. Yes, the list format predisposes you to just fill it in without spending too much time thinking about it. Yes, it seems hard to believe that you should devote time to crafting the perfect 150-character description of every activity on the list when you've got essays to write!

But don't let the list format cause you to underestimate the importance of this particular component of your application. The activities list is the admissions officer's first look at who you are outside the classroom. It is the foundation for the admissions officer's evaluation of you on the extracurricular dimension (see chapters 3 and 5). If you are thinking like an admissions officer (Ivey Strategy #2), you know that your activities list needs to convey your story (Ivey Strategy #3) and leave the admissions officer with a general sense of how you stack up on the core four (Ivey Strategy #4)—what your passions are, what talents you have, where you've shown initiative, and what you've done that has had impact. So how do you do that?

> ### Parent Tip: You Are Not an Administrative Assistant
>
> Parents, eager to be supportive of their children and do what they can to help, often insert themselves at this point in the application process and volunteer to be the typist. Although the impulse is understandable, we discourage parents from functioning as their children's administrative assistant. The college admissions process is an opportunity for students to develop skills that they will need in the near future and beyond. You will not be at college with them, where they will need to handle all sorts of administrative tasks on their own, including typing papers and other schoolwork. Because your ultimate goal is to equip your children to function on their own at college, you should seize this opportunity to cultivate an important skill. It gives your children practice while you are still on the scene providing guidance and support.

Happily for you, the activities list is a great place where you can work smarter, not harder (Ivey Strategy #1), because you have already determined your story and prepared a résumé. Armed with these two tools, you can produce a quality activities list in very short order.

Activities Tip #1: Decide Which Activities to List

This step is critical, because it is the step that will ensure that you highlight the right activities. You know that the right activities are the ones that convey your story and demonstrate the core four—passion, talent, initiative, and impact. (That means you also know what *shouldn't* make the cut.)

So take out your story and your résumé. What activities do you name in your story? What activities are shown on your résumé? Make a quick list or take a highlighter and highlight the activities, just so you can see what you are working with. In all likelihood, these are your right activities (for you!), and they will appear on your list. Easy, huh? Yes, it really is—because you have already done the work.

Activities Tip #2: Include *All* the Activities That Convey Your Story and Speak to the Core Four

Make sure you have captured all of your significant activities between your story and your résumé. Occasionally, we discover that applicants have failed to include nontraditional activities because they assume those activities don't count for the purposes of the activities list. But in the world of college admissions, activities reach beyond school-related clubs, team sports, and paid employment, so think broadly about your activities. If you spend your time doing something that is important to your story *and* if it demonstrates your passion, talent, initiative, or impact, then do list it even if it takes a little bit of effort to figure out how to translate what you've done into an entry on the list.

Here's an example. John was spending a lot of time with his grandmother while he was in high school. He had promised his grandfather that he would look after his grandmother after his college grandfather was gone. When John's grandfather died in the summer after John's tenth grade year, John dropped all of his activities except baseball so that he could make time for his grandmother. He went to her house at least four times a week, every week of the year, except when his family went on vacation. During his visits, he sat with her, talked with her, made dinner for her, and helped her with medications and household chores. That's how John was spending most of his free time, but should he really put that on his activity list?

The answer is yes! His relationship with his grandparents was a part of his story, and once he thought about it, he recognized that he had exhibited initiative and made an impact by caring for his grandmother, so he added it to his activities list. He felt validated when he found "family responsibility" listed as an activity in the drop-down menu of activities on the Common Application. That's an example of what we mean when we say to think broadly about activities.

Activities Tip #3: Focus on Quality, Not Quantity

Present a typical applicant with an activities list grid with ten rows on it and here is what happens. You inventory your activities. If you come up with ten, you relax, and list all ten. If you don't come up with ten, you panic and start trying to come up with filler activities. You know you have to come up with ten because there are ten rows to fill. Then you start convincing yourself that no one is going to be admitted who doesn't have ten. Then you panic some more and decide that you should list *more* than ten because that is what it is going to take to stand out.

What we have just described is the death spiral of applicant logic. *You have stopped thinking like an admissions officer and started thinking like an applicant.* So come back from the edge and put yourself back in the mind-set of an admissions officer again. An admissions officer is all about *quality*, not quantity. Who would you rate more highly on the activities dimension: the world-ranked, Olympic gold medal holder in downhill skiing who has only that one activity or the joiner who belongs to ten different clubs ranging from French Club to Board Game Society? If you apply applicant logic, then the joiner beats the skier by a landslide—ten to one. But you know better. An admissions officer doesn't evaluate on the activities dimension that way. The skier gets the higher activity rating because the skier can demonstrate the core four—passion, talent, initiative, and impact—whereas the joiner can simply fill all ten rows on the list.

Activities Tip #4: Don't Just *Fill In* the Space Available; *Use* the Space Available

But what if you don't have ten activities to list? Should you really just leave the space blank? That seems stupid to you, right? Why not list something? You spent all those Saturday mornings doing Zumba classes, so why not list Zumba? *Because you sabotage yourself when you add activities just to fill out the list.* First, you fool no one. Admissions officers can easily separate the fillers from the activities that count. Second, you distract the admissions officer from focusing on the activities that actually do make you stand out. As you know, admissions officers can devote only so much time to each application. The seconds that the admissions officer spends reading about your Saturday morning Zumba workouts are seconds that the admissions officer could have spent reading about your activities that count. Finally, and most important, when you add filler activities, you invite the admissions officer to question your judgment, and that means that every piece of information you report in your application will be greeted with a certain skepticism. That's not a good way to stand out.

So, please, don't fill in the space. Make the form work for you by *using* the space instead. When you use the space, you sneak in more information about your primary activities; elaborate on passion, talent, initiative, or impact; and tell more of your story. It is usually pretty easy to use your space, even if you have fewer than ten activities to list. All you do is come up with a good (and meaningful) way to subdivide one of your primary activities into multiple activities.

Here's an example. Let's say that one of your primary activities has been theater, and in fact your story says you are all about theater. You've participated in eight school productions in one way or another. You've acted in four, you co-wrote and directed one, and you did set design for three. How many activities do you have?

One, three, or eight is the answer, depending on how you combine them. You could simply list a single activity: theater. But you could subdivide that activity into three meaningful activities: acting, writing and directing, and set designing— and give yourself a bit more space to describe these various experiences. If space allows, you could go even further and subdivide your theater experience into eight separate activities, one for each production. If you truly are all about theater then allowing theater activities to consume a huge portion of your list is completely consistent with the story you want to tell. When you do this, you *use* the space instead of *fill in* the space. That makes all the difference.

Activities Tip #5: Consolidate Like Activities Together if You Are Constrained by the Number of Entries on the List

Sometimes applicants find themselves with too few available entries. Although this doesn't happen often on the Common Application, it could happen on some of the other applications. Bethany (see sample résumé in chapter 4) found herself in this situation. She didn't know how to present her activities when she was faced with naming only six activities on her Georgetown application. As she saw it, she had eight activities at a minimum: blogger, novelist, reading tutor, hospital volunteer, mission worker, church member, K-Life member, camper. How was she supposed to choose six?

In fact, she actually had three big categories of activities: writing, community service, and religious activities, so she had some flexibility. Each of those big categories was important to her story, and in each of the categories, she could demonstrate passion, talent, initiative, and impact. Ultimately she decided she would list the following six activities: blogger, novelist, reading tutor, hospital volunteer, mission worker, religious activities (Church and K-Life). Problem solved!

Activities Tip #6: Order Your List

After you know which activities you are going to list, you must order that list. The Common Application and most others direct you to list the activities in order of importance to you. This should not be hard for you to do: you know what is important to you. Yet many of you second-guess yourselves here.

Here was Phoebe's conundrum. She had ordered poetry first on her list, but then she started hearing from lots of people, including an alum from her top-choice school, that what colleges cared most about was "leadership." She was president of the French Club, so shouldn't she list French Club first? We advised against listing French Club first. Here's why: writing poetry was a major part of Phoebe's story; French Club was not. Remember Ivey Strategy #3—tell your story. Sure, you can alter your story as you go, so Phoebe could choose to list French Club first and make French Club a bigger part of her story *if* it were true. But it wasn't.

The advice she was getting from people, including the alum, was well meaning but ill-informed. Sure, admissions officers care about leadership, but that is not all they care about or even the most important thing they consider when rating you on your activities. You know that: admissions officers care about the core four—passion, talent, initiative, and impact. Which of these activities demonstrated those best in Phoebe's case? Hands down it was writing poetry. She lived and breathed poetry, and it showed in the amount of time she devoted to it. She spent as much time on poetry-related activities every week as she did on all her other activities combined. She had real talent as a poet—she had published poems and had won a local teen Poetry Slam several times. She showed initiative with her poetry—she had sought out an online poetry writing group that she met with regularly, and she had amassed a portfolio of more than two hundred poems. Finally, her poetry had impact. It was something she shared with others through publication and performance, and it meant something to those who read or heard it. One girl had even told Phoebe that one of her poems convinced the girl to get help when she was considering suicide.

And what about being president of the French Club? Well, she had really only done it so she could impress her French teacher; the club met infrequently; and the biggest thing they had done since she had been a member was organize a crêpe station at the school's annual bake sale for charity. It was nowhere near as important to her as poetry, and it was Phoebe's job as an applicant to show that.

Finally, when in doubt, follow the instructions. The question asked that Phoebe list her activities in their order of importance to *her*. Why wouldn't she do that? Application questions are not designed to trick you. They are designed to give the admissions officer the information he or she wants. Asking you to order your activities in their order of importance to you is a way of getting you to answer two questions in one list: the admissions officer finds out both what you did *and* what was most important to you. Your preferences and priorities are a part of who you are, and that is what they are trying to figure out by the order. That's all, and that's plenty!

Activities Tip #7: Make the Most of the Space Available for Description

As described at the beginning of the chapter, Common App 4.0 gives you space for two hundred characters of description for each activity: a fifty-character space for positions held, honors won, letters earned, or employer, and a 150-character space for details and accomplishments. (You will find similar descriptive fields on other applications, and even if the character counts morph a bit over time, the following principles will still guide you.)

These two hundred characters are the key to creating a standout activities list. If you make the most of that character count, you can and will leave the admissions officer impressed by your story and convinced that you have the core four—passion, talent, initiative, and impact. Look to your résumé for what you might want to say about each of your activities. If you've followed our advice so far, you have already developed descriptions that demonstrate one or more of the core four, so start there. Now edit them to get within the two-hundred-character limits. Here is how we suggest you use the characters available:

- Use *no* characters—really, none!—to demonstrate passion. You have already conveyed passion simply by what you have chosen to list and the amount of time you have devoted. Here you are showing your passion directly. You don't also need to tell.

- Use the fifty characters available for positions held, honors won, and so on to demonstrate talent and initiative. For example, claim your black belt or list yourself as founder.

- Use the other 150 characters to say more about your initiative and to communicate your impact as directly and forcefully as you can. Look back to the descriptions on your résumé and pull out the kernels of information that represent initiative and impact. Remember that you display initiative when you make things happen for yourself or lead others. Did you start it? Did you lead it? Did you seek it out? Did you create the opportunity? That's initiative. Remember that you have impact when what you did mattered to you or to others. How have you been changed by your experiences? How have others benefitted from what you have done? What have you added to your classroom, your school, your community, the world? That's impact.

Activities Tip #8: Claim Your Impact

Most applicants see impact as an all-or-nothing proposition. Either they've had *huge* impact—composed classical music performed by YoYo Ma, made the Forbes 400 list thanks to a side business launched from a bedroom with only an iPhone, or have been ranked world champion in some sport—or they've had *no* impact. In all likelihood, neither is true. You are seventeen. You have done some things that have had less than a world-shaking impact on yourself and others. Claim it and be proud of what you have accomplished. You don't need to exaggerate it in an attempt to be the one in a million who has had huge impact, nor do you need to hide under a rock because you are not that one in a million. You have to stand out; you don't have to be a superhero.

Activities Tip #9: Print It Out

Once you have entered your descriptions, print the draft application or generate a print preview. What you see on the screen may not be what shows up on the printout. Conform your answer so that what you see on the screen and what you see on the printout are *identical*, and save yourself the headache of discovering that your top-choice college didn't actually see the information you entered all because the screen lied and your printed answer was actually cut off in mid-sentence. Trust the printed version. That is the data that will be transferred and seen by the admissions officer whether they are reading your application electronically or in hard copy.

EXAMPLES

Just to show you how easy it is to complete your activities list, we've given you activities lists for the five applicants you met in the résumé chapter (4). You'll also see how these applicants lifted almost directly from their résumés to fill in most of the information on the activities list. You should be able to do the same. Note that the information is listed in the order that it would be asked on the example application described at the beginning of the chapter, so it begins with the drop-down menu choice for the activity description, and concludes with the 150 characters of details and accomplishments.

Gabriella's Activities List (Résumé in Chapter 4)

Activity	Science/Math
Grades in which you participated	11
When during the year you participated	School Year
Time devoted	5 hours per week/36 weeks per year
Whether you intend to participate in college	Yes
Positions held, honors won, letters earned, or employer	Researcher/Competitor.
Details and accomplishments	Exhibit/present clean energy research at city & state science fairs; top 50 (city)/top 10% (state).
Activity	**Science/Math**
Grades in which you participated	10–12
When during the year you participated	School Year & Summer
Time devoted	3 hours per week/36 weeks per year
Whether you intend to participate in college	No
Positions held, honors won, letters earned, or employer	Founder and Chair. Project Sunshine.
Details and accomplishments	Founded club w/ goal to provide at least 5% of school's energy through solar panels; 1/2 way to goal.
Activity	**Music (Vocal)**
Grades in which you participated	9–12
When during the year you participated	School Year & Summer
Time devoted	3 hours per week/36 weeks per year
Whether you intend to participate in college	Yes
Positions held, honors won, letters earned, or employer	Alto II. Youth Choir.
Details and accomplishments	Perform monthly in Sunday worship services at Old St. Pat's Church.

Gabriella's Activities (continued)

Activity	Science/Math
Grades in which you participated	10
When during the year you participated	School Year
Time devoted	5 hours per week/36 weeks per year
Whether you intend to participate in college	Yes
Positions held, honors won, letters earned, or employer	Researcher/Competitor.
Details and accomplishments	Exhibit/present air pollution research at city & state science fairs; top 50 (city).
Activity	**Work (Unpaid)**
Grades in which you participated	10–11
When during the year you participated	Summer
Time devoted	35 hours per week/12 weeks per year
Whether you intend to participate in college	No
Positions held, honors won, letters earned, or employer	Volunteer. Peggy Notebaert Nature Museum.
Details and accomplishments	Completed outdoor restoration projects; helped build collections on field trips; installed exhibits.
Activity	**Science/Math**
Grades in which you participated	9
When during the year you participated	School Year
Time devoted	5 hours per week/36 weeks per year
Whether you intend to participate in college	Yes
Positions held, honors won, letters earned, or employer	Researcher/Competitor.
Details and accomplishments	Exhibit/present green home cleaners research at city science fairs.

(continued)

Gabriella's Activities (continued)

Activity	Work (Unpaid)
Grades in which you participated	9–12
When during the year you participated	Summer
Time devoted	40 hours per week/12 weeks per year
Whether you intend to participate in college	No
Positions held, honors won, letters earned, or employer	Intern. Chicago Center for Green Technology.
Details and accomplishments	Developed "Green Cleaning 101" program that more than 500 people have completed.
Activity	Music (Instrumental)
Grades in which you participated	9–12
When during the year you participated	School Year & Summer
Time devoted	5 hours per week/52 weeks per year
Whether you intend to participate in college	Yes
Positions held, honors won, letters earned, or employer	Pianist.
Details and accomplishments	Studied piano since age 6; play almost daily for fun.
Activity	Music (Vocal)
Grades in which you participated	9–12
When during the year you participated	School Year
Time devoted	5 hours per week/36 weeks per year
Whether you intend to participate in college	Yes
Positions held, honors won, letters earned, or employer	Alto II. School Choir.
Details and accomplishments	Perform in three concerts/yr; chosen as soloist for Spring 2012 concert.

Andrew's Activities List (Résumé in Chapter 4)

Activity	JV/Varsity Lacrosse
Grades in which you participated	9–12
When during the year you participated	School Year
Time devoted	15 hours per week/12 weeks per year
Whether you intend to participate in college	Yes
Positions held, honors won, letters earned, or employer	Capt (12); Varsity (9–12).
Details and accomplishments	Midfielder. Chosen All Conf (11); Acad All Amer (11); Top Rookie (9).
Activity	**Other Club/Activity**
Grades in which you participated	12
When during the year you participated	School Year
Time devoted	10 hrs per week/36 weeks per year
Whether you intend to participate in college	No
Positions held, honors won, letters earned, or employer	Proctor. Johnson-Doubleday Dorm.
Details and accomplishments	Chosen by faculty to provide day-to-day mentoring and help to 50 underclassmen in dorm.
Activity	**JV/Varsity Ice Hockey**
Grades in which you participated	9–12
When during the year you participated	School Year
Time devoted	15 hours per week/12 weeks per year
Whether you intend to participate in college	Yes
Positions held, honors won, letters earned, or employer	Capt (12); Varsity (11–12); JV (9–10).
Details and accomplishments	Center. Named All Conf (11); rec'd Sportsmanship Award (10–11).

(continued)

Andrew's Activities (continued)

Activity	Student Govt/Politics
Grades in which you participated	9–12
When during the year you participated	School Year
Time devoted	2 hrs per week/36 weeks per year
Whether you intend to participate in college	Yes
Positions held, honors won, letters earned, or employer	Class representative.
Details and accomplishments	Represent class interests on 10-member student council.
Activity	**Other Club/Activity**
Grades in which you participated	10–12
When during the year you participated	School Year
Time devoted	3 hrs per week/36 weeks per year
Whether you intend to participate in college	Yes
Positions held, honors won, letters earned, or employer	Tour guide.
Details and accomplishments	Lead campus tours for prospective students and distinguished visitors.
Activity	**Club/Other Sport**
Grades in which you participated	10–11
When during the year you participated	Summer
Time devoted	168 hours per week/3 weeks per year
Whether you intend to participate in college	No
Positions held, honors won, letters earned, or employer	Lacrosse player.
Details and accomplishments	Invited to train at The Elite 150 Lacrosse Camps.

Andrew's Activities (continued)

Activity	Other Club/Activity
Grades in which you participated	9–12
When during the year you participated	School Year & Summer
Time devoted	1 hour per week/52 weeks per year
Whether you intend to participate in college	Yes
Positions held, honors won, letters earned, or employer	3rd generation baseball card collector.
Details and accomplishments	Attend collector conventions with father & grandfather. Favorite card: Topps Chrome Red Refractor Kevin Youkilis.
Activity	Student Govt/Politics
Grades in which you participated	11–12
When during the year you participated	School Year
Time devoted	1 hr per week/36 weeks per year
Whether you intend to participate in college	No
Positions held, honors won, letters earned, or employer	Member, Academics Committee.
Details and accomplishments	Created a summer research fellowship program for students.
Activity	Student Govt/Politics
Grades in which you participated	9–10
When during the year you participated	School Year
Time devoted	1 hr per week/36 weeks per year
Whether you intend to participate in college	No
Positions held, honors won, letters earned, or employer	Member, PR Committee.
Details and accomplishments	Developed "Event Tweet"; promotes events; keeps both boarding/day students better informed.

Bethany's Activities List (Résumé in Chapter 4)

Activity	Religious
Grades in which you participated	9–12
When during the year you participated	School Year & Summer
Time devoted	3 hours per week/52 weeks per year
Whether you intend to participate in college	Yes
Positions held, honors won, letters earned, or employer	Member. Bellevue Baptist Church.
Details and accomplishments	Lifelong member. Attend weekly worship and Sunday School w/ family.
Activity	**Journalism/Publications**
Grades in which you participated	9–12
When during the year you participated	School Year & Summer
Time devoted	3 hours per week/52 weeks per year
Whether you intend to participate in college	No
Positions held, honors won, letters earned, or employer	Blogger. www.BethanysBlog.com.
Details and accomplishments	Write blog on home-schooling from the kid's perspective; more than 250 posts and 1200 visitors.
Activity	**Community Service (Volunteer)**
Grades in which you participated	9–12
When during the year you participated	Summer
Time devoted	168 hours per week/6 weeks per year
Whether you intend to participate in college	Yes
Positions held, honors won, letters earned, or employer	Mission worker. Good Things Orphanage, Malawi.

Bethany's Activities (continued)

Details and accomplishments	Help girls ages 6–12 with schoolwork & maintain pen pal relationship w/ 2 girls that our family sponsors.
Activity	**Other Club/Activity**
Grades in which you participated	9–12
When during the year you participated	Summer
Time devoted	168 hours per week/4 weeks per year
Whether you intend to participate in college	No
Positions held, honors won, letters earned, or employer	Camper. Kanakuk Kamps.
Details and accomplishments	Attended Christian camp from age 10; served as CIT and camp officer in final year.
Activity	**Community Service (Volunteer)**
Grades in which you participated	11
When during the year you participated	Summer
Time devoted	40 hours per week/12 weeks per year
Whether you intend to participate in college	No
Positions held, honors won, letters earned, or employer	Volunteer. St. Jude Children's Hospital.
Details and accomplishments	1/30 chosen; helped patients who received stem cell/bone marrow transplants; helped w/ clinical studies.
Activity	**Community Service (Volunteer)**
Grades in which you participated	10–12
When during the year you participated	School Year & Summer
Time devoted	2 hours per week/50 weeks per year
Whether you intend to participate in college	No

(*continued*)

Bethany's Activities (continued)

Positions held, honors won, letters earned, or employer	Reading tutor. Haven House.
Details and accomplishments	Meet weekly with adult with autism (Laura) and help her improve her reading and vocabulary.
Activity	**Community Service (Volunteer)**
Grades in which you participated	9–12
When during the year you participated	School Year
Time devoted	5 hours per week/36 weeks per year
Whether you intend to participate in college	No
Positions held, honors won, letters earned, or employer	At-home volunteer. St. Jude Children's Hospital.
Details and accomplishments	Produce craft kits, sew mask straps & do other projects for patients' care and comfort.
Activity	**Religious**
Grades in which you participated	11–12
When during the year you participated	School Year
Time devoted	3 hours per week/52 weeks per year
Whether you intend to participate in college	No
Positions held, honors won, letters earned, or employer	Girls council member. Bellevue Baptist Church.
Details and accomplishments	Chosen by youth ministry team and Pastor; help plan/lead events; "big sister" to 7th grade girls.
Activity	**Religious**
Grades in which you participated	9–12
When during the year you participated	School Year
Time devoted	3 hours per week/36 weeks per year

Bethany's Activities (continued)

Whether you intend to participate in college	No
Positions held, honors won, letters earned, or employer	Member. K-Life Klub.
Details and accomplishments	Attend a weekly bible study & monthly worship and fellowship events.
Activity	**Journalism/Publications**
Grades in which you participated	9–12
When during the year you participated	School Year
Time devoted	20 hours per week/4 weeks per year
Whether you intend to participate in college	Yes
Positions held, honors won, letters earned, or employer	Novelist/short story writer.
Details and accomplishments	Write novel yearly during Natl Novel Writing Mo.; published short story (online mag, www.teenwriters.org).

Rodney's Activities List (Résumé in Chapter 4)

Activity	Theater/Drama
Grades in which you participated	9–12
When during the year you participated	School Year
Time devoted	5 hours per week/36 weeks per year
Whether you intend to participate in college	Yes
Positions held, honors won, letters earned, or employer	Actor/singer/dancer. School Productions.
Details and accomplishments	Performed in 6 musical theater productions; lead actor, soloist, or lead dancer in 5.
Activity	**Theater/Drama**
Grades in which you participated	9–10
When during the year you participated	Summer
Time devoted	20 hours per week/6 weeks per year
Whether you intend to participate in college	Yes
Positions held, honors won, letters earned, or employer	Actor/singer/dancer. Local Company X Productions.
Details and accomplishments	Cast by audition/performed in 2 musical theater productions for well-known SoCal theater co.
Activity	**Theater/Drama**
Grades in which you participated	11
When during the year you participated	Summer
Time devoted	168 hours per week/7 weeks per year
Whether you intend to participate in college	No
Positions held, honors won, letters earned, or employer	Student. Northwestern Musical Theatre Program.

Rodney's Activities (continued)

Details and accomplishments	Attended 7-week by-invitation-only intensive pgm; produced original musical theater production.
Activity	**Theater/Drama**
Grades in which you participated	9–12
When during the year you participated	School Year
Time devoted	2 hours per week/36 weeks per year
Whether you intend to participate in college	Yes
Positions held, honors won, letters earned, or employer	Acting student.
Details and accomplishments	Work with private acting coach, Ima Star, to develop my craft.
Activity	**Music (Vocal)**
Grades in which you participated	9–12
When during the year you participated	School Year
Time devoted	2 hours per week/36 weeks per year
Whether you intend to participate in college	Yes
Positions held, honors won, letters earned, or employer	Voice student.
Details and accomplishments	Work with renowned voice coach, Yoo Sing, to develop my voice.
Activity	**Dance**
Grades in which you participated	9–12
When during the year you participated	School Year
Time devoted	4 hours per week/36 weeks per year
Whether you intend to participate in college	Yes

(continued)

Rodney's Activities (continued)

Positions held, honors won, letters earned, or employer	Dance student. Fame Dance Studio.
Details and accomplishments	Study ballet, hip hop, tap & jazz; perform in annual recitals.
Activity	**Theater/Drama**
Grades in which you participated	9, 11
When during the year you participated	School Year
Time devoted	5 hours per week/6 weeks per year
Whether you intend to participate in college	Yes
Positions held, honors won, letters earned, or employer	Set designer. School Productions.
Details and accomplishments	Designed sets for two theater productions.
Activity	**Theater/Drama**
Grades in which you participated	9, 10
When during the year you participated	School Year
Time devoted	5 hours per week/6 weeks per year
Whether you intend to participate in college	Yes
Positions held, honors won, letters earned, or employer	Technical crew. School Productions.
Details and accomplishments	Served as stage manager for one production and worked on lighting crew for another.

Jacqueline's Activities List (Résumé in Chapter 4)

Activity	Debate/Speech
Grades in which you participated	12 (Jacqueline must convert to US grades.)
When during the year you participated	School Year
Time devoted	5 hours per week/36 weeks per year
Whether you intend to participate in college	No
Positions held, honors won, letters earned, or employer	Team captain. Model United Nations.
Details and accomplishments	Chosen to lead team; will organize participation in 3 conferences.

Activity	Debate/Speech
Grades in which you participated	10–11 (Jacqueline must convert to US grades.)
When during the year you participated	School Year
Time devoted	5 hours per week/36 weeks per year
Whether you intend to participate in college	No
Positions held, honors won, letters earned, or employer	Member. Swiss National Debate Team.
Details and accomplishments	Competed at 2 World Schools Debating Championships; ranked one of top 100 speakers (11).

Activity	Career Oriented
Grades in which you participated	11 (Jacqueline must convert to US grades.)
When during the year you participated	Summer
Time devoted	40 hours per week/8 weeks per year
Whether you intend to participate in college	No
Positions held, honors won, letters earned, or employer	Marketing intern. Get Help Now Hotline.

(continued)

Jacqueline's Activities (continued)

Details and accomplishments	Designed social media campaign to inform victims of human trafficking about Hotline/ services.
Activity	**Debate/Speech**
Grades in which you participated	9–11 (Jacqueline must convert to US grades.)
When during the year you participated	School Year
Time devoted	5 hours per week/36 weeks per year
Whether you intend to participate in college	No
Positions held, honors won, letters earned, or employer	Team member. Model United Nations.
Details and accomplishments	Attended 9 MUN conferences to date; awarded best speaker at Hungary Conf.
Activity	**Debate/Speech**
Grades in which you participated	9–12 (Jacqueline must convert to US grades.)
When during the year you participated	School Year
Time devoted	5 hours per week/36 weeks per year
Whether you intend to participate in college	No
Positions held, honors won, letters earned, or employer	Member. School debate team.
Details and accomplishments	Compete in Parliamentary style debate at World Schools Debating Society tournaments.
Activity	**Career Oriented**
Grades in which you participated	10 (Jacqueline must convert to US grades.)
When during the year you participated	Summer
Time devoted	40 hours per week/6 weeks per year
Whether you intend to participate in college	No

Jacqueline's Activities (continued)

Positions held, honors won, letters earned, or employer	Banking intern. Mirabaud & Cie.
Details and accomplishments	1/5 interns; rotated thru 3 areas of bank; designed investment portfolio that banker used with client.
Activity	**Other Club/Activity**
Grades in which you participated	9 (Jacqueline must convert to US grades.)
When during the year you participated	Summer
Time devoted	168 hours per week/4 weeks per year
Whether you intend to participate in college	No
Positions held, honors won, letters earned, or employer	Attendee. Global Youth Leadership Conference.
Details and accomplishments	Invited participant; intensive study of leadership; met world leaders in business, law, govt, media.

FIVE WAYS TO STAY WITHIN THE CHARACTER LIMIT

1. Pick the one to two most important things to communicate. You don't have space to list every debate tournament you won, but you can say "placed 1st at 27 tournaments."

2. Use phrases, not full sentences. The description is not a mini-essay.

3. Start each phrase with a verb that signals initiative or impact. For example, *started* signals initiative and *benefitted* signals impact. There are many more, so use the ones that work for each particular activity or experience, but use ones that do their part to convey your core points.

4. Use well-recognized or easily decoded abbreviations. Shortening words is fine in this context as long as the admissions officer can interpret it quickly. If you aren't sure, test it by having a parent or teacher read it and see if they understand right away. One warning: admissions officers are not teenagers, so assume they are not necessarily in the know about the abbreviations you use with your friends. That's why you ask a parent or teacher if they can decipher what you have written.

5. Quantify whenever possible and appropriate. Numbers use few characters and demonstrate real impact. "Raised $5000, enough to feed 50 children for a month" is much more compelling than "Raised money to feed hungry children in Africa."

CHAPTER 9

Really Short Answer Questions

A really short answer question is a question that demands an answer no longer than a text message (160 characters) or a Facebook post (420 characters). That means that you should be able to *own* these questions—they are tailor-made for your generation.

Yet, as it turns out, owning these questions is not so easy for most of you because you just can't figure out how to approach these questions. You are sure that there is a trick to them, because you can't believe that an admissions officer really cares about your favorite movie. Even if the admissions officer cares, you are pretty sure no one ever got into a top college listing the *Toy Story* trilogy as his favorite movie. Just what does the admissions officer want from you?

The admissions officer wants insight into who you are as a person. They craft the really short answer questions in such a way that they hope they can bypass your false personalities—the personality you project to seem cool, the personality you show to teachers or parents in order to get on their good sides, and the personality you *think* will appeal to an admissions officer. Admissions officers really, truly want to know who *you* are. They do want to know things such as your favorite movie, or what you do with a free afternoon, or your nutty idea for a gadget because these things give them a window into your genuine personality.

TEN STANDARDS: THE MOST FREQUENTLY ASKED REALLY SHORT ANSWER QUESTIONS

Really short answer questions vary more than any other kind of question on college applications, so a complete list of them is out-of-date the minute it appears. But there are some that regularly appear on multiple college applications year after year. We call these the *standards*.

- Favorites books or authors
- Favorite musician or artist
- Favorite movie
- Favorite keepsake or memento
- Favorite food
- What historical moment or event do you wish you could have witnessed?
- Dream job
- The greatest challenge facing society today is . . .
- What question would you ask on a college application?
- Describe yourself in three words.

That means that if you really are thinking like an admissions officer (Ivey Strategy #2), you *do* answer "*Toy Story* trilogy" in response to the "your favorite movie" really short answer question. You are not worried about having the right answer because you are focused on having an authentic answer.

We know that you doubt us because virtually all applicants deep down believe that their genuine personality is not really enough to get them into the college of their dreams. But that belief is nothing but an (understandable) insecurity. Stay focused on what admissions officers want—your authentic answer—and you will avoid the death spiral of anxiety that leads you to list *A Clockwork Orange* as your favorite movie, even though you have never seen it, because you Googled "most intelligent movie" and it got lots of hits. We can guarantee that you won't be able to fool the admissions officer into believing that *A Clockwork Orange* is your favorite movie, because it won't align with anything else on your application. You will be spotted as a pretender and blow it, because the only thing admissions officers are evaluating with these questions is authenticity. The trick to the really short answer questions? Be yourself.

Okay, fine. You agree to "be yourself." But just how do you do that in this context? Our advice (as always): start with your story (Ivey Strategy #3). Your story is chock-full of inspiration and material for your answers to these questions. For example, one of the most commonly asked really short answer questions is "name three words that describe you." That is a total softball question for you—you only have to look to sentence four of your story to find them.

But your story also gives you guidance regarding *any* really short answer questions. Your answers to these questions can be used either to emphasize a particular theme in your application or to bring out something about yourself that hasn't yet made it into your application. For example, you might want to emphasize your passion for French literature throughout your application. If so, the favorite book question is made for you. Your answer will surely be a piece of French literature. Or you might want to reveal your silly side (something that is a real part of you and that everyone you showed your story to agreed rang true) because the rest of your application is super serious. In that case, you pick the question about the gadget that needs inventing because it allows you to show this side of you. You answer, "a Groucho Marx app—hold your phone to your face, and you have a moustache and a thousand witty remarks at your disposal." Don't let well-meaning grown-ups talk you out of that genuine answer because as former admissions officers, we can promise you that your real answer is much more effective than giving the inauthentic answer that only an old person would give. (That's also our reminder to you that you don't have to be totally serious in your application at all times. Quirky can be fine if it's genuine and not over-the-top weird.)

As you can see, starting with your story makes answering these really short answer questions easier—yet another example of working smarter, not harder. (Ivey Strategy #1). It also makes it far more likely that you will come up with authentic answers to these questions. After all, your story is *your* story. If you find yourself giving an answer to these questions that doesn't align at all with your story, then you know you have strayed into dangerous territory. Return to your story and you'll be back on track. Moreover, if you work from your story, all of the really short answers you give will seamlessly weave themselves into the whole of your application. No matter how random the question, your answer will lead the admissions officer back to your story and what makes you a standout applicant.

Before we give you examples that show you how Angelina, Justin, and Nancy took their stories and generated their really short answers, we do have some important tips for making sure you come up with the very best really short answers.

REALLY SHORT ANSWER TIP #1: SHOW UP READY TO PLAY

The really short answer questions are not intended to be work; they are intended to be play. We know it's hard to imagine that anything related to your college application is "play," but these questions really are. You will have the most success with these questions if you play with them when you are well rested, relaxed, and in a pretty good mood.

REALLY SHORT ANSWER TIP #2: DECLARE YOURSELF

Many of the really short answer questions ask questions that are simply about having an opinion or a preference. So have one. Don't hedge. Don't waffle. Don't spin. Just declare yourself. There is no right or wrong, better or worse, good or bad favorite food. But an inability to *name* a favorite food suggests that you are not going to last ten seconds at college, because that suggests you can't think for yourself or form an opinion.

REALLY SHORT ANSWER TIP #3: DISTINGUISH YOURSELF WITH DETAILS

As you work your way through these questions, you will quickly discover that it's the details that distinguish a great answer from a merely good one. For example, how do you answer the question "three things I would take to a desert island"? You could answer "music, chocolate, and sunscreen." That is a decent answer. But you could also answer "my guitar so I could make music, a lifetime supply of M&Ms in my favorite color hot pink, and a trillion tubes of Banana Boat

Waterproof SPF 50 because I come in only two colors—white and red." Which answer has more personality? You guessed it, the second. What gives it personality? The details.

REALLY SHORT ANSWER TIP #4: CHOOSE WIDE OR DEEP

Some really short answer questions ask for lists. With lists, you will be most successful if you choose up front whether to go wide or deep. The wide approach would be to create a list that has variety; the deep approach would be to create a list that is focused. Either works. What does not work is to try to do both within one answer. So choose.

REALLY SHORT ANSWER TIP #5: GO BIG OR GO HOME

The really short answer questions invite you to unleash your imagination and be bold. Words such as *dream* and *fantasy*, which appear frequently in these questions, are your cue. It is all well and good that your goal is to be a lawyer, but you need to push it a bit further when you are asked to name your dream job. If you want to be a Supreme Court Justice, say so. If you want to work with asylum seekers, say so. Think big and aim high (and not just for your applications!).

REALLY SHORT ANSWER TIP #6: PERSONALIZE THE CLICHÉ

Many of the really short answer questions will elicit answers that are not unique to you. In fact, a huge percentage of applicants in any given year will give essentially the same answer to some of these questions. (These things come in waves. We still remember the six thousand times that teenaged girls told us their favorite movie was *Amélie*. Now it's something else, and you can probably guess.) That is because college-bound teenagers are, in fact, more alike in their experiences, viewpoints, and preferences than they are different. That is true of any subset of the population. For example, 40 percent of people worldwide name blue as their favorite color. So if you are answering these questions honestly and authentically, your answers are probably going to overlap considerably with many other college applicants in the same year.

Your answer runs the risk of sounding like nothing more than a cliché unless you *personalize* it in some way. Let's say you are in that 40 percent, and blue is your favorite color. How do you personalize that answer? You could contextualize it: "My favorite color is the blue of my mother's eyes." You could make it more specific: "My favorite color is royal blue." You could explain it: "My favorite color is blue because I am red-green color blind, and blue is the only color that I see as others see it." You have an infinite number of ways to personalize your answers.

Parent Tip: Use These Questions to Have Some Fun Conversations with Your Child

The really short answer questions lend themselves to a brainstorming-style conversation with your child. It can often be a fun interlude during a time when parent-child communication is usually somewhat strained. Follow the general principles of brainstorming by generating ideas quickly; welcoming the unusual, silly, and ridiculous ideas along with the more serious ideas; and withholding any judgment or criticism of the generated ideas. By the end of the conversation, you will likely discover that you have just gotten an important window into your child's current thinking about college and life. Resist any temptation you have to follow up with further conversation about your child's actual answers to the questions. Most parents' instincts about the "best" answers are off—you lean toward the goody-goody answers. These answers squelch your child's authenticity and that authenticity is exactly what admissions officers reward.

REALLY SHORT ANSWER TIP #7: WATCH THE TONE

Tone can be problematic with the really short answers. Answers that you think convey your sophistication can come across as arrogant. Answers meant to display your dry wit can come across as dark or disturbing. You don't want the admissions officer to come away with the wrong impression thanks to your really short answers. The best way to ensure that your tone is just right is to ask someone who knows you well to read all of your really short answers together. You've struck the right tone if the person reading the answers starts smiling and responds, "That's so you!"

EXAMPLES
Angelina

A few important things to know about me before you read my application is that I consider myself a Venezuelan but I have lived all over the world and currently reside in London, where my family landed just as I was starting high school. As a student, I am most interested by the subjects that delve into people's stories and cultures—literature, languages, and history. Outside the classroom, I spend most of my time doing Model United Nations and making music. I sing in multiple choirs and do musical theatre and I am a serious pianist. Close friends and family describe me as creative, persistent (stubborn), and "all about people". Right now, I imagine that I will become a cultural anthropologist, a psychologist, or a sociologist; in other words, I will do something that has to do with people and cultures.

Her Really Short Answers

Your favorite book: always changing, currently *Nothing to Envy: Ordinary Lives in North Korea*

Your favorite website: Facebook

Your favorite recording: Mercedes Se Está Bañando

Your favorite source of inspiration: Time at home in Venezuela

Your favorite line from a movie or book (and its title):

"Many years later, as he faced the firing squad, General Aureliano Buendia was to remember that distant afternoon when his father took him to discover ice. At that time Macondo was a village of twenty adobe houses, built on the bank of a river of clear water that ran along a bed of polished stones, which were white and enormous, like prehistoric eggs." *One Hundred Years of Solitude*

Your favorite movie: *Princess Bride*

Two adjectives your friends would use to describe you: creative, persistent

Your favorite keepsake or memento: My wooden Franciscan cross

Your favorite word: Supercalifragilisticexpialidocious

Justin

A few important things to know about me before you read my application are that I am an only child and lots of people make a big deal about the fact that I have accomplished so much in spite of having lost 70% of my hearing due to a childhood illness. As a student, I am a scientist type who likes to test everything in the lab, and I enjoy chemistry, biology, and physics equally. Outside the classroom, I play ice hockey (varsity starter on top ranked team in California), work with disabled kids (who face way bigger challenges than a hearing loss), and do lots of things with my church. Close friends and family describe me as quick-witted, kind, and tough. Right now, I imagine I will be a research scientist or an engineer.

His Really Short Answers

Name your favorite books, authors, films, and/or musical artists: *Einstein's Dreams*; all of the Sherlock Holmes stories; *the Great Gatsby*; all of the Harry Potter books; *1984*; *Into the Wild*; *The Usual Suspects*; *Gladiator*; *Braveheart*; *Talladega Nights*; *Anchorman*; *Forrest Gump*

What newspapers, magazines, and/or websites do you enjoy? facebook.com; sporcle.com; twitter.com; espn.com; wikipedia.com; the *New York Times*; the *Boston Globe*; *Time Magazine*; *Sports Illustrated Magazine*

What is the most significant challenge that society faces today? Finding an alternative source of energy to fossil fuels.

How did you spend your last two summers? Hockey training, volunteering with Special Olympics, and rock climbing.

What were your favorite events (e.g., performances, exhibits, sporting events, etc.) this past year? Salvador Dalí exhibit; Super Bowl XLV watched in our family room in the company of 15 buddies and my dad; and the fireworks show over the Charles River in Boston for the 4th of July.

What historical moment or event do you wish you could have witnessed? The "Miracle on Ice" during the 1980 Winter Olympics, ranked the #1 sports moment of the 20th century by *Sports Illustrated*—with front row seats so I could be in the center of the excitement.

What five words best describe you? Tough, curious, kind, open, quick-witted

Nancy (Remember her from Chapter 3?)

A few important things to know about me before you read my application are that I am a city girl, having been raised in Manhattan, and that I'm named for Nancy Drew, of teenage girl detective fame. As a student, I've always done well because I'm the kind of person who just loves learning, but I didn't speak that much in class because I was a bit shy—that is until 10th grade when I got furious when a group of loud mouth boys were dominating the discussion and then I found my voice! Outside the classroom, I read contemporary fiction, write short stories and poetry (two of my stories and one of my pieces of poetry have been published in anthologies by a major publishing house), and participate in drama club and school plays. Close friends and family describe me as thoughtful, creative, and passionate about words. Right now, I imagine that I will be a writer (and hopefully make enough money that I won't have to live with my parents).

Her Really Short Answers

Dream job: Poet Laureate

Most overrated superhero: Batman—doesn't actually have any SUPER powers, just a cool car, house, and sycophantic sidekick.

Most underrated superhero: Wonder Woman—has multiple SUPER powers, the Lasso of Truth and some amazing indestructible bracelets (got to love a woman with great fashion accessories).

Former kindergarten fear: Pin the Tail on the Donkey—who wants to be blindfolded and out of control?

Favorite movie: I'd rather read.

Favorite place to be or thing to do: Writing in my journal while sitting on the steps of the public library and sipping a Starbucks Frappuccino.

Advice for adults: Nurture the creativity of the next generation by giving kids more unstructured time to play and explore.

Gadget that needs inventing: A device that captures your thoughts and dreams in living color as you sleep.

CHAPTER 10

Short Answer Questions

The most frequently asked short answer question is some variation of the following:

> Please briefly tell us more about one of your extracurricular activities or a volunteer or work experience. (1,000 characters or less)

For those of you who have been working your way through this book chapter by chapter, this short answer question will be easy to answer. But if you have skipped the chapters on your story, your résumé, or your activities list, we suggest you go back to them now. Writing your answer to this kind of question before you have done those things will be harder than it needs to be. Remember Ivey Strategy #1—work smarter, not harder. If you are already equipped with your story, your résumé, and your activities list, then read on for how to write a stand-out answer to this short answer question as well as any others you encounter.

As always, we believe it helps if you think like an admissions officer before you begin composing your answer (Ivey Strategy #2). Let's eavesdrop on a conversation between two admissions officers to get a sense of how they think about one applicant's response to a typical short answer question about extracurricular activities (the applicant's name is Jaime):

Admissions Officer One: Hey, ready for a bit of a reading break? I could go for a frozen yogurt about now.

Admissions Officer Two: That sounds great. I just about hit the wall with my last applicant.

Admissions Officer One: Why?

Admissions Officer Two: I was just so disappointed by his answer to the short answer question about his extracurriculars. I was prepared to love this kid. He was student council president at this high school in my region. When I was there for the college fair, I heard a lot about how active the student council was and also about some great projects the previous president had led. I was hoping this kid would be more of the same. And he might be, but who knows? He pretty much just gave me the job description for a student council president. So nothing there. No initiative. No impact. No nothing. It pretty much tanked his extracurricular rating.

Admissions Officer One: I hate it when I see kids sabotage themselves. I don't get why they don't spend a little more time on the short answers.

By this point, we hope that nothing about this conversation surprises you because you are becoming expert in thinking like an admissions officer. You also know that the keys to this particular short answer question lie in Ivey Strategies #3 and #4: tell your story and focus on the core four. You know that what the admissions officer is looking for is an answer that conveys an aspect of your story and that demonstrates passion, talent, initiative, and impact.

Often it's the answers to the short answer questions that separate the true standout applicants from the LMOs, and that is why almost every college application throws some short answer questions into the mix. If you really want to submit a standout application, you need to master the art of the short answer and you need to give them the same kind of attention you give to the other components of the application. These are just as important as the full-length essay, and they can have a big impact.

We define a short answer question as any question that you are asked to answer in one to three hundred words. The Common Application has eliminated its short answer question with the introduction of Common App 4.0, but on many college-specific writing supplements to the Common Application, there is at least one short answer question. And MIT, which does not use the Common Application, has nothing but short answer questions on its application. For the typical applicant who applies to ten selective colleges, you can assume that you will have anywhere from two to fifteen short answer questions to answer. Whew.

Parent Tip: Try Your Hand at a Few Answers

Pick three or four of the short answer questions that your child has to answer on his or her college applications and come up with your own answers—answers that are about you, not about your child. Work to conform your answers to the guidelines and tips we give and be sure that your answers would be compelling to an admissions officer! There is nothing that you can do that will give you greater empathy for your child in the application process than this! It is quite humbling to discover just how hard it is.

As you begin working on your answers to these questions, the most important thing to understand is that *your short answers are not mini-essays*. Although the basic rules of writing still apply, writing a short answer is a different task than writing an essay. Just as poetry is not just prose that rhymes, short answers are not just short essays. That is why we have developed a set of tips specific to the short answer questions.

SHORT ANSWER TIP #1: ANSWER THE QUESTION

Colleges spend a lot of time deciding what questions to ask. Read the question carefully and make sure you answer *the question that is asked*. If the college asks you to elaborate on two activities, then don't write about one or three; write about two. If the college asks you to address what about their academic program appeals to you, then write about the cool major; don't write about what you love about the college's location.

The best topics for any short answer question are those that will punch up or call out one of the key themes of your story (Ivey Strategy #3). For example, if your story is "I'm a leader," and you have an opportunity to expand on an extracurricular activity in a short answer, pick an activity in which you were a leader and write about that, rather than writing about being a great team member on the tennis team (even if you love tennis more than life itself).

SHORT ANSWER TIP #2: MAKE ONE WELL-DEVELOPED POINT *ONLY*

There are really two tips in one here. First, make only one point. Second, develop the one point you make well.

For any question that relates to an extracurricular activity or work experience, your well-developed point is all about demonstrating the core four—passion, talent, initiative, and impact. Just by choosing one of your many activities as the subject of your answer, you convey where your passion lies. But passion alone is not enough. You need to complement it with at least two of the other three core four. (Very few activities allow for you to speak to all four, so three might be the best you can do!) Here are some questions to help you figure out how to find talent, initiative, and impact:

- Is your activity something you did to cultivate your talent? (passion, talent, and initiative)

- Do you have a talent you have shared? (passion, talent, and impact)

- Did you make something happen that had a demonstrable positive impact on others? (passion, initiative, and impact)

SHORT ANSWER TIP #3: BE SPECIFIC

Details distinguish you from everyone else, and they make your answer come alive. Can you see the difference details make in the following two short answers?

Too general: Competitive swing dancing is my passion. I practice every week and compete in 6 competitions per year. Last year, I placed at all of them. This year, I hope to win at least one of the 6. I know that means more practice, but I am willing to practice as hard as necessary to be a champion.

Much better: I want to be a swing dance champion. That's why I spent 8 hours last weekend working on nothing but leading turns. At my last swing dance competition, I placed but didn't win, because I lost style points for turns that "lacked finesse." I'm confident that by the next competition, I'll be the winner who is noted for his "style."

As you are composing any short answer, look for details that don't show up elsewhere in your application. Do not waste your precious words in the short answer restating what you've already said.

SHORT ANSWER TIP #4: SHOWCASE YOUR VOCABULARY

Using exactly the right word is important in the short answers because every word counts. Your thesaurus can be helpful here, *if* you use it to identify words that convey your message more precisely or more robustly. But before you pluck a word from the thesaurus and substitute it for the word you had, make sure you understand the distinctions between the two words. That means you also need to look them up in the dictionary. For example, although you might assume that *loathe* and *despise* mean the same thing, they do not. *Loathe* conveys that you disliked it intensely. *Despise* conveys that you looked down on it with contempt. Which are you trying to say? That you disliked it or had contempt for it? That kind of nuance matters.

For a short answer focused on an activity, you can use your language to reinforce your focus on the core four. For example, to emphasize your passion, you can choose words that pack a passion punch to convey your enthusiasm, excitement, and love of the activity. (No *loathe* or *despise* belongs here!)

SHORT ANSWER TIP #5: OBSERVE THE GRAMMATICAL RULES FOR FORMAL WRITING

In the context of a college application, you should assume that the grammatical rules for formal writing apply. Short answers are not Facebook status posts. They are not outlines or lists. They are full-fledged, written answers. That means you should use full sentences and proper punctuation.

Now that you have the short answer tips in mind, let's revisit Jaime's short answer (the subject of the conversation between admissions officers at the beginning of the chapter) and see how he could have applied these tips to produce a standout short answer.

Before

I was proud to be elected president of the student council at my high school; it is a major honor to lead a school of more than 4000 students. During the campaign, I focused on issues that were really important to students, and I am determined to fulfill all of my campaign promises before I leave office this spring. As President, I conduct weekly meetings of the 16 person student council, and I am determined that we will work together to complete some significant projects. I also organize monthly meetings between the four officers and the school principal to discuss issues and student concerns. There have been some intra-school tensions between various groups, and that is often one of our topics of conversation. I want to be the kind of president who brings the school together and leaves it better than I found it. (826 characters)

After

Thrilled to be elected to President of the school's student council, I was determined to fulfill my campaign promise to get a student lounge. We had some intra-school tensions between groups that I believed could be eased if students had a place where they could just hang out. I needed a plan, so I sought out help from a family friend who led big real estate construction teams. Armed with the plan, I divided the student council into three work groups—designers, DIYers, and fundraisers. The designers came up with a brilliant design that converted a basement classroom, the fundraisers raised the $15,000 we needed to make it comfortable, and the DIYers painted and decorated the space. We started in March, worked through the summer and when school opened in the fall, we had our new student lounge! Already, tensions have eased and the school community is coming together. (879 characters)

His after answer is pretty different from his before answer, isn't it? The after answer portrays Jaime as a can-do leader who has passion, initiative, and impact to spare. The after answer would not have sent that poor admissions officer into despair; it would have made that admissions officer rejoice.

CHAPTER 11

Essay Questions

A re you terrified of the college application essays? You're not alone. Most applicants are, and your anxiety is understandable. You know that there are lots of applicants with credentials as good as yours and that you must produce a standout application in order to be admitted. You fully appreciate that standout essays are necessary to a standout application. No wonder you're anxious!

But let's keep the task in perspective. A college application essay is generally no more than a two-page, double-spaced essay about a subject that you know really well—yourself. It may not be the easiest writing assignment ever, but it is not the hardest either. You absolutely can do it. In fact, there is no reason why every applicant can't produce a great college application essay. We are going to walk you through it and give you all the tips you need, from picking a topic to polishing your finished product.

PICKING A TOPIC

Do your applications give you a choice of topics for your essay? They might; they might not. If you don't have a choice, then skip this section and move on to next one about producing a draft. If you do have a choice, then you might be having a hard time choosing among the topics available. You want to make exactly the right choice, but perhaps you can't figure out which one that is. If you are having trouble choosing, you are probably caught in one of these two infinite loops:

Infinite Loop #1: You Can't Choose One from the Given Set

The college application invites you to choose one topic from a given set of topics. This is the format for the Common Application and many others. You debate the pros and cons of each topic, but it never quite feels as if any one of them is the right topic.

Infinite Loop #2: You Can't Generate a Topic of Your Choice

The college application invites you to write on a topic of your choice, but given this freedom, you have an even more difficult time. You generate idea after idea but discard each for one reason or another, only to finally decide on one and then discover it on some list of worst possible essay topics, and it's back to the drawing board.

Escaping from these infinite loops and generating the best topic for yourself is actually pretty easy once you know a few tips and tricks.

Topic Tip #1: Remind Yourself That the Real Topic of All of the Essay Questions Is You

No matter what the stated topic is, it is nothing more than a frame, a launching pad, or a prompt to get you to write about the real topic, which is *you*.

Consult the application that has the list of possible topics for your essay. Now quickly scan the topics looking for the words *you* and *your*. We are willing to bet that every topic has the word *you* or *your* embedded in the question itself or in the instructions preceding it. Why? Because *you* are the real topic of every single essay on a college application.

This is true no matter how random, obscure, or hard the essay question may seem. It is even true for the University of Chicago's legendary "stump the student" style questions. Consider for example, these two topics found on recent University of Chicago applications:

- 1. "What does Play-Doh™ have to do with Plato?"—The 2011 University of Chicago Scavenger Hunt List.

Every May, the University of Chicago hosts the world's largest scavenger hunt. As part of this year's hunt, students raced to find the shortest path between two seemingly unrelated things by traveling through Wikipedia articles. Wikipedia is so passé. Without the help of everyone's favorite collaborative Internet encyclopedia, show us your own unique path from Play-Doh to Plato.

(Inspired by Ayla Amon, AB'10, Daniel Citron, AB'09, and Benjamin Umans, AB'10) [University of Chicago Supplement to the Common Application, 2011–12]

- "Find *x*." [University of Chicago Supplement to the Common Application, 2010–11]

At first blush, neither of these questions seems to have anything to do with *you*. But if you read the last phrase in the Play-Doh to Plato question, it is right there in black and white. What is the real question? "Show us *your own unique path* from Play-Doh to Plato." That is absolutely about *you*.

But what about "Find *x*"? There is no *you* in that one. Or is there? Your English teacher would probably gently remind you that there is an implied *you* in front of every imperative statement. So what is the real topic? "[*You*] find *x*." In the world of college application essays, it really is all about *you*.

If *you* are the real topic of every single essay question, then you can relax already. You cannot go wrong in your topic selection. You *will* choose the right topic as long as you remember that whatever the topic is: it's all about *you*.

Topic Tip #2: Use Your Story as Your Guide for Choosing

Now that you know the real topic of every essay question is *you*, you can do a better analysis of the choices you have. Because your goal in your application is to tell your story (Ivey Strategy #3), your story is your guide. Referring back and forth between your story and your choices for topics, identify the best choice using these three guidelines:

- Choose the topic that speaks to your *most essential* qualities or your *most formative* experiences. This is particularly true when it comes to the personal essay on the Common Application or any other essay that is the one and only essay on the application. The one and only essay is the focal point of your whole application, so make sure you use it to tell your story because there is no better place to do so.

- Choose the topic that seems easiest to write about and easiest to make your own. Is there a topic that relates directly to some part of your story? Then it should be easy to write about, and the content will stay naturally focused on you. Don't make the mistake of eliminating a topic just because it seems easy (and you therefore think it can't be right). Exactly the opposite is true. If you've written your story properly, the topic *should* seem easy to write about.

- Choose the topic that reveals something about your story that you haven't been able to tell elsewhere in the application. What part of your story has not been fully told?

In other words, which topic really allows you to tell your story best? That's the right topic!

Topic Tip #3: Use Your Story to Generate Topics for the Topic of Your Choice Option

A topic of your choice option invites you to really zero in on the real topic—*you*. Where can you find ideas for generating your own topics? Your story has all the topics you could ever wish for embedded within it, if you just look.

Going sentence by sentence through your story, challenge yourself to come up with at least five possible topics for your essay. That is only one topic per sentence, so this exercise is completely doable. Remember Tom from chapter 3? Here is his story again:

> A few important things to know about me before you read my application are that I'm the oldest child in a very close-knit family and that I would be the first person in my family to leave the state to go to college. As a student, I'm into science, and inspired by physicist Richard Feynman; I've even done summer courses in astrophysics just for fun. Outside the classroom, I play drums in a garage band and water polo. Close friends and family describe me as curious, smart, responsible, and funny (once you get my brand of humor). Right now, I imagine myself as a physicist who makes some miraculous scientific breakthrough.

And here are the ten topics he came up with based on his story:

- Sunday lunch—a weekly tradition involving my entire extended family (a group of 20+)
- Declining economy in my home state and why that propels me out-of-state for college
- Why Richard Feynman, famous physicist and author, is my fount of inspiration
- Why I think space exploration must continue and be better funded
- How I got a paying gig for my garage band
- My famous "eggbeater kick" (a kick used in water polo to tread water)
- The language my friends and I invented (inspired by the language created for the Dune novels) for "confidential communiqués"
- My continuing pursuit of the solution to an "impossible math problem" I got in 10th grade
- Nanotechnology is where the miraculous breakthroughs will come from
- Science fiction is a great source of ideas for a future physicist (invisible cloaks would be great)

See, there's a lot to choose from, just from his story!

Topic Tip #4: Choose the Topic That Allows You to Tell Your Story and Produce Your Best Essay, Even if It Is the More Conventional Topic Rather Than the "Stump the Student" Topic

Among the topic choices some applications offer you, you might find what we call *stump the student* questions along with more conventional ones. Some applicants are under the mistaken impression that choosing the stump the student topic is the right choice, because the stump the student topic is the hardest question. In other words, they think they get points for choosing the topic, even if the essay they produce is lacking. Wrong. Admissions officers evaluate the essay you produce, period. So choose the topic that allows you to tell your story and produce your best essay. If you have no idea how to tackle the Dr. Seuss–inspired question but you know exactly what do with "What makes you happy?" (two questions on the Tufts supplement to the Common Application for 2012–13), then by all means write about what makes you happy and leave *Green Eggs and Ham* for someone else.

Topic Tip #5: Seek Advice before You Choose a Topic That Is Intensely Personal and Sensitive

You may be considering a topic that is intensely personal and sensitive. Perhaps you have confronted a particularly difficult situation at home, been the victim of a crime, or have a physical or mental disability. If you are considering such a topic, analyze the pros and cons in confidence with a trusted and mature advisor—one of your parents, your school-based college counselor, an independent college counselor, or another counseling professional. Pick this kind of topic only if both of the following are true:

- You have grappled with and already reached some kind of resolution or made some kind of peace with it. You should be able to write and talk about the issue clearly and without significant emotional upset to yourself. The college application process isn't therapy and shouldn't be therapy. It's not the right place to work through difficult emotional challenges.

- You consider it a primary element of your story. You are the boss of your own story, and you get to determine what makes the cut. You don't have to make this topic the whole focal point of your application unless you want it to be. Believe it or not, even something as fundamental as struggling with gender identity might not make it into an applicant's story, depending on what he or she considers most important about him- or herself. Everyone is different, so don't feel obligated to push a particular topic to the top of the list (or the top of your story) just because other people might put it there. Do you *define* yourself in some important way by this personal or sensitive issue? If not, you really, truly don't have to write about it in your main essay.

If you decide you do want to write about a personal or sensitive topic, consider whether it is best used as your primary personal essay or as a brief statement in the Additional Information section (see chapter 15). If you can address this topic in the Additional Information section, then you can make it a part of your story but not the focus of your application. In many situations, this is the best option, because it allows you to tell more of your story.

Topic Tip #6: Choose a Different Topic for Each Short Answer and Essay on a Single Application

Sometimes there are two questions on a single application that overlap in terms of the possible topics for your response. For example, the essay question on the Common Application asks you to "Recount an incident or time when you experienced failure. How did it affect you, and what lessons did you learn?"(Common Application 2013–14) and the college-specific writing supplement asks you to "Describe an experience that sparked your interest in mathematics, science or engineering" (Harvey Mudd Supplement to the Common Application 2012–13). You have a great story to tell about trying to build a robot, and it was both an incident when you experienced failure and an experience that sparked your interest in engineering. What do you do?

Use that story as the subject of only one of these essays. You should see every short answer or essay question as an opportunity to reveal something new about yourself to the admissions officer. Repeating yourself suggests that there is only one thing to know about you. But you know that is not the case. Go back to the topics available on the application and consult your story. What are the other possibilities?

You could choose a different topic for the Common Application (there are four others!), or you could describe a different experience in your Harvey Mudd essay. Either way, the key is to choose two different topics that are equally important to conveying your story (Ivey Strategy #3).

But what if you really, really want to use the robot story in your Common Application essay because you want to make sure that every college reads that essay? That means you have to choose it for the Common Application essay, because you can only create one version of the Common Application, right?

Wrong. You can actually create *alternate versions* of the Common Application, so you could have one version that uses the robot story in the essay on the Common Application and another version that has a different essay for the Common Application and that uses the robot story for the Harvey Mudd essay. For more information about alternate versions, consult chapter 21.

WRITING THE ESSAY

Now that you have your topics, you might be sitting there telling yourself you need to start writing, and yet (if you're like many people) you don't. We're going to guess that the reason you haven't started writing is that you aren't exactly sure how to go about turning your topic into an essay.

That's perfectly understandable! If you are like most applicants, your nonfiction writing experience can be summed up like this: you have written lots and lots of papers, reports, exams, and the like (expository writing), and you have little or no personal essay writing experience. In other words, you know how to write a mean essay analyzing Lady Macbeth, but you have no idea how to write a personal essay.

Guess what? It is not nearly as big a problem as you might think. The good news is that you can indeed write. You know the fundamentals; you just aren't sure how to apply them to your college application essays. But we can show you how. Once we do, do we have your word that you will buckle down and start writing? Good. Because that's the only way it is going to happen!

Even though you've heard us say over and over again that you should work smarter, not harder (Ivey Strategy #1), working smart can still involve a lot of work. In the case of the essay, it means multiple drafts. Sorry! If there's one thing we've seen over and over again among college applicants, it's that they aren't expecting to write so many drafts of their essays. They assume they can just knock out one draft, have their mom or English teacher read it, make a few tweaks here and there, and then treat it as done.

But we have to break the news to you that the best college application essays we've seen went through many more drafts than that. That doesn't make your job harder, necessarily. (Writing your college essay is not rocket science, really.) It just means that the essay is a work in progress for longer than you would have assumed, and it's going to change a lot more between your first and final drafts than you were expecting.

So before you start writing, read this section of the chapter straight through, then write a first draft. Then reread this section, and make notes about what you need to revise. Make your revisions and then reread this section again to take notes on your next round of revisions. Keep revising and checking your drafts against this section until you have a final draft that stands up to our checklist at the end of the "Your Final Draft" section. In our experience, it usually takes *at least two rounds of revisions* before you have a final draft. Don't shortchange yourself in the revising process. All great writing requires multiple drafts, and yours will be no exception.

As you write and revise, your most important job is to focus on the one essential element that all great personal essays share, and that brings us to the final Ivey Strategy:

Ivey Strategy #7: Show, don't tell.

Why is showing so effective? If you show the admissions officer something about you, the admissions officer actually has a direct experience of it. Direct experiences are far more memorable and far more convincing. Showing is the best way to influence the admissions officer in your favor, and that's why all great personal essays show, rather than tell. Yours will, too, if you follow our tips.

Writing Tip #1: Ditch the Five-Paragraph Structure

We know that you have been taught to use the standard five-paragraph structure for your writing in school, and that it has served you well there. You've been taught to start with an introduction (paragraph one), make three points (paragraphs two through four), and then wrap it up with a conclusion (paragraph five). In other words, you tell them what you are about to tell them, then you tell them, and then you tell them what you just told them. Wonderful as the standard five-paragraph structure may be for certain purposes, it is guaranteed to produce *deathly dull* college application essays. So ditch it. We mean it.

So how should you organize your essay instead? The most important thing to remember is that you are telling a *story*. A story has a beginning, a middle, and an end (for the Classics buffs among you, this insight goes all the way back to Aristotle), so structure your essay around that model instead. That means you need to think carefully about where your essay will begin and where your essay will end and what changed in your story in between. Begin with an opener that *grabs* the reader and end with a closer that *releases* the reader. Under no circumstances should you use an introduction that is a preview of the essay or a conclusion that is a summary of the essay. That is the five-paragraph standard essay coming back from the grave. Kill it.

Writing Tip #2: Make Your Essay Flow

An essay that flows well carries the reader effortlessly from one idea to the next. For the admissions officer who reads thousands of applications very quickly, an essay that flows well is a delight to read and always makes a positive impression.

Pay close attention to make sure that there is a logical order from sentence to sentence and paragraph to paragraph. The first sentence should lead to the second sentence, which leads to the third sentence, and so on. The first paragraph should lead to the second paragraph, which leads to the third paragraph, and so on.

Once you have a logical order established, concentrate on your transitions from paragraph to paragraph. Your paragraphs should relate and connect to each other in such a way that the admissions officer never stumbles, gets lost, or has to reread to figure out where he or she is in the essay. Good transitions smooth the essay out. Keep working and reworking them. And make sure to read all your drafts out loud as you're revising them. You'll *hear* bumpy transitions (and bumpy writing more generally) long before you *see* them.

Writing Tip #3: Be Memorable by Keeping the Content Focused on You

You've picked a great topic, and you're fiddling with the best structure and flow, but that's not enough! If you stop and think like an admissions officer (Ivey Strategy #2), you'll realize that your essay also has to make an impression. It has to be memorable—not just in the moment but weeks later when the admissions officer is in a committee meeting and is summarizing you for his colleagues and may even be trying to persuade doubting colleagues to admit you. An admissions officer can't do that if he can't really remember what you wrote about.

We know what you are thinking now. "There is no way my essay will be memorable. I haven't cured cancer, become a gazillionaire by creating a mobile app, or had my first novel published." Well, you are wrong. We have read thousands of essays throughout our careers, and some of the most memorable essays were about daily life, tiny achievements, and ordinary events. Really? Yes, really. One of Alison's favorites was an ode to a tropical fish. One of Anna's favorites was about a particular mathematical equation as a metaphor for romantic relationships. Memorable content *stands out*—not necessarily because the subject matter is earth-shaking but because of the way you reflect on the topic or the experience, or the voice you use, or the way the essay gives the reader some insight into how your mind works, or what makes you tick.

In other words, memorable content is about *you* (because as you know *you* are the topic of the essay). So as you are writing, make sure you are keeping the content focused on you. If you are writing about a person who influenced you, check to make sure the focus isn't shifting from you to the influential person. If you are writing about a significant experience in your life and it has a pretty complicated plot line, make sure the plot line doesn't take over from your reflection about why it was significant to you.

Writing Tip #4: Show Your Story

Remember that your overall goal for your entire application is to tell your story (Ivey Strategy #3), but here we want you to focus on showing your story (Ivey Strategy #7). How do you show your story? You must connect the essay topic to your story. So sit down with your story and your essay topic and look for connections. Finding connections might be straightforward or it might be a bit trickier, particularly when it comes to a stump the student topic.

Here's an example. Valentina was having trouble making that kind of connection between her essay topic and her story when she was working on this essay for Princeton:

> *Using the following quotation from "The Moral Obligations of Living in a Democratic Society" as a starting point, tell us about an event or experience that helped you define one of your values or changed how you approach the world.*
>
> Empathy is not simply a matter of trying to imagine what others are going through, but having the will to muster

enough courage to do something about it. In a way, empathy is predicated upon hope.

—**Cornel West, Class of 1943 University Professor in the Center for African American Studies, Princeton University**

Valentina hit pay dirt with the first sentence in her story: "A few important things to know about me before you read my application are that my family immigrated to the US from Russia when I was 13, and that was the defining event of my life." Here are all the connections that she found.

"an event or experience" —> "immigrating from Russia"

"define" —> "defining event of my life"

"values" —> immigrated to US —> why? —> freedom, opportunity

"changed" —> "defining event of my life" —> everything changed for me

"what others are going through" —> immigrating —> connects me to other immigrants

She also found connections between the key words and ideas and other parts of her story. For example, she saw the phrase "having the will" in the essay question and noticed that one of the adjectives she had used to describe herself was *determined*. She also saw that the phrase "courage to do something about it" was connected to her life aspiration to work for the United Nations Refugee Agency, which in turn was motivated by her own experience of feeling displaced from her home country. Valentina could now write a fabulous essay, one that was both personal and memorable and that actually answered the question.

Writing Tip #5: Have a Voice and Use It

Your writing voice is what makes your essay distinctively yours. It is a combination of word choice, tone, and rhythm. Just as someone can recognize you from your speaking voice, someone should be able to recognize you from your writing voice as well. Admissions officers yearn for voice in the personal essays. Voice makes the personal essays interesting, fresh, and alive. Voice gives a personal essay authenticity, and the admissions officer feels as if she is getting to know the real you.

Parent Tip: Being the Right Kind of Editor

Editing your child's college application essays is tricky business. You have to be quite restrained in your editing to make sure that you don't take over the essay. It is particularly important that you don't eliminate your child's voice from his or her essay. Teenagers do not sound like their parents, and admissions officers can spot a parent's language and turn of phrase a mile away. And it's the teenager's voice that the admissions officer wants to hear, not yours. Parents are often prone to taking out the lively, quirky, "teenager-y" bits and trying to make the essay sound more serious and sophisticated. The end result is usually deathly boring for these purposes. So resist the temptation to substitute your own voice for your child's. You might not be substituting it intentionally, but it can happen incrementally over successive rounds of edits. You are almost guaranteed to make the essay worse rather than better if you start trying to "fix" or "improve" the voice.

Writing Tip #6: Use Vivid Language

Bring your essay to life with language that is rich in meaning and descriptive detail. Choose words that invoke one of the five senses (seeing, hearing, touching, tasting, or smelling) and words that give your essay momentum. In particular, we encourage you to let your *verbs* do the heavy lifting. Why? For two reasons.

First, verbs show, they don't tell (Ivey Strategy #7). If you are going to get the most from your verbs, you should consider whether you have used the best verb for the task in each and every sentence. We all tend to fall back on the most common verb for a particular action, but the most common verb does not always convey as much as we would like. Take, for instance, the verb *to ask*. What are other verbs that you might use for *ask*? A quick check of the thesaurus yields lots of choices, and it quickly becomes obvious that the choices do, in fact, have subtle nuances. If you are being polite and decorous, you can *ask, question, inquire, request,* or *query*. If you are being a bit of a detective, you could *demand, interrogate,* or *examine*. If you are totally desperate, you *beg, plead,* or *beseech*. See how easy it is to use verbs to convey a lot of information in one word? Good. We beseech you to use verbs.

Second, verbs are less likely to lead you into the danger zone of million-dollar words. All too often applicants are eager to impress with their vocabularies, so they use the thesaurus, just as we did when coming up with alternatives for *ask*.

But rather than searching for accuracy, they are looking for obscurity—the million-dollar word that, they hope, will dazzle the admissions officer. The problem is, those words don't dazzle. Instead they come across as exactly what they are—inept attempts to impress. Million-dollar words also rob your essay of voice because they are not words that you would ever actually use. To make things worse, many applicants misuse their favorite million-dollar word and convey something they didn't really intend. It's better to stick with good old-fashioned five-dollar words.

Writing Tip #7: Strike the Right Tone

The right tone for an essay is friendly and informal, and it matches the question in terms of seriousness. The admissions officer should feel as if he or she is having a conversation with you while you both chugalug some coffee at Starbucks.

A *friendly* tone leaves the admissions officer liking you and wanting to admit you. We suspect you know what friendly is and isn't but just in case: friendly is *not* offensive or angry. There is no room for arrogance, negative judgments, insults, whining, or sarcasm.

An *informal* tone is the just right midpoint between formal and casual. Formal writing is for academic assignments and papers. Casual writing is for e-mails, Facebook posts, and text messages. Informal writing is the just right in between and is perfect for the personal essay. It isn't as fussy as formal writing and allows for a lighter, conversational feel, but it isn't so light and conversational that it sounds sloppy or dashed off. Sometimes the easiest way to test your writing to see if it is informal is to consider how the writing sounds when you read it aloud. Does it sound like a presentation you would make in one of your classes? If so, it is probably too formal. Take it down a notch. Does it sound like an exchange you might have with a friend as you are making plans for the weekend? If so, it is probably too casual. Take it up a notch.

This advice may be counterintuitive to some of you. Parents are often surprised to find out that essays aren't meant to sound formal. Applicants from other cultures are also not used to submitting anything less than formal writing. But when you are sending your essays to admissions officers at US colleges, formal is not the way to go. If they wanted a term paper, they would ask for one. They don't. And yes, it's even fine to use contractions (*don't* instead of *do not*) and other things you wouldn't do in more formal writing.

It's just as important to make sure you match the tone of your essay to the tone of the question. We know that some of you are tempted to go for a "creative" mismatch in an effort to be funny or clever, but that rarely works. A serious question calls for a serious answer. A lighthearted question calls for a lighthearted answer.

Writing Tip #8: Pay Attention to Rhythm

All writing has a rhythm to it. An interesting rhythm enlivens the writing, and it also directs the reader where to pay closest attention. It will keep the admissions officer engaged, and it will make it easy for the admissions officer to get what you want to say. To make the rhythm of your essay interesting, you must have variety. Too much of any one thing makes for a boring essay, so change it up.

For example, vary the length and structure of your sentences and paragraphs. We all tend to be creatures of habit when we write. Maybe all your sentences are long but your paragraphs are really short. Or maybe you like to start every sentence with a prepositional phrase or you always use compound sentences. Whatever your habits are, break them so that your writing has sufficient variety. And finally, aim for a rhythm that aligns more closely to conversations than lectures or academic papers.

Writing Tip #9: Don't Procrastinate

Writing is a process that takes time. No one gets it right in a first draft. *No one.* Don't leave the writing until D-Day (deadline day) because you tell yourself you work best under pressure. You don't. Even if you are a fast writer, it takes time to do the revising and polishing necessary for a great essay. Your writing will also benefit if you stick it in a drawer for a while and take a mental break from it. Coming back to it with a fresh pair of eyes can work wonders.

Writing Tip #10: Get an Editor

Even the best writers swear by their editors. That's why we encourage you to get an editor. If you are working with an independent counselor, that person will likely serve as your editor (among other roles). If you are not working with one, you can probably identify several possible editors who can push you to improve your essay: an English teacher, a tutor in the writing clinic, an advisor to the school newspaper, your school-based college counselor, a family friend, a mentor. Ideally, you are looking for someone who is

- A good writer

- Nice, and also honest, with feedback

- Willing to devote some time to working with you

Writing Tip #11: Slay Your Writer's Block

If you find yourself stuck, here are some tricks you can try:

- Borrow from filmmakers and do the scenes out of order. There is no rule that you have to write your essay in any particular order. Jump to some part of the essay that you find easy to write and write it. Then come back to the parts you are finding hard to write. Sometimes the easiest place to start is the middle, and you can work out from there.

- Talk your essay using voice recognition software. If talking comes easier than writing, there are lots of tools and apps that will translate what you say into typed text.

- Write in microbursts. Sit down and write whatever you can for fifteen minutes, then stop. Do something else for thirty minutes, and then come back to the writing. Write for another fifteen minutes. Then stop and do something else for thirty minutes. Repeat until you are rolling.

Writing Tip #12: Be Ruthless

There comes a time when your essay is almost done, and you have to start cutting instead of adding. You'll turn your essay from good to great if you show no mercy in the cutting process.

- If you exceed the word limit by 10 percent or more, you can't eliminate just a word here and a phrase there. You must eliminate a whole point or idea. Pick which one to eliminate and then cut everything related to it.

- Take out all of the side journeys in the essay. Your detour might be interesting, but you do not have the luxury of detours in a two-page, five-hundred-word essay. Take them out.

- Eliminate repetitions. When people get excited about an idea, they often like to repeat it and make the same point in different ways. You do not have room to repeat yourself in an essay of this length. Make your point once and eliminate the repetitions.

- Cut the empty calories. Believe it or not, there are usually lots of words, sentences, and even paragraphs that don't say much at all. These are the empty calories of writing, and they make your writing fat and flabby. Go through your essay word by word, sentence by sentence, and demand of each one, "Is this word or sentence necessary?"

- Let go of your favorite phrases or sentences. People fall in love with particular phrases or sentences in their writing and rarely consider them for elimination when editing. But sometimes that favorite phrase or sentence is not really actually essential or helpful to the essay. Try editing it out and see what happens. You may be surprised to see that taking it out improves your essay overall.

YOUR FINAL DRAFT

Even the best writers on earth have trouble knowing when they are done. Sometimes their editors have to tell them to stop futzing with revisions and put the (virtual) pen down. How do you know when you're done? You have a final draft and are ready to move on when you can check off each of the following:

- ☐ Your essay has a beginning, a middle, and an end and uses an organizational structure other than the standard five-paragraph structure.

- ☐ Your essay flows—from sentence to sentence and from paragraph to paragraph—logically and smoothly.

- ☐ Your essay has content that is memorable because it is focused on the real topic—*you*.

- ☐ Your essay shows (not tells) one or more central elements of your story.

- ☐ Your essay uses vivid language.

- ☐ Your essay has a tone that is friendly and conversational and that matches the essay question in terms of seriousness.

- ☐ Your essay has an interesting rhythm. (You must read your essay aloud for this.)

- ☐ Your essay feels done.

At this point, you have a final draft that has all of the makings of a great essay, but it isn't quite there yet. In order for your final draft to become the great essay it is destined to be, you must do one more thing: *proofread*.

Proofreading Tip #1: Proofread for More Than Typos

When you are finalizing an essay, the proofreading you should do is more than just proofreading for typos. You are looking for all errors that fall into the category of grammatical or spelling errors. We suggest that you use the following checklist to proofread for one category of errors at a time:

- ☐ Check paragraph breaks.
- ☐ Check subject-verb agreement.
- ☐ Check verb tenses for shifting tenses or incorrect tenses.
- ☐ Check pronoun-referent agreement
- ☐ Check for pronoun-antecedent clarity and agreement.
- ☐ Check punctuation.
- ☐ Check spelling.

Done well, proofreading takes some time, and it is best done when you are fresh and awake. So do not leave proofreading to the last minute or do it at the end of a long session. When you do sit down to proofread, use tricks to force yourself to proofread carefully. Some of our favorites are to read your essay aloud, cover the writing with a piece of paper so you can see only one line or sentence at a time, or read it backward, word for word.

Proofreading Tip #2: Do Not Overrely on Spellcheck

Word processing programs are wonderful but they are also fallible. You must take the time to review your essay for yourself. We assume that you know the rules of grammar and know how to check spelling. If you don't, you need to learn now. Ask your English teacher for help and make use of online tools such as dictionary .com. A special note to international students: make sure your word processing software is set to "US (English)" or "UK (English)" grammar and spelling rules.

If you have it set to another language, your word processing software will not give you any proofreading help.

Proofreading Tip #3: Break Grammatical Rules Only for a Higher Purpose

Great writers routinely break grammatical rules, but they do so for a particular rhetorical effect that they are trying to achieve. It's fine if you do that, but in that case make sure it's obvious to the reader that it was intentional and not just a careless error. Proceed with caution and quadruple-check the rest of your essay to ensure that it is error free so that the admissions officer knows you do, in fact, know the rules of grammar.

 THE SEVEN DEADLY SINS OF PERSONAL ESSAYS

Sin #1: Your personal essay is not your work. Your essay is expected to be your work, and if an admissions officer figures out that your essay is not your work, she will reject you. Don't hire out your essay. Don't copy or mimic a sample essay you find online (or in this book!). Don't let a well-meaning editor (such as your mom or dad) rewrite it or tweak it beyond all recognition. Write your personal essay yourself.

Sin #2: Your personal essay is not an essay. Essays are specific forms of writing. You are asked to write an essay, so write an essay. Don't write a poem. Don't write a screenplay. Don't write an academic treatise. Don't write an autobiography. Write an essay.

Sin #3: Your personal essay is not personal. Your personal essay is supposed to be about *you*.

Sin #4: Your personal essay is not specific enough. Your essay must be specific enough to be about you and *only* you. You are not the first, last, or only applicant who will write about your mom or dad when you pick the essay question asking you to write about a person who has had a significant influence on you. In fact, thousands of applicants will do just that every year. And that is perfectly fine, as long as your essay is distinctive enough that it wouldn't work equally well for some other applicant.

(*continued*)

Sin #5: Your personal essay is off-putting or worrisome. Admissions officers read all components of an application with an eye for the applicant who is off in some way that could be threatening or disruptive in a college community. Diatribes don't sit well with admissions officers, nor do personal essays that are just plain creepy (like an in-depth discussion of your fascination with serial murderers).

Sin #6: Your personal essay exceeds the stated word limit. Word limits used to be more of a suggestion than a strict requirement. But online applications have made it much easier for colleges to enforce the word and character limits, so most of the time, you simply can't exceed the stated word limit. But even if you can, you should adhere to any stated word limit. It is disrespectful to simply ignore the directions you have been given. Regardless of how well written your thousand-word essay is, if you were asked to write five hundred words, you will be penalized for disrespecting those instructions. So follow the directions. Distill and clarify your thinking, and your writing, until your essay is within the word limits.

Sin #7: Your personal essay is not well written. Misused words, grammatical errors, and typos are simply not acceptable. Your personal essay should be your best piece of writing ever. It should deserve an A++ from the most critical English teacher you have ever had (but make sure she understands that you're not meant to be writing in term-paper language). Polish it until it becomes that A++ essay.

SAMPLE ESSAYS

Following are some sample essays for you to take a look at. They take different approaches, as you'll see, and they come from different types of applicants.

See how they have different voices and different stories and allow us to get a sense of each person without actually meeting him or her? Of course, it goes without saying that you should not copy these sample essays, mimic them, or borrow from them. But do let yourself be inspired by the range and the possibilities that you see here.

Sample Essay #1
Describe . . . a historical figure . . . who has had an influence on you and explain [his/her] influence. (Common Application 2012–13)

Laser guns. Space ships. Nanobots. Wormholes. The science fiction I consumed was full of these wonderful figments of imagination. The more I read, the more I wondered, "Are they possible?" The answer, I learned, may lie in the bizarre field of physics known as quantum mechanics.

Wanting to know more, I asked my Physics teacher, "What is a good, easily understandable book to read about quantum mechanics?" "Try *The Character Of Physical Law* by Richard Feynman," he answered thoughtfully. And so I did. Not only was it a great introduction to the world of science, it was also the beginning of my love affair with Richard Feynman.

Over the next few months, I delved into his life. I read his autobiographical collection of stories, *Surely You're Joking Mr. Feynman*. I couldn't believe it but as I read it, I just sat there, laughing uncontrollably—reading and re-reading the passage of how he contemplated hopping backwards up the stairs in front of the king of Sweden after accepting the Nobel prize. I dragged my parents to a play based on Feynman's famous lectures to students. I attended a two-week national physics seminar largely because it included a lecture on Feynman's work on quantum electrodynamics. As of this fall, I have devoured more than a half dozen books by and about Feynman, seen the play, and studied countless of his lectures. Yet, I still want more.

So I ask myself . . . what is it about Feynman that so captivates me?

Truth be told, it isn't Feynman the brilliant scientist that has kept me spellbound after all this time: it is Feynman the man. Feynman had this amazing gift for enjoying life. He made friends everywhere he went and they ranged from artist to mathematician to Las Vegas showgirl. He was a musician who composed music for a ballet in San Francisco and played the skillful frigideira in a Brazilian samba band. He was a painter who liked to paint nudes. Why, he even discussed dice and poker with the infamous Nick the Greek.

Prior to discovering Feynman, I subscribed to the cliché that all scientists were unalterably dull. Feynman convinced me otherwise and persuaded me that I could become a scientist without becoming a bore. I can get lost in the minutiae of calculus but also enjoy a good joke and love good company. I can be a nerd and have close friends that aren't. I can take time off from "deep thinking" and play the drums or read a good book.

No wonder I love Richard Feynman. Even if he didn't exactly answer my question about whether faster-than-light travel is possible, he has inspired me to "calculate for myself," keep asking questions, and live life fully and extravagantly. That is enough.

Sample Essay #2

Given your personal background, describe an experience that illustrates what you would bring to the diversity in a college community. (Common Application 2012–13)

I scan down the list of available checkboxes. Where is the one that describes me? I can't find it. I look again. Why isn't there one for me? It is the 21st century and I know there are lots of people like me, so why isn't there a checkbox for us? It would be simple really. Just add a checkbox under citizenship that says "world" and a checkbox under race/ethnicity that says "all of the above." But it seems the checkboxes haven't caught up to reality, so I find it incumbent upon me to add some explanation in order to adequately describe myself.

I hold a Kenyan passport, and have been brought up there. Undoubtedly Kenya is home and my upbringing there has shaped me. Only someone raised in Kenya would be equally comfortable responding to being charged by a wild animal while walking barefoot on safari, handling massive waves on a beach or knowing what to do when power is cut unexpectedly for extended periods. Furthermore, in Kenya, I learned to be friendly with everyone no matter their position in society—from the people on the street to the President and everyone in between.

Although Kenya is home, it is not the only country where I have lived or attended school and it is not the only culture that has shaped me. My mother is of Middle Eastern descent and I lived and attended school in Cairo, Egypt for five years. As a result, I feel equally at home in Arab countries since I speak Arabic, I am Muslim, and know the customs and practices of Arab culture. While living in Egypt, I learned the habits of Arab generosity. Arabs give as much as they can without expecting anything in return; they constantly help friends, family, and people in need. I myself am now someone who gives freely and without hesitation whenever I encounter someone in need, be it a friend, family member, or fellow human.

I began living in England when my parents determined that my best opportunity for the highest quality secondary education was at a boarding school there. In many ways, it was easy for me to adapt to living there. English is my first language and I speak it with a British accent because Kenya is historically linked to the British Empire. At school or on the streets of London, I could easily pass for just another Brit. And I've found myself oddly suited to the life of a Brit—how else do I explain my passion for clay pigeon shooting, my love for fish and chips in the pub for lunch, or my bizarre fondness for shopping in the rain?

Kenyan, Arab, or British? Each is true but none is fully descriptive. And honestly, my racial/ethnic identity is equally complex with a plausible claim to African, Arab, and Indian. You see my dilemma with the checkboxes and I am not alone. From my experience living in numerous countries and attending five international schools, I would have to say that many people in the world aren't all that well served by the checkboxes; each of us is a particular blend of our "checkbox" identities, a racial-ethnic-national mix that both reflects and transcends our ancestry and citizenship. So check me a citizen of the "world," with its corresponding "all of the above" blend of race and ethnicity.

Sample Essay #3

Evaluate a significant experience . . . and its impact on you. (Common Application 2012–13)

Looking out of the back window of the car as the ferry departs from the dock, I feel myself begin to relax completely and unwind. Soon I'll be walking through the door of a weathered, but solid, house on Islesboro, a small island off the central coast of Maine. This house has been my second home my whole life, since my Dad inherited it from a great uncle before I was born. I love it there.

I reach for my phone to answer a text, but then I remember that once the ferry pulls away, there is no cell service or internet. I'm "disconnected." I wonder to myself how I'll communicate with friends this summer. I suppose I could resort to the ancient technology of postcards. What would they say?

June 30

Wait until you see the new fire pit. I dreamed it up as a project yesterday when my sisters and I were sitting around bored beyond belief. It turned out to be a little more work than I'd guessed, mostly because we had to use ancient tools. I had to clear the site, which was covered in waist high grass, with a SCYTHE and a PUSH MOWER. Brutal, especially since both were pretty rusty. It kept me and my sisters busy all day, but the fire, s'mores, and stars twinkling overhead made for a perfect reward. Wonder what I'll come up with to do next?

July 7

Best 4th of July ever. As always, we started the day with the "big parade"—10 floats and some locals. Then we had a cookout and the afternoon to ourselves. The whole family convened at our house for the amazing dinner feast of lobsters and steak. We gather around an enormous table in our barn. This year I counted 18 relatives around the table devouring the food and laughing over stories. After we stuffed ourselves, we walked down to the beach and watched the fireworks. Not any great display; in fact, they were kind of lame, as fireworks go. But, somehow a perfect ending to this annual family tradition.

July 12

The great "All Ball" tournament is just ending. All Ball, a mix of field hockey and soccer with a twist, is an Aldrich family favorite because we invented it. The rules of the game are fairly simple. The players split into two teams. Each player is given a stick-like object (e.g. Lacrosse Stick, Whiffle-Ball Bat), which must remain in the player's hands at all times. The object of the game is to shoot the ball past the goalie, using the stick or your feet, to get a point. Beyond these basics, there are no other rules—no out of bounds and no penalties except for hitting to the face. It is truly a great game.

I'm awakened from my postcard daydream by a jolt when the ferry reaches the dock. As we edge forward off the ferry and onto the island, I realize that summers on Islesboro have made me who I am. They have awakened my ingenuity, deepened my connections to family, and given me an appreciation for both work and play. I can't wait for this one to begin. I urge my Dad to drive just a bit faster and I am the first one to jump out of the car and make it into the house. The official start to another magical summer.

Sample Essay #4

Tell us about a[n] . . . accomplishment that is important to you. What about that . . . accomplishment makes you proud and how does it relate to the person you are? (University of California 2012–2013)

"Elisa, hold up, I have something for you!" I yelled down the hallway while reaching into my backpack. Pulling out a CD, I admired my work as she walked over to me: the label I had designed was on it in just the right way and a crisp image of her smiling face and my watermark looked back at me. Still overwhelmed by the fact that I had a real photography business with its own watermark, I beamed as the CD passed from my hands to hers. Looking up from her new possession, her eyes sparkled in a way that was nearly impossible to capture with a camera, although I had worked relentlessly until I was able to feature it in her senior portraits. Thanking me, she gave me a quick hug and ran off to her next class as I found an even greater smile sliding across my face.

I didn't actually set out to start up a portrait photography business. But I am a well-known photographer in my school and when a friend asked if I would do her senior portraits, I seized the opportunity. As the daughter of a mother who is an entrepreneur, I had grown up learning how to start up and operate a profitable business. I knew there was a need for someone who would produce good senior portraits at a reasonable price because I knew the competition in town and frankly they just weren't very good and they were quite expensive. So I jumped into business by saying yes to that first request. Within weeks, I was solidly booked and I was doing things like creating a watermark and packaging for my product.

I was committed to producing senior portraits of the highest quality. After all, your senior portrait is immortalized in the yearbook forever. I knew that the secret to producing a really high quality senior portrait for each client would require manipulation of the image using computer software (since the photographs were all digital). I have heard people say that it is the raw image captured by the camera that tells the truth, but I don't believe that. Raw images only document reality, they don't reveal truths. In the case of senior portraits, I edit the raw images to highlight the physical or personal characteristics that I find so captivating and that are really the essence of that person. A person is not that blemish on the upper left cheek; instead the person is the glowing smile and soft beach hair or the warm brown eyes and heavenly cheekbones. A person is not the fly away hairs, but the full laugh frozen in mid-moment and at the center of the frame. So, this is what I spend the long hours working to achieve: an image that highlights the truth that I see, not an image that merely documents a person's face.

Although my business has been quite successful, I'm not sure yet whether I will keep it operating and build an ongoing business in portrait photography or whether I will shut it down now that senior portrait season has passed. Regardless, the experience has been beyond my wildest dreams. I love that I was given the opportunity to show the beauty I see in my classmates to the world through senior portraits. For the artist in me, that is the ultimate satisfaction.

Sample Essay #5

Evaluate a[n] . . . achievement and its impact on you. (Common Application 2012–13)

When an idea popped into my head about starting a club for everyone who loves math as much as I do, I couldn't resist. I knew my classmates would go for it. We've been together in a very small advanced math class since eighth grade and have formed a common bond. We know the joys and the sorrows that come from solving the impossibly hard problem or being challenged by a perplexing derivative. We work together and we have fun. In fact, we are proud to say that we love math!

When I shared my idea for a Mathletes club, my class was all for it. Immediately we began brainstorming with our teacher and planned some events for the upcoming year. One of our major goals for the club was to find a way to spread the love for math to as many other students in our school as possible. In order to do that, we knew we needed to be strategic about introducing the club to the school.

We began to create the invitation that we would place in the lockers of every potential "Mathlete". The invitation read:

Place: $\dfrac{x-11}{10}+\dfrac{x+9}{12}=20$ $f(x)$ $\begin{cases} -2x+10, & 1\le x\le 3 \\ 2x-2, & 3<x\le 4 \\ 10-x, & 4<x\le 6 \\ \dfrac{4}{3}x-4, & 6<x\le 9 \end{cases}$

Month: $f(x)=\dfrac{1}{2}(x^2-3)-30$

        Solve for $f(9)$

Day: $a=64;\ n=2$

        What is the nth root of a?

Time: $\dfrac{6\left(144\frac{1}{2}\right)}{2\left(9\frac{1}{2}\right)}$

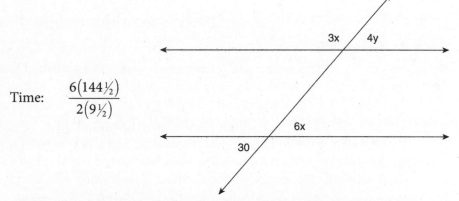

For the true Mathlete, this was a simple enough equation to solve and when she solved it, she knew that she was supposed to come to room 111 on September 8th at 12:50 to learn more about Mathletes. The invitations created quite a buzz in our school, so it seemed we were off to a promising start.

When the day of our first meeting arrived, I was ecstatic when I walked into the room to find about 30 girls—almost everyone we had invited. Since that first meeting, Mathletes has evolved into a strong, successful club with weekly math practice sessions that always attract a good crowd. We enter online competitions and we race each other in solving math problems. Some of us also entered competitions, such as "Who Wants to be a Mathematician?" in which we were given the chance to win prize money. We've even gone on field trips together; my personal favorite has been seeing the play, *Eureka!* about Einstein and various math principles.

It has been wonderfully satisfying for me that a random idea that popped into my head in math class could turn into a real club full of enthusiastic members. But beyond the satisfaction of having a real club comes the satisfaction of spreading the love of math. Thanks to the efforts of Mathletes, there are Mathlete shirts, chants, and talk about math is common in our hallways. Best of all students see math as fun and exciting. That's a legacy that makes Mathletes one of my proudest accomplishments.

Sample Essay #6

Discuss your favorite place to get lost. (University of Virginia Supplement to the Common Application 2012–13)

In my math and science classes, my brain functions like a well-oiled machine as I focus my efforts on finding the one and only right answer. But in art class, I allow myself the pleasure of getting lost; in the splatter painted, disorganized, even chaotic, art room, I can escape the machinations of my analytical brain and let my creative brain take over.

I started taking art in seventh grade. My initial approach to art was much like my approach to math and science—an attempt at perfection. I loved producing still lifes because I could focus on rendering each detail completely accurately. But as my pieces became more abstract, I realized that I could approach art differently. One day in portfolio class, my teacher walked up to my painting and smacked a big gob of white paint on the middle of my piece. "Go with it," she said. And so I did.

From that day forward, art class was the place where I could forget about getting it right and instead get lost in a world I created, expressing my own wonderfully "unstill life."

Sample Essay #7

What is your favorite ride at the amusement park? How does this reflect your approach to life? (Emory Supplement to the Common Application 2011–12)

Although my idea of fun has changed significantly since I was in grade school, I will never deny that amusement parks can be extremely fun. Over the past decade, my family and I took a countless number of trips to Disney World and there was one ride that I made sure to hit each visit—Buzz Lightyear's Space Ranger Spin. And I always insisted that my Dad ride it with me.

The concept of the ride is simple—you and another person sit in a rotating "spaceship" with laser guns, and as the "spaceship" progresses throughout the ride, it is your job to shoot the greatest number of targets possible; whoever has the most points at the end of the ride wins. As a child, this ride was always my favorite, but I never thought about why until now.

As I think about it, I realize that it does in fact reflect a lot about my everyday approach to life. To begin with, I'm ultra-competitive in everything I do, from academics to athletics. I love to compete and win, especially when I face opponents I admire and respect. I'm not ruthless or unsportsmanlike, but I am focused and determined. At Disney World, it was definitely my goal to beat my Dad—my most worthy and perpetual opponent. Since I strive to be the kind of man my Dad is, when I can do something as well or better than he does, I know I am succeeding, even if it is just shooting the most targets on an amusement park ride.

Beyond outshooting my Dad, the ultimate high for me on the ride came at the end when Buzz Lightyear thanks us for helping him to save his planet from the evil Emperor Zurg. Whenever I heard those words, whether I had beaten my Dad or not, I felt like an accomplished hero. For all of my life, I have had the desire to do something spectacular, to be a hero. As a child, I was satisfied that by helping Buzz save the planet, I was, in fact, doing something pretty spectacular. Now, of course, I realize that I'll have to do something in the "real world" if I want to achieve that dream. But I still have that same desire to be an accomplished individual and to do big things with my life, like make major breakthroughs in medicine or science that help end suffering for lots of people.

As silly as it may seem, Buzz Lightyear's Space Ranger Spin is probably as good an expression of my approach to life as anything. In fact, I might have to convince my Dad to have one more go just before I leave for college . . .

Sample Essay #8

Tell us about an intellectual experience, project, class, or book that has influenced or inspired you. (Brown Supplement to the Common Application 2010–11)

As an Egyptian, I am a citizen of a country at the heart of both Arab-Israeli conflict and peace efforts and I am a witness to the hardships the conflict continues to bring. I have always been intrigued by the course of the conflict, frequently posing questions about decisions made in the past and assessing decisions being made in the present. It was for that reason that I chose to write my IB Extended Essay, my biggest yet research paper, on the current conflicts between the Palestinians and Israel.

The challenge of this project was really, truly understanding the mind-sets of both the Palestinians and Israelis. As a Middle Eastern Muslim, I can easily comprehend the mind-set of the Palestinians, many of whom share the same culture, customs, and religion as I do, but I do not have a similar window into the mind-set of Israelis. Though I have travelled worldwide, and Israel and Egypt are neighbours, I have never been to Israel or had a meaningful relationship with an Israeli.

Seeking a better understanding of the Israeli mind-set became my quest. I interviewed noted leaders, such as the Head of the Arab League, H.E. Amr Moussa, and Egyptian Ambassador to Israel Mohamed El Bassiouny. But as interesting and helpful as these interviews were, they did not illuminate me. Ultimately, it was the work of a lesser known scholar that was transformative and gave me the window into the Israeli mind-set that I needed. Reading Dr. Rita Rogers' dissertation *"The Emotional Climate in Israeli Society"*, I learned that there is not a singular Israeli mind-set, but instead there are multiple mind-sets arising from the radical cultural and political differences amongst Israelis. Dr. Rogers linked these conflicting mind-sets to the larger conflict in the Middle East by arguing that Israel maintained its internal social cohesion through the presence of a common enemy.

Her paper satisfied my original quest to get some insight into the Israeli mind-set, but it also made me question my initial assumptions about the conflict and gave me new questions to ponder. I now had to consider the function of the presence of a common enemy for Israel. Was it a political tool? Was it a distraction that keeps internal social clashes from surfacing? Although some of my questions were answered as my research progressed, particularly those in relation to the current Palestinian-Israel conflict, many of them continue to linger. But discovering Dr. Rogers' scholarship and wrestling with the questions it raised validated my belief that understanding the "other's" mind-set is critical to an informed understanding of the world. I expect to spend my life striving to listen, discover and understand the other, so that I can build bridges between peoples, cultures and nations.

Sample Essay #9

Think about a subject or topic that you love. It can be something you have studied in school or on your own, but something about which you have really enjoyed learning. What first intrigued you about the subject and what have you found to be most fascinating? In what ways have you shared what you have learned with others? (Bucknell Supplement to the Common Application, 2011–12)

I got glasses in 7th grade and they did their job—I could see. But I was completely perplexed by how putting two pieces of glass in front of your eyes would improve your vision until I took Physics in 11th grade. My Physics teacher explained to us the concept of eyeglasses. He taught us that the light passes through the lenses and refracts at such an angle so that the beams of light will cross on your retina, thus allowing a clear image to be produced and sent to your brain to be processed. Awesome.

Sometime later, I got the answer to another question that had stumped me. Why do people look like they have teeny, tiny legs when you see them reflected in water at a certain angle? Turns out, it too is all about refraction. When the light hits the water it bends at such an angle that causes your eyes to see an image in a spot other than where the object truly is and distorts the object. The image your eyes see is not what is there. Even more awesome.

All of this stuff fascinated me. Physics was so interesting to me that I just assumed everybody was as interested in it as I was. I would come home after school, and I would ramble on about what I learned in Physics today. My parents were surprised and pleased, since until I took Physics, I never talked much about my day or what I had learned. But my sisters were a bit irritated because I would corner them and force them to watch as I re-created experiments we had done in class. But I loved it and couldn't be contained.

So when I got to put my Physics knowledge to work in the service of neighborhood "extreme sports" it was about the best day ever. My friend, who was also taking Physics, and I decided to add a jump to our sledding hill, just to make it a little more dangerous and entertaining. We determined the angle for the jump's slope, roughly calculated the horizontal and vertical velocities of the rider and approximated where he/she would land, and designed it so the rider's landing would be cushioned with fresh powder (or so we hoped). Much to our delight (and amazement)—it worked! The jump delivered each rider on or fairly close to the predicted landing spot.

These experiences have only whetted my appetite for more Physics. I look forward to the day when I can understand the complexity of fiber optics (a bit more advanced than eyeglasses or light on a lake) and design things with bigger world impact than a sled jump. But, for now, I'm content to have discovered a subject that gives me answers to questions that perplex me, offers solutions to real world problems, and is just plain awesome.

Sample Essay #10

There is a Quaker saying: "Let your life speak." Describe the environment in which you were raised—your family, home, neighborhood, or community—and how it influenced the person you are today. (Tufts Supplement to the Common Application 2012–13)

Compassionate. Talkative. Sensitive. Understanding. Relational. No, I'm not describing my mother—I'm describing myself. Although I hate to assign a gender to personality qualities, I have to note that many of these qualities are traditionally labeled feminine. Rarely are they used to describe a teenage male, especially one who is a varsity linebacker on a 4A football team in Georgia. So how did I come to acquire these "feminine" qualities (qualities that I actually value in myself as much or more than some of my traditional "masculine" qualities)?

I believe I've developed these qualities, in part, because of the world that I come from—a world in which my family is central and my family is dominated by females, particularly in my generation. In my immediate family, I am one of three—the other two? Girls. Beyond my immediate family, I have six female cousins. How many male cousins? Zip. Zero. None. So if you're keeping count, you now realize that in my daily life, it's me and two girls, and at family gatherings it's me and eight girls. Like I said, dominated by females. Think of all the time that I have spent in the company of these girls and it is pretty obvious that I couldn't help but learn from them. Their ways of doing things rubbed off on me and over time I've developed them into some of my most defining personal qualities.

But contrary to what one might expect, developing my "feminine" virtues has not come at the expense of my "masculinity." If anything, I am more aware of being a male because I am surrounded by females. I'm comfortable with how I've integrated the "feminine" qualities given to me by my family with the "masculine" qualities that have been mine from birth. It is this combination of qualities that defines who I am.

CHAPTER 12

"Why College X?" Questions

You will discover that a majority of colleges have some version of a "Why College X?" question on their applications, although the specific wording of the question varies considerably. Some, such as Columbia's, are quite straightforward:

> Please tell us what you find most appealing about Columbia and why.
> **—Columbia Supplement to the Common Application, 2012–13 (300 words)**

Others, such as Oberlin's, are more complex:

> Given your interests, values and goals, explain why Oberlin College will help you grow (as a student and a person) during your undergraduate years.
> **—Oberlin College Supplement to the Common Application, 2012–13 (300 words)**

Most suggest an answer in the longer short answer range (250 to 300 words), but some allow for an essay that's as long as the personal essay (250 to 500 words).

Regardless of the exact wording of the question or the type of answer required (short answer or essay), the fundamental question you must address is why you consider College X a good match for you. Although this should be an easy question to answer well, 90 percent of applicants' answers are bad, and a good 30 percent are truly horrible.

In fact, many admissions officers consider this part of the application the most painful to read because so many applicants blow it so badly. Tim offers a good example of the typical bad answer to a "Why College X?" question.

> My passion for biology is the chief reason why I want to attend Duke. I know that Duke has one of the strongest biology programs in the nation and is one of the top research universities in the world. I know that the outstanding faculty would challenge me to develop my critical thinking and research skills and that I would be in classes with students who share my interest in learning and my passion for the sciences. The other reason why I want to attend Duke is its emphasis on the balance between academics and social life. I have been an active and involved in all kinds of activities during high school and I want to continue that in college. It seems like I will be able to do that at Northwestern. I know that there are lots of opportunities to participate in club or intramural sports. I want to join a fraternity at Duke and I hope I will find some way to become a leader. I will definitely be an enthusiastic contributor to the huge tradition of school spirit at big sports events and annual traditions. Work hard, play hard. That's my motto and that's why Duke is the perfect place for me.

Can you think like an admissions officer (Ivey Strategy #2) and come up with the list of things Tim did wrong in his answer? We suspect so, but just in case you are still perfecting your ability to think like an admissions officer, here's what the inner monologue would look like in the admissions officer's head:

> Mr. Near-Perfect Math/Science SAT scores (800 on Math on the SAT, 780 and 800 on the Physics and Calculus SAT Subject Tests, respectively) really let me down with his short answers and essay. His response to the "Why Duke?" question was particularly lame.

He couldn't articulate any specific reason beyond Duke's reputation and the frat and party scene. It's all "blah, blah, blah." Of course, that is the hazard of writing a generic answer to this question and then trying to customize it with a little find-and-replace action, as is obvious from his failure to find and replace Duke for Northwestern throughout the answer. Too bad he couldn't even exhibit enough enthusiasm for Duke to proofread his application. Altogether, I'm guessing Duke is not at the top of his list. Although I'm sure he could do the work here, there are plenty of others with his academic profile who actually want to come to Duke. My vote: deny.

How do you avoid being Tim? You use Ivey Strategies #1, #2, and #5: you work smarter instead of harder, you think like an admissions officer, and you sweat the details. And you make sure you use the following tips.

DEVELOP THE RIGHT CONTENT

Most applicants don't consider why admissions officers ask the "Why College X?" question in the first place, and therefore their answer is not really designed to tell admissions officers what they want to know. But by now you've been thinking like an admissions officer for a while (Ivey Strategy #2) and you can probably guess. What do admissions officers want to know? Two things. They want to know something about your goals and how College X will help you achieve them. They also want to know whether you have a genuine interest in College X (see chapter 5's discussion of the importance of demonstrated interest).

Now while you are thinking like an admissions officer, take another look at Tim's essay. You probably have almost the same reaction the admissions officer did. Yes, Tim did articulate some goals, but they were mostly about his sports and social life, and he didn't really connect them to Duke in particular. Instead, he basically indicated that he'd be happy at any highly ranked college that has club sports and a Greek system. He also failed to convey any genuine interest in Duke because he said nothing that was specific to Duke, and of course the admissions officer knew that Duke was not high enough on his list for Tim to have invested the basic effort to proofread his application.

Your "Why College X?" essays will be much better than Tim's because you are going to speak to what admissions officers want to know. Here are a few tips for developing your own content.

Content Tip #1: Do Have Goals

You don't have to have figured out your life goals before you apply to college, but you do need to have some goals for college itself. What is it that you actually want to get out of the college experience? Check out the last sentence of your story—you have articulated some goals there. Start with those career goals and work backward. What do you need to do in college to put you on the path to that career? If you don't have career goals yet, look to sentence two of your story—your academic interests—and start from there. Add some goals for other things about college life that excite you, but make your academic goals front and center (college is after all, first and foremost, an academic enterprise).

Parent Tip: Help Your Child Take the Long View

It is really hard for your child to take the long view of his or her life right now. All your child can think about is getting in. That's why coming up with goals for college can be quite difficult. But you have the advantage of perspective that comes with age and experience. You know that getting in is really more of a beginning than an end. Help your child see that, too. Here are some ideas for how to do that:

- Change the conversation with your child from the college application process to the experience of college itself. Ask your child questions about what he or she wants to accomplish at college. What is his or her bucket list for college—the ten must-have experiences? Find out what your child imagines happening in his or her first semester at college. The last semester? Invite your child to map the path from college to his or her dream life.

- Temper your child's belief (and maybe your own) that getting into College X secures a perfect and happy future with some reality checks. We all know that being admitted to college goes on no one's résumé—it is graduating from college that counts. And we also all know that what you *do* with the opportunities you encounter in college is at least as important as what opportunities the college offers.

Content Tip #2: Connect College X to Your Goals

It's not enough to say that there's a connection between the two—you have to show it (Ivey Strategy #7). Back up your assertion with examples and reasons. For example, if you want to have internships during college, and College X offers a top-notch internship program, then include that in your answer.

Content Tip #3: Avoid Goals That Are Pageant Answers or Animal House Answers

Pageant answers are goals that are so lofty ("world peace") or so banal ("balance between academic and social life") that no admissions officer thinks they're real. They come across as goals found on some website entitled "Goals That Will Impress Adults." *Animal House answers* are goals that reveal that you have one overarching goal for college: to party. It is fine to have goals related to your social life, and you can even include a goal of this nature in your answer, as long as it is not your only or dominant goal.

Content Tip #4: Do Your Research

Do you know enough about College X that you can demonstrate genuine interest? What makes College X different from the other colleges of its kind? What are the signature programs at College X? What is College X's motto and how does that come through in its culture? Show your interest by showing that you actually know something about College X.

Content Tip #5: Be Specific and Personal

It is not enough to identify what makes College X interesting in general; you need to specify why College X is interesting to you in particular. Maybe it's the massive library where you could get lost in the stacks. Maybe it's the dining hall with vegan options. Maybe it's the creative writing instructor who happens to be your favorite author. Whatever it is, name it. (In case you were wondering, being interested in the college because of its ranking is not specific or personal. That may be why you're applying, but it is not enough and not terribly interesting to the college. Do your research and figure out the reasons why it ranks in *your top ten*. That's what will impress admissions officers.)

USE A TEMPLATE

Tim, of Duke-Northwestern fame, thought he *was* working smarter instead of harder (Ivey Strategy #1). He thought that writing one answer and then using the find-and-replace function to swap out the school names was doing exactly that. It sure did reduce his writing time considerably! But was he really working smarter? Not so much. In fact, we'd say that Tim's approach is a good example of working dumber.

In order to be able to use the find-and-replace tool, Tim had to make his answer generic enough to fit every college on his list. That basically guaranteed that he would not produce a high-quality answer. A generic answer violates everything we've just said about content. His *one* essay, even customized with the college's name, couldn't possibly answer the question asked or be specific. As we noted at the beginning of this chapter, the "Why College X?" questions vary considerably in their specific wording. They are not all the same question, so you can't use the same answer. It's not smart to sacrifice quality in an effort to do less work. (To make matters worse, Tim also failed in executing his tactic by being sloppy with find and replace.)

There is a better way to approach these questions—a way that truly is working smarter, not harder, and that is to *use a template*. A template will result in an answer that follows a predetermined pattern for answering the question, but the details you fill in will vary from school to school. To help you see what a template is like, we've provided outlines for three samples, each with slightly different approaches.

Template #1: The Week in the Life Template

Imagine a week in your life at College X.

- Describe the classes you'd be taking (real ones from course catalog), your major, and any special programs you're pursuing, such as internships.

- Talk about the activities you'd be involved with outside the classroom—clubs, teams, college sports fandom, and so on.

- Describe what makes college life at College X so very sweet. The great outdoors? Its educational philosophy? Its traditions? And so on.

Template #2: Burning Qualities Template

Think back to your visits to the school or research you've done. Describe the three to five burning qualities of that college that made you want to add it to your list. We've given you some prompts that will elicit the burning qualities, but there are a gazillion that would work. What keeps this template answer from reading like blah, blah, blah is using prompts that are more conversational in tone.

- I knew College X was for me when . . .
- I only got more excited after . . .
- The minute I saw, heard, felt, learned . . . College X became my top-choice college.
- I wasn't sure about College X until . . .
- The only real concern I had about College X was put to rest when . . .
- College X is the one and only college where . . .

Template #3: Gets Me Where I'm Going Template

Describe your goals for life after college and explain how College X is instrumental to your achieving those goals. We recommend this approach only if you have specific life goals *and* the college offers something distinctively suited to achieving those goals.

- Describe your life goal(s).
- Articulate the path you have mapped out for achieving those goals.
- Explain why College X offers a distinctive program or opportunity that is critical to your achieving your goals.

Whatever template you use or come up with on your own, here are some tips to follow *in order*.

Template Tip #1: Determine Whether You Are Creating a Short Answer Template or an Essay Template or Both

Remember that a short answer and an essay are not the same thing, and we've given you different guidelines and tips for each. Refer back to chapter 10 if you are working on a short answer template and chapter 11 if you are working on an essay template.

Template Tip #2: Choose an Organizational Structure for Your Template Answer

A template is largely defined by its structure. For example, you might choose a story as your structure (as template tip #1 does), or you might choose a narrated list as your structure, or come up with some other organizational structure entirely. Whatever your structure, make sure it aligns well with your content.

Template Tip #3: Draft and Test Your Template

Draft the template as a set of fill-in-the-blank sentences and then test it by filling in those blanks for one college on your list. Does it work? Does it include the content that you developed? Or is it not really working as well as you thought it would? You may need to refine your template a few times before it starts coming together.

CHECK YOUR FACTS AND PROOFREAD

Tim's answer went from bad to worse because he failed to sweat the details (Ivey Strategy #5). You know better. In fact, you know that the details can work in your favor. They can take your answer from good to great if you pay attention to them.

First, make sure to double-check your facts. Whatever you say about College X needs to be true about College X. Take the time to verify everything that you have said, and get it right. That is how you impress the admissions officer that you really do know College X. For example, if your answer says you want to major in biology at Brown, you've blown your chance to impress because Brown doesn't have majors; Brown has concentrations. So your answer should say you want to *concentrate* in biology at Brown. Sure, majors and concentrations are basically the same thing, but using Brown's terminology shows that you have really done your homework about Brown, and that demonstrates your genuine interest in Brown. Little details like that can take your answer from good to great.

And we'll bang this drum one more time: *proofread!* Errors will count against you, and proofreading is the only way to make your answer error free.

TIM'S ANSWER REWORKED

If Tim had employed the Ivey Strategies, using a good template, he could have transformed his "Why College X?" answer into a great one. Here are ways he could have used the templates and the tips and made his answers stand out.

Duke's Question

If you are applying to Trinity College of Arts & Sciences, please discuss why you consider Duke a good match for you. Is there something in particular at Duke that attracts you? Please limit your response to one or two paragraphs. (Duke Supplement to the Common Application, 2012–13)

   Note: In the following answers, the words in italics are the words or sentences that filled in the blanks on Tim's template answer for Duke.

Using Template #1: A Week in the Life

As I walk out of *Biology 89S (my first year seminar)*, I realize that *Duke* is everything I had hoped for academically. Sure, some people might think that *being fascinated by how finches prove Darwin's theory of evolution* is pretty nerdy but I am a bit nerdy when it comes to biology. *In this seminar*, there are other students who are as interested as I am, and we get into great discussions. There is no way I could have had this kind of experience if I were *in a standard Intro Biology lecture class*. And thanks to *Duke's* support for undergraduate research, *I've already secured a lab assistant position for next semester in Volkan Lab (the fruit fly lab)—fruit flies are where the action is when it comes to genetics*. Since I intend to become a geneticist and work on big scientific breakthroughs, getting to *work with fruit flies in a real lab as a first year* is a dream come true for me.

Of course, I don't spend all my time studying *finches* or experimenting with *fruit flies*. I joined the ice hockey *club team* right away. I've played ice hockey since I was old enough to skate, and I was not looking forward to hanging up my skates when I got to college. A *club* team that actually competes *in a real conference* was the answer. The best part for me is that I'm one of the stars of the team: twelve years of Michigan winters pay off! Come *January*, I'll be rushing for a fraternity. Almost all of the men in my father's family have been Kappa Sigs for several generations. They all name their fraternity experience as one of the best parts of college, and my Dad's best friends are guys from his pledge class. So I really want to continue the tradition. *But I confess to being happy that there are no frat houses at Duke. I like that you can live with your brothers, but also be right at the center of the campus.* Yes, *Duke* was in fact the perfect choice for me, both academically and personally.

Using Template #2: Burning Qualities

Duke first got my attention when I learned *about all the opportunities for students to learn from and work alongside world-recognized faculty*. Since I am committed to becoming a world-renowned geneticist myself, I know how important it is *to have these opportunities early*. At *Duke*, I can *start with a first-year seminar taught by one of the full-time faculty in the department—like the course on Darwin's Finches taught by Professor Donohue. As one of only 15 students in the class, I will really get a chance to know the professor in a way that just isn't possible in a giant lecture class.* I have also learned *that, at Duke, undergraduates really do get to do research as early as their first year. I found more than 30 opportunities on the Duke List for research positions in biology, including one in a fruit fly lab—and fruit flies are where the action is when it comes to cutting edge research in genetics, so that would be an exciting thing for me to do.*

But even as attractive as *these academic opportunities* are, I wasn't completely sold on *Duke* until I found out about *the club* ice hockey team, and how the Greek system operates there. I've played ice hockey since I was old enough to skate and I was not looking forward to hanging up my skates when I got to college. A *club* team that *actually competes in a real conference* was the answer. After *e-mailing with the team captain*, I am convinced that I will enjoy playing ice hockey as a *club* sport at *Duke*. As for the Greek system,

I was really impressed *by two things: a January rush and no frat houses.* Because almost all of the men in my father's family have been Kappa Sigs for several generations, and because they name their fraternity experience as one of the best parts of college, I really want to join a fraternity (hopefully Kappa Sig). But I know fraternities can have their downsides, especially if *you rush right away or you move into a frat house off campus.* Since neither happens at *Duke*, it feels as if I will get all of the positives of Greek life without any of the negatives. Unparalleled and distinctive opportunities that seem tailor made for me—that is why I want to attend *Duke*.

Using Template #3: Gets Me Where I Am Going

My goal in life is to become a world-renowned geneticist, while still being a somewhat normal guy who has a life outside the lab too. Some people would probably say that it is arrogant of me to think I could achieve this goal. But I subscribe to the philosophy of Ralph Waldo Emerson, "We aim above the mark to hit the mark." After doing some research into the lives of world-renowned scientists, I have discovered that the path to my goal lies in going to college, then going on to graduate school for a Ph.D., then doing post-doctoral research and then finally getting a faculty appointment or R&D position in industry where I research and publish until my staggering breakthroughs result in my gaining fame and recognition throughout the world. That makes college the next step on the way to my goal. From what I can tell, at college I should learn from faculty who are recognized as the best in their fields and where I can do some meaningful research, publish, and present as an undergrad. If I want to be a normal guy too, then the college also needs to offer me an enjoyable life outside the classroom and the lab.

Duke offers everything I need and want both as a developing geneticist and as a normal guy. Not only do I have access *to lecture courses* with world-renowned faculty, I actually *will be able to take seminar courses* from them and work alongside them in the lab starting *in my first year.* For example, I can take *first-year seminars taught by full-time Biology faculty—like the seminar offered on Darwin's Finches taught by Professor Donohue. As one of only 15 students in the class, I will really get a chance to know the professor in a way that just isn't possible in a giant lecture class.* I can also do research *as early as my first year.* I have set my sights on working *in a fruit fly lab during college, because fruit flies are where the action is when it comes to cutting edge research in genetics.* When I looked for research positions open to undergraduates at *Duke*, I found *more than 30 opportunities, including one in a fruit fly lab.* When I am not learning or researching, I can, in fact, be a normal guy at *Duke*. I can play ice hockey on the *club* team, continuing with a sport I've played since I was old enough to skate. I can also rush a fraternity and, if all goes well, continue a multi-generation family tradition by pledging Kappa Sig. Almost all of the men in my father's family have been Kappa Sigs and they all name their fraternity experience as one of the best parts of college, so I want it to be a part of my college experience too. Serious student and scientist by day, ice hockey player and frat boy by night: *Duke* is the college where that is possible, and that's why it is the college for me.

CHAPTER 13

Disciplinary and Criminal Background Questions

At the end of every college application lurk two questions that every applicant wants to be able to answer "no" to and breeze on by: the questions about disciplinary and criminal histories. The first question will ask you if you have been in trouble at any school you have attended since ninth grade, and the second question will ask you if you have been in trouble with the law.

If you have encountered either sort of trouble, then you cannot breeze on by these questions. You absolutely do have to sweat the details (Ivey Strategy #5) because you can't wish that history away, and you have to deal with it if you are going to have any hope of admission to a selective college.

You probably already understand that having a disciplinary or criminal record reduces your chances for admission dramatically at a selective college. But many applicants do not really understand exactly why. They have trouble thinking like an admissions officer (Ivey Strategy #2) because they are so anchored in their own points of view about their particular situation. But if you are going to make a case for admission, you really do have to understand why admissions officers take any disciplinary or criminal record so very seriously. We know because we've been admissions officers, and we've had to read these kinds of disclosures and make some hard admissions decisions around them, so we are going to share what we know with you frankly and directly so that you can report about this part of your background in the most constructive way possible.

All admissions officers are keenly aware of their responsibilities as gatekeepers for the college and its community. We certainly were and you would be, too. Think about it. You would not want to be the admissions officer who admitted the student who ended up going on a killing spree, would you? Or the student who became a famous researcher but then turned out to have fabricated his lab results? And if you had known in advance that that student had a previous history of dodgy behavior by virtue of his disciplinary record, how much worse would that look for you as the admissions officer (and the college)? Of course, very few applications raise concerns as extreme as these two examples but some do. And those are the kinds of situations that every admissions officer has in the back of her mind when an applicant shows up with a disciplinary or criminal record.

Admissions officers are very reluctant to offer admission to anyone who could harm the college or its community in any way—be it something as dramatic and serious as killing another member of the community or be it a smaller but still hurtful action that taints the academic integrity of the college or diminishes the reputation of the college in any way. Applicants with a disciplinary or criminal record have a demonstrated history of behavior that has damaged their previous communities, and for that reason, they are high-risk admits as far as admissions officers are concerned.

But admissions officers can and do admit applicants despite disciplinary or criminal records. We both did, and other admissions officers have, too. In fact, some of the most inspiring applications we have read came from applicants who presented clear and convincing cases that they had earned a second chance. They demonstrated that they had learned from their mistakes and persuaded us that they would make a positive contribution to our academic communities and beyond.

We will not sugarcoat, though. If you have a disciplinary or criminal record, you have a big hurdle to overcome in order to be admitted to a selective college. If you are up for the challenge, we are going to show you how to increase your odds of clearing that hurdle.

Most important, if you are going to be admitted in spite of a disciplinary or criminal record, the admissions officer must have reason to believe that you will never, ever, be in serious trouble again. The foundation of your case—and you are indeed making a case and an argument on your own behalf—must be the *subsequent actions* you have taken and lessons you have learned. Here are tips on how to show, not tell (Ivey Strategy #7) that you have put the past behind you and that you are ready, willing, and able to make a positive contribution to the college community.

Records Tip #1: Change Your Behavior

Bad behavior got you into trouble. The only way you are going to get and stay out of trouble is to change your behavior. In all likelihood, in order to change your behavior, you will have to address some underlying problems or issues in your life. What problems or issues precipitated you getting in trouble in the first place? Whatever they are, you must deal with them. Did you cheat on an exam because you couldn't handle the pressure to perform? Then you'll have to figure out more constructive ways to handle pressure (because pressure doesn't go away once you graduate from high school). Do you have a substance abuse problem? Get sober. Did you get an in-school suspension because you hit another student? Learn to control your temper. Did you get caught shoplifting because you wanted to be accepted within a group that wore clothes you couldn't afford? Find a different way to get the clothes, or find a different group to hang with.

Until you change your behavior, you have not really addressed exactly those things that will concern an admissions officer. If the bad behavior persists or the underlying problems and issues are not resolved, then you will be a repeat offender. And that means you are inadmissible. Period. So do what it takes to change your behavior, because if you haven't changed your behavior by the time you apply, an admissions officer will not take a chance on you.

Parent Tip: Look Forward, not Backward

Parents find themselves in a very difficult situation when their child gets into serious trouble during high school. We hear from parents in this situation that they are very unclear about what they can and should do to help their children navigate their way through the trouble to the other side. They don't want to be too strict, and they don't want to be too lenient. In practice, finding the right

(continued)

---

sweet spot is tricky. We use these guidelines to help parents devise strategies in these types of situations.

First, get help. This is not the time to go it alone or do it yourself—for either you or your child. Nor is it a time when you are in the best position to be your child's primary advisor. It is virtually impossible for a loving parent to see these emotionally charged and high-stakes situations clearly, and your child is certainly not equipped to manage without good counsel from an adult.

Second, "the only way round is through" (thank you, Robert Frost). Like it or not, there is no way round this situation; there is only a way through it. So support your child in moving through it without suffering from disproportionate consequences. For example, is there a way that the trouble can be resolved without creating a permanent record for your child? That is often possible both in school and criminal proceedings. (Judges often have a fair amount of discretion in juvenile sentencing.) Being able to have a record expunged after a certain period gives your child a fresh start at a defined point in the future. Some graduate school applications and professional certification boards might still ask about expunged records, but expungement is better than nothing, and just being able to say that something is expunged often helps.

Third, replace the phrase *get back on track* with *chart a new course* in your conversations with your child. Metaphors are great tools for giving people guidance in difficult situations. Although *get back on track* is the metaphor that we hear most frequently from applicants and parents, it is not descriptive or helpful here. *Get back on track* implies that there is only one track leading to admission at a selective college (and success in life), but that is not the case. Your child is now on a different track, but that does not mean the destination needs to change. By contrast, *chart a new course* acknowledges that the circumstances have forced a new course, but it also assumes that there are multiple courses to the same destination. And whereas *get back on track* implies a return to a previous state that no longer exists, *chart a new course* acknowledges the new reality and orients to the future. Your child has encountered trouble, and there is no going back to the pretrouble world, but there is going forward to a post-trouble world.

Records Tip #2: Build an After Record

Once you have changed your behavior, you need to *prove* that you have really changed. You need to build enough of a record so that an admissions officer can believe that you had a problem in the past but that you have addressed it, and that you will not ever have that problem again. Time is your friend in this case. The longer the period of time between your bad behavior and your application, the better.

As a general rule, you need at least a year to build an after record that is sufficient. However, that window can vary considerably depending on the circumstances. For example, if you are serving a probated sentence for a crime, you may have to wait out your probation period before you can build a sufficient after record.

Records Tip #3: Disclose What You Are Required to Disclose

The disclosure questions on college applications are not meant to be confessionals. You are not being asked to belabor every time you were reprimanded by a teacher at school or every prank you ever pulled. Rather, the disclosure questions are designed to elicit disclosure of the times when you have been in *serious* trouble. Read the questions carefully and see if the problems you have had are serious enough to require disclosure.

When it comes to disciplinary records at school, here are the general guidelines we give to applicants about what they must disclose:

- Disclose any incident at school that resulted in one of these disciplinary actions: probation, suspension, removal, dismissal, or expulsion.

- Disclose any incident at school that is a part of your permanent record and is noted on your transcript.

- Disclose any incident at school that will be disclosed by your counselor on the school report.

When it comes to criminal records, we advise that applicants consult with a lawyer about what to disclose. The words used in the questions about criminal backgrounds have technical legal meanings, and the meanings can vary from state to state and jurisdiction to jurisdiction. Don't guess at what you have to disclose.

(You don't want to overdisclose or underdisclose.) Be sure to give your lawyer the exact language on each application because each disclosure requirement may be different.

Records Tip #4: Explain in a Supplemental Essay

Most applications will ask that you provide some additional information about any disciplinary or criminal record you have to disclose. Some give you further instructions about what information to include; others do not. You should, of course, follow whatever instructions you are given. But regardless of the instructions or lack of instructions, you should think like an admissions officer (Ivey Strategy #2) and remember to show, not tell (Ivey Strategy #7) as you put together your supplemental essay. If you are thinking like an admissions officer, you know that your essay must *persuade* the admissions officer that you have earned a second chance. And if you remember to show, not tell, then you are going to write a supplemental essay that demonstrates your worthiness through the *content, tone,* and *specificity* of your essay.

We recommend that your supplemental essay consist of three parts. The first part should be a straightforward presentation of the facts. Avoid excuse making or trying to justify your bad behavior. Just describe what happened. As you are presenting the facts, your tone should be neutral. Avoid any language that sounds defensive or blame shifting. Also avoid any language that sounds like you are trying to evade responsibility or that you are being technically accurate but not truthful. You want to leave the admissions officer with the sense that he or she has gotten the whole story and that you have taken full responsibility for your actions. If the admissions officer feels as if you are hiding anything or trying to shirk responsibility, he will doubt that you have learned from your mistakes and will consider you likely to repeat your bad behavior. In that case, you will be denied.

The second part of the essay should address what actions you have taken to repair the damage you did, detail your after record of good behavior, and demonstrate that you have changed your behavior permanently. Implicitly, you are also demonstrating that you now have better *judgment.* Did you make payment to the store for the item you stole? Did you apologize to the person you intimidated and degraded in a derogatory e-mail that you sent to the whole school? What actions have you taken to address the underlying problems that precipitated your bad behavior? What evidence is there that you have been on good behavior for a significant period of time? Put every fact that supports your case in this second part of your essay; *show* that you have truly changed and grown up.

The third and final part of the essay should be what you have learned from the whole experience. You must be specific here. For example, if you were suspended from school for getting questions on a test ahead of time, what have you learned about what constitutes cheating? And how will you handle it in the future when people ask for an advance peak at the questions for a test you have already taken but they have not?

Records Tip #5: Add Credibility with Supporting Documentation

You can add credibility to the case you are making by providing supporting documentation for the admissions officer to evaluate. This documentation is another way of showing, not telling (Ivey Strategy #7). Gather any documentation that can validate what you have reported in your supplemental essay or that can offer another trustworthy person's endorsement of how much you have changed.

For example, it would go a long way with the admissions officer if you can get a recommendation from the teacher who turned you in for cheating, in which she explains how you won back her trust and how she then selected you as one of her exam proctors. It really helps when a third party (someone other than you) can validate your turnaround. Likewise, you could provide documentation of your successful completion of the community service project you undertook to restore the parts of the park you destroyed when you careened through it in an off-road vehicle while drunk. That, too, would help make your case to the admissions officer.

Records Tip #6: Don't Make Your Disciplinary or Criminal Record the Focus of Your Application

You must have a story to tell that is bigger than the bad stuff. Look back to your story (Ivey Strategy #3) and focus your application on these positive things about you. For example, you should focus your personal essay on how you led the basketball team to its first-ever state championship, not on your criminal conviction. Discuss the criminal conviction in your supplemental essay instead.

Records Tip #7: Schedule a Personal Interview with an Admissions Officer if Possible

A personal encounter can be very persuasive and can go a long way to convincing the admissions officer to take a chance on you, so if you have an opportunity to interview with an admissions officer, seize it! Focus the interview on all the good things about you, but also take some part of the interview to address your disciplinary or criminal record. If the admissions officer does not raise questions about it, you should call it to his or her attention. (She's going to find out eventually anyway, so you may as well deal with it in person rather than just in writing.) Let the admissions officer ask all the questions he or she has. If you handle those questions well, you will have helped your case considerably.

Records Tip #8: Consider Your Alternatives before Forging Ahead with Plan A

Like it or not, a disciplinary or criminal record can make plan A so unlikely that you are better off pursuing plan B, C, or D. Many applicants with records are so eager to get past their problems that they lose sight of their ultimate goals and don't take the time to consider alternative paths that would position them better to reach those goals. If your ultimate goal is to get a degree from a selective college, then there are a few alternatives you should consider:

- *Plan B:* Delay your application for a year. Do a postgraduate year or take a gap year and apply during that year instead of your twelfth grade year. It will give you one more year to build your after record.

- *Plan C:* Start at another college and then pursue transferring. If you need more than a year of time to build your after record, then consider starting college at a less selective college and then applying to a more selective college as a transfer student. In addition to giving you more time to build your after record, this option also gives you a chance to cultivate recommenders who only know you after. You effectively get to prove yourself at an easier college.

- *Plan D:* Leave the most selective colleges for graduate school. If things have gone way wrong, then you may need to focus your energies on building your after record at a college that will be less intense. If you do well there, then you can return to the world of selective colleges for graduate school. College is *not* your last chance at a top university.

Records Tip #9: Update Your Application if You Encounter Trouble after You Submit It

Some applicants are under the mistaken impression that once they have submitted their applications, they are home free. Wrong. You are under an ongoing obligation to update your application should anything change postsubmission. That means if you get in the kind of trouble you would have been required to disclose before you submitted your application, you have to update your application and disclose it when it happens. This obligation continues up until the day you enroll at the college. Furthermore, your high school counselor has a similar obligation and will make at least two updates to the school report throughout the year. So there is no way for you to hide. If you do encounter trouble in your senior year, then you should definitely consider your alternatives before forging ahead with plan A (see records tip #8). You should also give serious thought to withdrawing your application before a decision is made. Once a college has denied you, and that denial is, at least in part, linked to a disciplinary or criminal record, it is virtually impossible to reapply and be accepted. If, however, you withdraw yourself from consideration, you will be able to start with a clean slate if and when you reapply.

CHAPTER 14

Miscellaneous Other Questions

Believe it or not, the preceding chapters have not addressed every single question you will find on your application. There are still more. They show up in different places and can be lumped together in odd ways. They range from questions about your career interests to your intentions regarding financial aid to whether you are applying Early Action or Early Decision.

These questions seem like trivial, can't-go-wrong questions to most applicants. But if you are thinking like an admissions officer (Ivey Strategy #2), you realize that no question on your application is trivial. Admissions officers don't have time for trivial questions. Every question on your application serves a specific purpose, and every answer you give will be used in some way. So before you blithely answer the trivial, can't-go-wrong questions, we want to give you some insight into the various questions: why they are being asked and how admissions officers will use them.

QUESTIONS THAT GET YOUR APPLICATION INTO THE RIGHT PILE

You probably haven't given much thought to the administrative chores involved in sorting thousands of applications in the right piles for evaluation. But we can tell you (as can anyone who has worked in admissions) that applications have to go into the right piles.

What do we mean when we say *right piles?* We mean that your application has made it to the people who will evaluate it. We use the language *piles,* because back in the dark ages of paper applications, there were literally piles of applications that would be delivered to a particular admissions officer or to a particular admissions team for evaluation. Now it is probably more accurate to refer to a *queue,* because the piles now usually exist as a set of queued electronic files. But the chore is the same: your application comes in and needs to be delivered to the right people for evaluation.

Obviously, you want your application to get into the right pile. For example, you want your Early Decision application to be evaluated in the Early Decision round. And you want your application to the Engineering School to be sent to the Engineering School's admissions team, not the admissions team evaluating applications to the College of Arts and Sciences. To ensure that your application gets into the right pile, pay attention to the following questions and make sure your answers reflect your intentions properly.

College

Here you are indicating the name of the college for which you are completing these questions. (*Note:* On the Common Application, you simply need to confirm the selection that has already been filled in for you.)

Divisions within the College

If the college to which you are applying requires you to apply to a *particular division (sometimes called a* school) *within the college,* you will usually find a question about asking you which school you are applying to. Make sure you select the right school at the college so that your application goes to the School of Engineering and not to the School of Agricultural Sciences. And be sure to double-check that the program you want is actually housed at that division. Assume nothing, and make sure to check on the college's website. Theater might be housed in the School of the Arts at one college but in the School of Communications at another.

Programs and Majors

This can be the most confusing of all the questions asked on a college application, even though it is not intended to be. The important thing for you to do with the college where you are applying is to figure out whether you have to be admitted into a specific program or major (in addition to being considered for admission to the college overall).

If the college does require you to be admitted to both the program or major *and* the college, then this question is a *right pile* question. For example, if you want to be admitted to the studio art program at a particular college, your application might need to end up in the studio art program pile *in addition* to the general admission pile. However, if the college does not restrict admission to particular programs and majors, then you should treat these questions the same as academic interests questions; more on those in the following section of the chapter.

The most important advice we can give you for these questions is the following: *Don't try to outfox the system.* Once applicants understand the concept of the piles and that there are varying levels of selectivity for different divisions, programs, or majors at a particular college, they sometimes think that they might be able to outfox the system. Their reasoning goes like this: "I need to get myself into the pile that has the highest chance for admission. I know that there is a higher chance of admission to program A than to program B at that college. So even though I want to study at program B, I will apply to program A. Then once I'm in program A, I'll just switch from program A to program B."

But guess what? You won't be the first applicant to think of that. So do you think colleges really allow it to work that way? Of course not. You can't just hop from program to program or from major to major at colleges where entry to the particular school, program, or major is restricted. It can be done but it is not easy. (You typically have to apply like any other transfer student to make the switch.) So if you really want to study at program B, then apply to program B.

Entry Term

This is where you indicate when you intend to start college. Don't accidentally check *spring* if you want your application to be evaluated for the fall term.

Decision Plan

Early Action, Early Decision, or Regular Decision? Early Action One or Two? Early Decision One or Two? The best thing to do is to make this question the *last one you answer* before you submit. Once you have submitted, the only way to undo it is to contact the colleges directly. Avoid that scenario.

Full Time, Degree Seeking

Are you applying for the full-time program, and are you seeking a degree? Unless you are applying for a part-time or nondegree program, then your answer to both of these questions is "yes."

ACADEMIC AND CAREER INTERESTS

For a variety of reasons, there are questions that applicants consider irrelevant to telling their story (Ivey Strategy #3), when they are anything but. Two of those types of questions are questions about your academic and career interests. Seize them!

Academic Interests

What interests you right now? We hope you are actually interested in something of an academic nature; otherwise, college is going to be bleak for you. So name your genuine academic interest rather than squandering the opportunity by giving a nonanswer answer like *undecided*. Look at your story and see if there are some obvious academic interests. List those. Alternatively, pick your favorite class this term and list that as an academic interest. And don't be afraid to pick a third academic interest that is a total wild card—something that interests you but that you really know little about. That is, by definition, an interest. So list that.

And don't get freaked that you are committing yourself to a particular course of study when you choose academic interests. You aren't. At least you aren't with your answer to a true academic interest question (see the section previously in the chapter about programs and majors questions that do mean you are making commitments). It is simply a question about your interests.

Career Interests

You may also be given an opportunity to indicate your career interests. Answering this question should be ridiculously easy: all you have to do is refer back to the last sentence of your story. But what if you left that sentence out of your story because you don't really know yet? You have a couple of options.

Explore Some Career Interests

You can go online and do a little research into careers. In fact, you will find tools to do this on the College Board's website (www.collegeboard.org) as well as many colleges' websites. You can see what resources are offered by your high school's counseling office. In most cases, your school will offer you some assistance either through personal counseling or some sort of self-guided exploration. You should be able to identify several potential careers for yourself. And remember, you are simply indicating interest; these answers do not bind you to anything for life or even for the following year!

Answer *Undecided* or *Unknown*

When it comes to the question about career interests, we think it is okay to choose *undecided* or *unknown*, even though we said you shouldn't do that in the question about academic interests. At this point in your life, you have enough experience as a student that you can and should express some preferences about what academic subjects you enjoy and will perhaps pursue as majors in college. But you might not yet have enough experience to draw on when it comes to determining your career interests. In that case, it's fine to answer *undecided* or *unknown*. It will not be held against you.

As you consider your answers to academic and career interest questions, here are some tips to guide you.

Interests Tip #1: Align Your Interests Answers with Your Story and with Each Other

If your story is that you are a science type who wants to become a doctor, then your academic interests should probably be in the sciences and your career interests should include medicine. You are not trying to show the wide breadth and range of your interests here; you are trying to tell your story (Ivey Strategy #3).

Interests Tip #2: There Are No Right Answers to the Interests Questions

Students are often under the mistaken impression that there are right and wrong academic or career interests, that the right interests get you in, and the wrong interests keep you out. But that's not how it works. Admissions officers are not looking for a particular answer to these questions; they are simply curious about whether you have an answer. If you do, that gives the admissions officer one more piece of information to use in building a profile of who you are.

QUESTIONS THAT CHANGE YOUR CHANCES OF ADMISSION

As you already know, admissions officers consider factors beyond the core three dimensions (academic, extracurricular, and personal) when making admissions decisions. The four most common additional factors are demographics, demonstrated interest, ability to pay, and flags on your file (see chapter 5). The questions we cover in this section all relate to these additional kinds of factors (although most of the questions related to demographics are covered in chapter 6, and we won't revisit them here).

Residency Questions (Demographic Factor)

Because public colleges have a mission to educate the citizens of the state where the college is located, all public colleges give preferential treatment to state residents in the admissions process. Some private colleges also give preferential treatment to residents of particular states (usually for some financial reason).

Consequently, you will find questions about your residency status on many college applications. These questions will inquire about where you were born, where you have resided, and how long you lived in the state. For many of you, residency is simply a given; you have always resided in the same state. However, for some of you, residency may be more complicated. Perhaps you have divorced parents who live in different states and share custody, so you have a plausible claim to residency in two states. If you have any special circumstances regarding residency, and your residency matters, then you should definitely do your research and find out what your residency is and how you should answer the residency questions to your best advantage.

Demonstrated Interest Questions

You will also find questions on many applications that relate to your demonstrated interest in the college. These are the questions such as, "How did you learn about the college?" or "Have you visited the college?"

Parent Tip: The College Visit That Matters

At some colleges on your child's list, demonstrated interest might be a factor in admissions decisions (see chapter 5), and at those colleges, a visit matters. It is counted in your child's favor, so try to schedule visits to those colleges. The best time for those visits is sometime in the summer before or early in the fall of the senior (twelfth grade) year. Obviously, visits can be expensive and difficult to arrange, so before you scramble to arrange visits for every college on the list, do some double-checking to make sure that demonstrated interest really is a factor (the college websites will usually tell you, and if they don't, call the admissions office to find out).

It is sometimes difficult to distinguish demonstrated interest questions, which are evaluative and will be considered by the admissions officer when making his or her decision, and marketing questions, which are nonevaluative and will not be considered by the admissions officer when making his or her decision. Common Application 4.0 specifically prohibits colleges from asking marketing questions, so if you encounter a question on the Common App or on a college's writing supplement that asks anything about your contact with the college or interest in the college, you should assume it is a demonstrated interest question and that your answer may influence the decision on your application. On other applications, take the better-safe-than-sorry approach and assume that all of these questions count.

Why do colleges consider your demonstrated interest? Because it matters to the college's ranking and reputation. Here's how. Applicants with higher demonstrated interest are more likely to say "yes" if offered admission, which means the college has a higher yield (the percentage of students who accept their offers of admission). The higher the college's yield, the fewer offers of admission the college has to make. The fewer offers the college makes, the higher the college's selectivity rating and the higher the selectivity rating, the higher the college's ranking and reputation.

The bottom line for your purposes? The higher your demonstrated interest, the better your chances for admission, so you want to make the most of whatever you have done that demonstrates your interest. Answer all of these questions with that goal in mind. Give more than a one-word answer, when possible. Take advantage of opportunities over the next few months to do things that will enable you to answer more of these questions with positive proof that you are definitely interested. For example, do go to the college fair, and do meet with the admissions representative who comes to your school.

The Fake Demonstrated Interest Question

One question that you may see on applications is, "Where else are you applying to college?" Colleges love to know where else applicants are applying, because it can help their marketing efforts if they know who their competition is. Some applicants assume that this is a demonstrated interest question and worry about their answers to it. But this is a pure marketing question and does not bear on your admission to the college. Given the prohibition on marketing questions by colleges using Common Application 4.0, we expect this question to disappear from many college applications. For those where it does appear, we recommend that you give a polite but very general answer such as, "I'm applying to nine other colleges," or "I intend to apply to five to eight colleges with strong programs in engineering."

Need-Based Financial Aid Questions

Colleges might ask you questions about your intentions regarding applying for need-based financial aid. It is simply a "yes" or "no" question that inquires whether you intend to apply for need-based financial aid. Most applicants assume that it is a purely administrative question that allows the admissions office to coordinate with the financial aid office. That is indeed one purpose of the question. But for some colleges, as we explained in chapter 5, your ability to pay will be factored into the admissions decision. By definition, a student who has the ability to pay the tuition does not qualify for need-based financial aid because such aid will be awarded only if the student has financial need. Colleges therefore describe their policies with regard to ability to pay as *need blind* or *need aware*. At need-blind colleges, the need for financial aid *is not* considered in the admissions process. At need-aware colleges, the need for financial aid *is* considered in the admissions process. Some colleges are need blind until decisions are being made about the wait list and then they become need aware. The best way to find out the college's policy is to ask directly; most will be forthcoming. If they do not clearly answer that they are a need-blind college, then assume the college is need aware.

If the college is need aware, then how you answer this financial aid question can change your chances for admission. Your chances will be higher if you answer "no." Obviously, if you do need financial aid, then you have to answer the question "yes." But if you have the luxury of a choice, then you might be better off (for admissions purposes) answering the question "no."

(Note that colleges may also ask you about your intention to apply for merit-based financial aid. That *is* purely an administrative question, so we do not address it here and you should simply answer it.)

Legacy or Child of Faculty or Staff Questions (Flags on the File)

Most colleges ask whether you are related to anyone who either attended the college or works for the college in order to determine if you have what they call *legacy status.* If you do, then your file may be flagged for preferential treatment in the application process. As we have already explained in chapter 5, how much this particular flag changes your chances of admission varies considerably depending on the college's policies. Regardless of the amount of benefit you will get from this flag on your file, you should scour your family tree for people with relationships to the colleges where you are applying. List them all. The only time you should decline to name a person is if that person brought shame to the college or the relationship between that person and the college ended on a very bad note. In that case, it is probably better to keep that relationship to yourself. (Although most colleges will be far more concerned about you than your ancestors, why go there?)

CHAPTER 15

Additional Information Questions

Near the end of almost every college application, you will find a fairly innocuous question that goes something like this: "Do you have anything to add?"

How do most applicants handle that question? They skip it unless they have been instructed elsewhere in the application that they are required to explain something. That is a huge mistake and a squandered opportunity. That little, innocuous-looking question is an opportunity for any applicant who really wants to produce a standout application.

This question *invites* you to make the form work for you (Ivey Strategy #6). It gives you the opportunity you need to explain and to supplement. It is the catch-all that saves you from the limitations of the rest of the application. So what do you have to add? The answer is: you might have *plenty*. Here is a checklist you can go through to figure out what might be beneficial to add so you can make the form work for you!

Be aware that one of the more controversial changes made in Common App 4.0 was the strict character limit placed on the Additional Information section. You can no longer upload documents here, which prevents you from including your résumé and significantly constrains your ability to add an additional essay. So as you work through this checklist, be aware of the limits imposed on the Additional Information question on whatever application you are completing.

REQUIRED EXPLANATIONS

As you have worked your way through the application, you may have discovered that you are required to explain certain responses. For example, if you were out of school for a term or longer, you are asked to give an explanation here (see chapter 7). If you have a disciplinary or criminal record, you must provide the details here (see chapter 13). Obviously, you must do what is required and explain when required to do so.

OPTIONAL EXPLANATIONS OR EXTRA INFORMATION

Beyond the explanations or information you are required to provide, you may have discovered that there are questions for which you wanted to explain further or give extra information, but the form did not permit it. For example, you might want to say more about a particular academic honor (see chapter 7) or you might want to list more or different family members than you could in response to the factual questions about your family (see chapter 6). The Additional Information question is your chance to offer these optional explanations and provide extra information. Make use of it!

SUPPLEMENTAL STATEMENTS OR ESSAYS

A supplemental statement or essay is occasionally warranted, but it should never be included "just because." Consider including a supplemental essay when you want to address some aspect of your story (Ivey Strategy #3) that you did not make the subject of your personal essay *and* when the Additional Information section provides you with sufficient opportunity to say what you need to say. When would that happen? As noted in chapter 11, this most often happens when you want to speak to a particular personal situation, but you do not want it to be the main focus of your application.

For example, Jay has a mild case of stuttering that shaped his character in some essential ways. It gave him compassion for others and motivated him to become a research scientist focused on finding ways to prevent and treat neurological disorders. But Jay did not want to make his stuttering the topic of his personal essay, because he had successfully regulated it, and it really hadn't been a big part of his life over the last several years. An admissions officer wouldn't really be able to understand who Jay was without knowing about this part of his background, so the perfect solution was a very brief supplemental essay that he included as additional information.

Reflect on your story and see if there is any critical component that you feel must be included but that shouldn't be the topic of your personal essay or another essay. If so, then determine whether you can fully address it in the Additional Information section. If so, then a supplemental essay is the solution for you, too!

YOUR RÉSUMÉ

That's right, your résumé. If you can upload a document, we suggest you submit your résumé even though you may have included much of the information on it elsewhere in the application. It can provide additional information that is really helpful to admissions officers, and for that reason it is generally welcomed by them. (See more about this in chapters 4 and 16.)

Here are a few tips to ensure that you make the Additional Information question work for you.

ADDITIONAL INFORMATION TIPS

Additional Information Tip #1: If You Are Asked to Upload a Document in Response to the Question, Combine All the Additional Information into a Single PDF Document

If the Additional Information question is a general one and it allows you to upload a document in response, you will probably be limited to a *single uploaded document*. So if you have more than one thing to add, then you need to combine them all into one document. We suggest that you put a table of contents on the first page of the document so that the admissions officer understands right away that you are including multiple items in one document. There will be limits on the size of the document and the format of the document so you will need to work within those limits. Once your document is complete, be sure to convert it to a PDF to avoid glitches that can arise with documents uploaded in other formats.

Additional Information Tip #2: Respect the College's Policies on Supplementary Materials in General

If the college says that they do not want an art portfolio, they do not want an art portfolio, and in that case you should not attach one in the Additional Information section either. (See more about supplementary materials in chapter 16.)

Additional Information Tip #3: Restrain Yourself When It Comes to Explanations Regarding Your Academic Record

Don't go overboard with the explanations (especially when it comes to your grades or test scores). If an explanation is required, give one, but don't use this section to explain common bumps in the road. *Examples:* that one B on your transcript or the lower test score on the science section of the ACT. Those situations do not require or need explanation. Yet often applicants obsess about every flaw or imperfection they see on their records, and they want to explain them. If you feel that impulse, resist it. No applicant is perfect. Admissions officers know that and are not seeking perfection. Your attempt to be perfect and explain away every flaw will only distract the admissions officer from seeing the best parts of you and make him or her worry about your stress levels!

Parent Tip: Restrain Yourself, Too

Parents sometimes are as guilty as their children when it comes to going overboard with explanations. It is often Mom or Dad who thinks that a paragraph about being a poor test taker is an important addition to the application. If you are one of these parents, you need to check yourself because too much explaining makes a bad impression and is sometimes worse than no explaining at all.

CHAPTER 16

Supplementary Materials

Back in the dark ages, when all applications were completed on paper and snail-mailed(!), the Common Application had just launched with fifteen intrepid participating colleges, and the number of applicants was approximately one-half of the total today. Back then, the conventional wisdom was that supplementary materials could make or break you. Hours and hours were devoted to thinking about how to send exactly the right supplementary materials. Stories (usually urban legends) circulated about the clever Cajun applicant from Louisiana who sent over a king's cake with her application baked inside it. (King's cake is served at Mardi Gras and usually has a trinket hidden inside.) Or how about the one about the applicant who sent a patent for a better mousetrap along with a prototype for use and testing by admissions officers?

But that was then and this is now. Applications are now completed online and submitted electronically, the Common Application is used by five hundred colleges, and the applicant pool is still growing thanks to the forward momentum of population growth and globalization. Supplementary materials are now considered much differently. The baked goods and mousetraps are now nothing but a *big headache* for admissions officers trying to process tens of thousands of applications. Instead of impressing admissions officers, baked goods and mouse-traps merely irritate. That's not what you want.

But just because baked goods and mousetraps are out doesn't mean that there is no place for supplementary materials. In fact, many of you will find that you should submit other supplementary materials. So what should you submit? This chapter will cover everything you need to know about preparing and submitting supplementary materials that help you rather than hurt you!

SUPPLEMENTARY MATERIALS DONE RIGHT

More is not always more. More is only more if it really truly *adds* something to your application.

Remember Ivey Strategy #3: the goal of your application is to tell a coherent and compelling story about yourself. Supplementary materials are where some applicants go astray and throw in the kitchen sink. They stick to their stories in the application itself but then decide they will throw in anything that could possibly matter in the supplementary materials.

Their reasoning goes like this: "I can't possibly know what the admissions officer really cares about, so why not add the stuff about scuba diving in the supplementary materials? Maybe I'll get lucky and land with the admissions officer who loves scuba diving more than life itself, and she'll be more impressed by my diving than anything else I reported. So I better just include it here; I'll just throw some more spaghetti at the wall and hope that some of it sticks."

But you know better. Random bits of information about you will not persuade an admissions officer to admit you. What gets you in is a coherent and compelling story about yourself. That story has to be focused and distilled. It does not include every single thing one might ever know about you, and admissions officers don't *want* to know every single thing about you. They only want to know the things that matter in their evaluation. Your story singles out those things, so you can trust it as your guide. If the supplementary materials don't relate to your story, then they don't belong anywhere in your application, including the supplementary materials.

Even if the supplementary materials relate to your story, they may not add much to your application except bulk. If you are thinking like an admissions officer (Ivey Strategy #2), you know that bulk doesn't help you. It is quality, not quantity, that counts. Unless your supplementary materials add new, different, or better information to your application, they are bulk. More of the same is not more.

Supplementary materials done right enhance your application. They show, rather than tell (Ivey Strategy #7) the admissions officer something about you that he wouldn't know otherwise. They call out and highlight something important about you, something that matters to admissions officers.

SUPPLEMENTARY MATERIALS TO CONSIDER

There are seven basic types of supplementary materials that you should consider as possibilities:

- Your résumé
- Arts portfolios
- Athletic statistics, clip reels, or other recruiting information
- Samples of academic work
- Abstracts of scientific research and scientific research papers
- Additional essays
- Newspaper clippings, certificates, or other documentation of accomplishments

Notice that all of these materials can be prepared and submitted in an electronic format, and that is one major factor that distinguishes them from the baked goods, mousetraps, and other supplementary materials of yore.

Which supplementary materials should you prepare and submit? Use these tips to guide you.

Supplement Tip #1: Submit if Required

Read the instructions and all parts of each application thoroughly to see if the application requires any supplementary materials. Look for any question asking you to address something in a required explanation or an Additional Information section or any instructions to submit something beyond the application itself. Sarah Lawrence, for example, requires that all applicants submit a sample of analytic writing. If you are applying to an arts program, it is likely that you will be asked to provide a portfolio of some sort. And don't overlook the questions that require you to write a brief explanation in certain circumstances, such as the requirement on the Common Application that you explain any interruptions in your education. (See more about required explanation questions in chapter 17.) Required supplementary materials are just that—required. So you should approach them as you would any other required element of the application. Deploy all of the Ivey Strategies and use the tips appropriate to the various types of supplementary materials to ensure that these materials are just as standout as every other part of your application.

Supplement Tip #2: Submit Nonrequired Supplementary Materials Only if They Are Welcomed and Considered by the College

Applicants often simply assume that any and all supplementary materials are welcomed and will be considered but that is not always the case. Do yourself a favor and do your research before you create optional supplementary materials. If you do your research, you are employing a key Ivey Strategy—working smarter, not harder (Ivey Strategy #1). There is no reason to spend precious time preparing optional supplementary materials that are not welcomed and will not even be considered.

Colleges don't pussyfoot around when it comes to communicating whether optional supplementary materials are welcomed or will be considered. You will find explicit language in their application instructions. The range of possibilities is captured by these instructions from Hamilton, Barnard, and Northwestern (note that these examples come from past application years; they may have changed their precise instructions by the time you apply):

- Hamilton College (welcomed and considered):

  You are invited to submit materials to document your special talent(s), e.g. tapes of individual music performances, slides of artwork, videos of theatre, dance or athletic performances, or samples of creative writing. We will return samples if you

include pre-stamped, self-addressed packing materials.
(Hamilton College Application Instructions)

- Barnard College (welcomed, may or may not be considered):

  Submit supplementary material (art, music, or creative writing) for review.

  Material should be submitted only when it represents a substantial amount of an applicant's time, dedication, and energy. Please note: Supplementary material will not be reviewed by Barnard faculty, and there is no guarantee it will be reviewed by the Admissions Committee. (Barnard College Application Instructions)

- Northwestern University (not welcomed, not considered):

  Unsolicited items, such as artwork or recordings (CDs, DVDs, videotapes, etc.), will not be accepted. (Northwestern University Application Instructions; boldface in the original)

It goes without saying that you should follow the instructions given by the college. Do not submit optional supplementary materials if they are not welcome.

What should you do if the materials are welcomed but may not be considered? That is a judgment call. If you are preparing the materials anyway, you might think, "Why not?" But you might have to make a choice about how to spend your limited time. You can either spend your time focusing on those parts of the application that will definitely be considered and making sure they are in the best possible shape or you can spend your time producing supplementary materials that may or may not be considered. In that case, it's pretty obvious that you should forego the supplementary materials.

Supplement Tip #3: If Possible, Submit Your Résumé

If you have followed our advice about how to create a résumé (chapter 4), your résumé should enhance your application. It absolutely, positively relates to your story and, in all likelihood, includes new, better, or different information than you have been able to include elsewhere in your application. This is particularly true with respect to your activities, especially if you were constrained by character limits on the activities list. If the college permits you to upload a résumé, do it!

In our experience, there is no college or admissions officer who does not welcome or consider a résumé if it is submitted. So uploading one can only benefit you.

Supplement Tip #4: Submit an Optional Arts Portfolio Only if You Have the Talent to Warrant It

Just because you have devoted a major part of your time to a particular endeavor doesn't necessarily mean you should submit a portfolio; you may simply be a dedicated and capable amateur or hobbyist. All of you—whether you are a great talent or dedicated amateur or hobbyist—have already conveyed your talent elsewhere in the application. It is after all part of the core four (passion, talent, initiative, and impact)—that's Ivey Strategy #4. The amateur or hobbyist should stop there.

If you include an arts portfolio, you are asserting that your talent rises to a different level, and you need to be able to back that up because your arts portfolio will be reviewed and evaluated by an expert independently of your application as a whole, and that evaluation will not be sugarcoated. If the expert evaluation comes back low, you have taken what could have been an amazing extracurricular rating and diminished it.

So before you sabotage yourself, get an expert opinion about your talent. Seek out the most impartial and ruthless expert you can find to evaluate your talent because that is also the kind of person who will be evaluating your arts portfolio. Now is not the time to get the opinion of someone who will be nice and emphasize the positive, puffing up your self-esteem and inflating your estimation of your own abilities. Now is the time to get the opinion of someone who will tell the unvarnished truth about your talent.

Parent Tip: Help Your Child Be Realistic about Talents

Your child may or may not have a realistic view of his or her artistic or athletic talents. If he or she has been exposed to or competed at the highest levels of talent, then it is more likely that he or she also has a realistic view. But for most applicants, including your child, his or her experience and feedback to date may have created a distorted sense of his or her talents. For example, your child may indeed be quite competent as an amateur pianist. She may have been playing since age three and had numerous recitals and other performances where she

---

received thundering applause and even a positive review in a local newspaper. But that doesn't mean that an artistic portfolio is warranted. Those would be reserved for the applicants whose talents are on par with someone who could realistically pursue a career as a concert pianist. Likewise, your child may be the most gifted football player in school history, but that doesn't mean that he is necessarily talented enough to be a recruited athlete for a serious Division I football team. (More than a million boys play football at the high school level, and there are fewer than fifteen thousand slots for Division I recruited athletes in football.) If your child has a distorted view of his or her talents, the absolute best thing you can do is support your child in getting an expert evaluation of his or her abilities from someone who can and will provide a more realistic assessment. That set of feedback is invaluable and will help your child considerably.

Supplement Tip #5: Send All Athletic Materials Directly to the Coach

There is no doubt that being a recruited athlete (as defined by NCAA rules) or even a sought-after athlete can enhance your chances for admission, but the way to become a recruited athlete is not by sending supplementary materials that document your athletic abilities to the admissions office because that is an unnecessary and untimely step in the process.

The way it works is this. The athletic recruiting process and the admissions process are two distinct processes that intersect in the fall of the year you are applying. The athletic recruiting process starts earlier and coaches are in charge. The admissions process starts later and the admissions officers are in charge. In the fall of the year you are applying (usually your senior year), the coaches will notify the admissions office about which applicants they would like to have as recruited athletes. The admissions office then evaluates your application with that in mind, which gives a big boost to your likelihood of admission.

So who needs to know what a phenomenal athlete you are? Who needs to get your statistics, clip reels, or other materials you have prepared in the hopes of being a recruited athlete? The coaches!

Because coaches do make their choices early in the fall of the year you are applying, we encourage applicants to contact coaches the year before that (usually your junior year). If you have not already been in touch with coaches, then make those direct contacts as soon as you can.

Supplement Tip #6: Do Submit Scientific Research Abstracts, but Make Sure They Can Be Understood by the Admissions Officer

If you are already a scientist in training and have conducted scientific research beyond the classroom requirements, then you have done things that many don't do until late in their undergraduate careers. You have a head start that suggests you have a promising future as one of the best and brightest scientists of the next generation. So you should absolutely include abstracts of your research as supplementary materials. But remember that an admissions officer must read and understand your abstracts if you are going to really wow her.

You should assume that the admissions officer is *not* a research scientist. You want to be suitably awe inspiring, but you also want the admissions officer to understand what you did and why it matters. The way to strike this balance is to use a format that is used by serious scientific researchers (the "big dogs"), and use language that can be understood by anyone. You can find formats for scientific abstracts by asking your research mentor or simply searching the Internet for samples. You can test whether the language you have used is understandable by asking some lay people (educated nonscientists) to read your abstract and give you some honest feedback about what they understand and don't understand. Parents are often good lay readers, as are English or History teachers.

Supplement Tip #7: Submit Samples of Academic Work Only if Required

There is really no reason to submit samples of your academic work unless they are required. The admissions officer is not going to review and evaluate it on its own academic merits unless that is part of the admissions process at that college. Here's an example.

It was hard for Brad to accept that his A+ paper on the literature of the Civil War South was not really worth submitting along with his application. His teacher had raved about his paper. It clearly showed that he was an excellent writer and a provocative thinker. He had even won an award for it. Brad thought this paper was especially helpful to his admissions case, because he hadn't always been such a great student in English, and he was sure this paper would counterbalance his bad grades from ninth and tenth grades.

We reminded Brad that admissions officers have very limited time to review every application, and that he needed to make his case in a way that consumed as little time as possible for the admissions officer. In other words, he needed to think like an admissions officer (Ivey Strategy #2). We pointed out that there were much better ways for Brad to make his case about his grades and his academic work than submitting a long paper and hoping the admissions officer would read it carefully.

First, Brad should get the teacher to write a recommendation and refer to his paper. The teacher's comments could be expanded to reflect on how far Brad had come as a student overall. That would do far more to counterbalance his early grades than a single grade on a single paper would. Second, he can highlight his success on his paper in both his résumé and in his honors and awards. The application and teacher's recommendation will be read by the admissions officer and will have a positive impact. That is a far better outcome than could be expected from the submission of the one paper, which is highly unlikely to be read.

Supplement Tip #8: Use Additional Essays Sparingly

Applicants often approach additional essays as an extra credit, but they are *not* extra credit. If you are thinking like an admissions officer (Ivey Strategy #2), you understand that the admissions officer is not evaluating your application file on *quantity* of essays produced but instead on *quality* of essays produced. You also understand that an applicant does herself no favors by adding unnecessary bulk to the application file. Therefore, unless you are an applicant whose circumstances warrant an additional essay as part of the Additional Information section (see chapter 15), we advise against it.

Supplement Tip #9: Don't Submit Newspaper Clippings, Certificates, and Other Documentation of That Sort

Some applicants (and many parents) have a scrapbooking mentality when it comes to supplementary materials. They want to include certificates from programs, newspaper articles written about them, and every possible sample of work they have done that has ever been recognized. But none of these supplementary materials really *add* anything; they simply provide evidence or backup for what you have already reported elsewhere, and you need to use your judgment about which parts of the application you choose to back up or document. It does not benefit you to be redundant.

Your application is not a scrapbook, so don't treat it like one, even when you are tempted to do so because the quality of your supplementary materials is high. Here's an example. Beatrice had some of the highest quality supplementary materials we had ever seen. The materials came in the form of a professionally produced PR media kit that Beatrice had prepared for use in her extraordinarily successful entrepreneurial venture. She designed and manufactured bags that she had sold to classmates and others through an Etsy website. When a celebrity bought one of her bags and was then photographed with the bag in a *People* magazine shoot, her business took off. She engaged a professional PR firm, and they worked with her to put together this PR media kit. It was very impressive. Part of Beatrice's success had come from her ability to self-promote, and she thought that the PR media kit would be a perfect set of supplementary materials. Yes or no?

No. Although presented in a sophisticated manner, the PR media kit was nothing more than a scrapbook in disguise. When Beatrice scrutinized the information contained within the PR media kit, she discovered that every piece of information in the kit had already been reported elsewhere in the application. We considered that a victory for Beatrice—she had used her talents at self-promotion and followed the Ivey Strategies in such a way that she didn't *need* the supplementary materials. Submitting them would be unnecessary and would only distract the admissions officer from the fabulous, standout application she already had. Beatrice wasn't trying to sell the admissions officer one of her bags; she was trying to get into college. There's a difference.

Supplement Tip #10: Allow Plenty of Time to Complete Your Supplementary Materials

Supplementary materials often take considerable time to prepare. Portfolios, CDs, websites, and the like usually can't be pulled together in an all-nighter or at the last minute. Start them early and allow yourself a lot of time to complete them. That's why the sample timeline (chapter 2) indicates that you should begin working on them as early as August before your senior year and continue working on them as you are completing the other components of the application.

Supplement Tip #11: Prepare the Supplementary Materials in the Required Format

Colleges that require or welcome supplementary materials typically specify the format they want for those materials. These specifications allow the colleges to process all that supplementary material as efficiently as possible, so it is critical that you follow their specifications. Failure to do so usually results in one or both of the following: your supplementary materials do not get to your application file in time or you acquire a negative reputation that follows you through the entire admission process. Obviously, neither is desirable. So follow Ivey Strategy #5 and sweat the details. You might end up having to prepare the same materials in multiple formats but that's just the way it is.

Supplement Tip #12: Label Everything with Your Name, Birth Date, Contact Information, and the Header *Application Supplement*

Supplementary materials are often submitted separately from other components of your application, and sometimes they are also stored separately from your application after arriving in the admissions office. You want to make sure that your supplementary materials make it into your file and then get sent to the right place and person for evaluation. Labeling your materials properly helps ensure that your supplementary materials don't get lost in the shuffle.

CHAPTER 17

Test Score Reports

If you are a typical applicant to a selective college, you have spent a huge part of the last several years focused on getting the best scores possible on your standardized tests. You have done hours of test prep and you have taken multiple tests. At this point, you need to shift your attention away from collecting test scores and turn your attention to presenting those test scores you have to your best advantage. When you're deciding what test scores to report, we have only one rule: report only those test scores *that are required or that help you.*

That's a pretty commonsense rule, don't you think? If a college requires that you report test scores, report them. If the test scores help you, report them. That's all there is to it. Of course, it does take a little research to determine what is required and a little analysis to determine what helps you. But once you have done the research and analysis, you will be able to decide which test scores to report with great confidence.

RESEARCH THE COLLEGES' TEST POLICIES

Every college sets its own test policies, including their policies for test score reporting, so you must determine what the policies are for each of the colleges on your list. We will help you do that by sharing some research tips.

Research Tip #1: Use the Requirements Grid

Each year, the Common Application produces what they call a *requirements grid*. You can find it on their website. The requirements grid specifies what tests are required and gives some brief description of the college's test policy. So go directly to the Common Application website and start there for all of the Common Application colleges on your list.

Research Tip #2: Focus on Four Pieces of Information

You do not need to know every single thing about a college's test policy in order to make decisions about what test scores to report. You only need to know the answers to these questions:

- Does the college require scores from standardized tests? If so, what test scores or combination of test scores will satisfy the standardized test requirements for the college?

- If you have taken tests beyond those that are required and want to submit those nonrequired scores, will the college consider them when evaluating your application?

- If you have taken a particular standardized test more than once, do you have to report all of your scores or can you choose which ones to report? The admissions lingo to describe the latter scenario is *score choice*, so that is the term to search for when you're doing your research.

- If you have taken a particular standardized test more than once and are reporting scores from more than one testing date, can you take the best subscores among those scores (for example, the critical reading score from one test, the math and writing scores from another test) and combine them into a single best score? The admissions lingo for this practice is called *superscore*, so that is the term to search for when doing your research.

Research Tip #3: Pay Close Attention to the Requirements for SAT Subject Tests

The policies can be a bit tricky here. Here are some examples:

- The college might specify which SAT subject tests must be submitted. For example, many engineering programs require a math and a science subject test.

- The college might specify which SAT subject tests cannot be submitted. For example, the college might not permit you to submit both Math 1 and Math 2.

- The college might require SAT subject tests in addition to the SAT reasoning test or ACT, or the college might require the SAT subject tests only if you take the SAT reasoning test but not if you take the ACT.

- The college might not require the SAT subject tests but they might recommend them. If you have some of these colleges on your list, see scenario #3 found later in this chapter for more guidance about how to handle that scenario.

Research Tip #4: Put the Information into a Chart That You'll Use When You Order the Reports

It is fairly easy to get confused about which college requires what if you have not done a good job documenting what you find in your research. The easiest format is the following chart:

	Test Scores Required	Test Scores Considered	Policy on Score Choice	Policy on Superscoring	Other Notes
College					
College					
College					

CHOOSE YOUR SCORES

Once you know the test policies of the colleges on your list, you can easily determine the choices you have by comparing the requirements to the test scores you have. You will likely only have a few choices available, and you may even discover that you have no choices at all. Typical choices would include the following:

- Choosing between multiple scores on the same test

- Choosing between scores from two different tests (for example, the SAT reasoning test versus the ACT)

- Choosing whether to report test scores at all

Make a list of the choices available to you.

Score Tip #1: Know When to Stop Taking Tests

Once you're looking at your choices for reporting your scores, you might wonder if you should take a different test or take the same test over again. Here is what we advise.

Consider taking a different test (or tests) if you have reason to believe you would perform considerably better and you have the time to adequately prepare. For example, if you have taken the SAT reasoning test twice and have not done well, you might consider taking the ACT. As a general rule, most applicants find that they perform about the same on both tests; however, a significant minority do perform better on one or the other. To find out if you are part of the significant minority, work a practice test and score it for yourself. Sign up only if your practice test shows you are likely to perform considerably better and you have the time to prepare adequately.

As to whether you should take the same test one more time, we apply the three strikes and you're out rule: if you have already taken this test three times, you are out. Your score is not likely to improve enough to make taking the test again worth the time and energy. If, however, you have taken the test only once or twice, then it is worth considering whether to take it again. But take it again only if you can prepare and have a plan for preparing differently and better than the previous times.

Score Tip #2: Don't Get Stuck in Analysis Paralysis

Sometimes there is no way to compare and determine what your best choices are. If you find yourself unable to compare choices, shift from trying to make your *best* choice to trying to make a *good* choice or trying to avoid a *bad* choice. You cannot go wrong with good choices or not bad choices. But you can absolutely go wrong if you do not make a thoughtful decision. So try for best but settle for good or not bad if best cannot be determined.

Score Tip #3: Focus on Getting In, Not Getting Credit

At this point, the *only* standardized test scores that should concern you are the scores that an admissions officer considers when deciding whether to admit you. Once you are enrolled in college, it may be the case that you benefit from reporting additional standardized test scores to the college. For example, you might receive credit for certain courses if you took the AP exam in that subject and received a score of 4 or better. Or maybe the requirement to take a certain number of math courses might be waived if you achieved a sufficiently high math score on the SAT reasoning test, the ACT, the SAT subject tests in math, or an AP math test. But *none* of that affects the *admissions* decision. Right now, keep your eyes on the prize—admission.

Now that you have a list of the choices available to you, you must choose. That takes us back to our rule—choose to report the test scores that help you. In many cases, it will be obvious which score helps you but there are several situations when it is not so obvious, and we spend the rest of the chapter walking you through the analysis of five different scenarios so you can learn how the thought process works.

Scenario #1: If You Have Multiple Scores for Either the SAT Reasoning Test or the ACT

Beth had taken the SAT reasoning test three times and these were her scores (CR is critical reading, MA is math, and WR is writing):

January junior year:	CR 630	MA 620	WR 600	Total: 1850
March junior year:	CR 630	MA 660	WR 580	Total: 1870
June junior year:	CR 630	MA 680	WR 560	Total: 1870

Note: we use the SAT reasoning test here, but the same analysis would apply to the ACT, except that the total on the ACT is the composite score, and the superscore is an average rather than a total.

Beth's question was simple. Which of these scores should she report?

Our first question to Beth was to find out if she had a choice about which score to report. In other words, what were the score-choice policies for the colleges on her list? Some of the colleges required that she report all of her scores; with those, she had no score choice. So her decision was made for those. She should report all of the scores.

But several of the colleges permitted her to choose which scores to report. So using our rule, she knew she wanted to submit only the scores that helped her. Deciding which scores helped her was a bit complicated for Beth because she didn't have one best score. Or did she?

Our second question to Beth was whether all of the colleges on her list considered the writing score on the SAT. As it turned out, a couple of them did not (that's noted as "SAT without writing" on the Common Application requirements grid). So for those colleges, Beth did have a best score, and it was June's test: they were her highest total and highest individual scores in both critical reading and math. For those colleges, she should submit only her June scores.

Our third question to Beth was to evaluate how much the difference in her writing scores really mattered. Was there any real difference between a 560, 580, and 600? Sure they were different scores, but would the 600 really put her in a different category of applicant than the 560? We directed her to take some time to get a more nuanced sense of these scores by looking at the percentiles. On the College Board website (they administer the SAT) or the ACT website, you can get data about how you compare to different pools of test takers.

For example, you can see how your scores compare to those of the same gender, race, or ethnicity. You can also see how your subscores compare. Admissions officers are intimately familiar with these nuances for test scores, so we advised Beth that in order to think like an admissions officer (Ivey Strategy #2), she should get this additional information before making her choices. Once Beth had that information, she knew that there was a big difference between a 560, a 580, and a 600—almost ten percentile points. Even the difference between a 580 and 600 was significant; it was the difference between being in the top 25 percent and the top 20 percent of all test takers. So reporting her 600 in writing would help her. That meant she should report her January *and* her June scores.

Our final question to Beth was whether any of her colleges superscored. Would any of the colleges on her list combine her best CR, MA, and WR scores into one total? If so, then she should report the scores from the tests that make up her superscore. What's Beth's superscore? CR 630 + MA 680 + WR 600 = 1910 total, and that's higher than the total of any of her individual tests (1850 and 1870). She discovered that three of her colleges did in fact superscore, so she should report the test scores (January and June) that resulted in the superscore.

Scenario #2: If You Have Both SAT Reasoning Test and ACT Scores

Sam has learned that he is required to submit scores from either the SAT reasoning test or the ACT with writing to nine of the ten colleges on his list. He has taken them both with the following results:

SAT: CR 760, MA 760, WR 640
ACT: 32 English, 36 Math, 33 Reading, 31 Science, 8 Writing, 33 Composite

Which score helps Sam the most? It is actually pretty tricky to compare scores between these two tests. However, college admissions officers do have tools that they use to compare them, and those tools are available to you if you know where to look.

The tool that the college admissions officers use to compare SAT reasoning test scores with ACT scores is called a *concordance table* and shows the equivalent score between the two tests. You can find the most up-to-date concordance table on either the College Board website (the agency that administers the SAT) or on the ACT website. (Search for "concordance table SAT ACT" to get to the right spot on either website; it is often tucked away on the sites in areas that applicants never visit.)

When Sam consulted the concordance table, he learned that his ACT composite score was actually a bit higher than his SAT total score. So in Sam's case, his best score was his ACT score, and he reported that one.

Scenario #3: If You Have Several SAT Subject Test Scores

Gloria had taken four SAT subject tests with the following results:

Literature	690
US History	700
Math Level 1	610
Spanish	800

She had two questions about which of these scores to report. First, at several colleges she was *required* to submit the results from two SAT subject tests, and she wanted to use her two top scores, but she was not sure if her Spanish score really counted because her first language was Spanish. As she was doing her research, she read on one college's website that the college would not consider a foreign language subject test score if the language was the applicant's first language. But there was nothing to that effect on other colleges' websites.

She raised a good question. This issue has only recently become a topic of discussion in college admissions. The policies are still very much in flux, so we gave her the following advice: use the US history and literature scores to fulfill her required SAT subject tests and *also* report her Spanish score as a third SAT subject test. The Spanish test score could not hurt her, and if the college will accept it, then she gets the benefit. Because there was some possible upside with no downside in submitting the Spanish score, that was the best way for her to go.

Second, she had one college on her list that did not require any SAT subject tests, but *strongly recommended* applicants to submit scores from three SAT subject tests. She also had several colleges on her list that would *consider* her SAT subject tests if submitted. Gloria was unclear about the difference between *strongly recommended* and *considered*. She was also unclear about how many of her test scores she should submit if she was going to submit.

Gloria was right to pick up on the possibility that there might be a distinction between colleges that strongly recommended and colleges that considered the SAT subject tests. *Strongly recommended* is admissions code language for *pretty much required*, whereas *considered* is admissions code language for *truly optional*. Now that the language is decoded, it is easier for Gloria to evaluate her choices.

At the college that strongly recommended Gloria submit scores from three SAT subject tests, we advised her to adapt our rule to read as follows: "Report only those test scores *that are pretty much required and that do not hurt you.*" She knows that three SAT subject tests are pretty much required, so the only question is whether submitting three SAT subject tests would hurt her.

To determine whether her SAT subject tests would hurt her, we advised Gloria to evaluate her performance on the SAT subject tests in light of her grades and her performance on the other standardized tests. In other words, consider how her SAT subject tests play into her story (Ivey Strategy #3). In Gloria's case, three of her SAT subject test scores aligned well with her grades and compared favorably to her other standardized test scores. The one SAT subject test score that was off was her Math 1 score. Gloria had very good grades in honors math courses and had a math subscore on her SAT reasoning test of 750, so her Math 1 score was not a score she would want to report. It could, in fact, hurt her by calling her grades and other standardized test score into question.

Based on this evaluation, for the schools that recommended SAT subject tests, Gloria submitted three SAT subject test scores: all but the Math 1 score. But note that if Gloria had had only three scores total, including her math score, she would have submitted only two scores, still leaving out the Math 1 score. She would have been better off submitting two scores that did not hurt her than submitting three with one that would hurt her.

At the colleges where the SAT subject tests are considered if submitted, we pointed Gloria back to the rule. Are these tests required? No. So her evaluation should strictly be about whether these tests help her. How can Gloria determine if these tests help her? Gloria would need to go back to Ivey Strategy #2 ("think like an admissions officer") and Ivey Strategy #3 ("tell your story").

Which of these test scores would help Gloria tell her story? Spanish might because her story did include her bicultural upbringing and her strong attachment to her Latina identity. Literature and US History both did; they were among her favorite subjects and she was leaning toward a major at college that would combine literature, history, and language in some way—perhaps anthropology, perhaps something interdisciplinary.

But Math 1? No way. She had done fine in math, but it was not a part of her story. So Gloria knew what her story was and how the SAT subject tests might be used to support her story, but how would her test scores be evaluated by an admissions officer?

Admissions officers look to test scores in their evaluation of the academic dimension (see chapter 5). Gloria's scores on her Spanish, literature, and US history tests compared quite favorably to her other test scores. (In general, you should expect your SAT subject tests to fall into the same range as your SAT reasoning tests, so if you have mid-600s on the SAT reasoning test as Gloria did, you should expect mid-600s on your SAT subject tests, too.) Because Gloria's scores all converged around the mid-600s, they served her well on the academic dimension, and they served to validate her abilities.

So given that all three scores support her story, and none of them would undermine her on the academic dimension, there was no reason to leave off any of those three scores. (If one of them would have undermined her academic dimension, that would have been a good reason to leave it off, even if it supported her story.)

Scenario # 4: If You Have to Choose between One of the Skills-Focused Tests (SAT Reasoning Test or ACT) and a Combination of Knowledge-Focused Tests (SAT Subject Tests, AP Tests, IB Tests, National Exams)

Blaine was applying to New York University (NYU), a college that has been on the leading edge of the test-flexible movement. NYU, like all test-flexible colleges, offers applicants a broad array of choices with regard to fulfilling the standardized testing requirements. Blaine appreciated having the choice of what tests to submit but he could not figure out how to compare all of the various options that NYU offered. In his particular case, he could elect to submit the SAT reasoning test *or* three AP exam scores.

There were, of course, many other options (the ACT with writing, SAT subject tests, IB exams, and national examinations among them) but Blaine had not taken those tests, so they were not meaningful choices for him. Blaine was careful to read the fine print and also knew that his three AP exams had to include one in literature or the humanities *and* one in math or science.

Blaine had the following test scores to choose among:

SAT: Total 2140 (CR 680, MA 740, WR 720)
APs: Art History 4, Calculus AB 5, English Language 4, Biology 4

How would Blaine even begin to compare his performance on the SAT versus his APs? Short answer: he couldn't. But he still had to make a decision, even though he couldn't know everything he would like to know before making it.

Blaine had to go back to the rule: *submit test scores that are required or that help you.* Blaine did not need to figure out which test is better in this case—the SAT reasoning test scores or the AP scores. He only had to figure out whether the scores would *help* him. As long as at least one set of test scores would help—either in telling his story or in some other way—he was good to go.

It took Blaine almost no time to do that analysis. He noted that both his SAT MA score and his AP Calculus AB score showed him to be the strong math student that he was. He also noted that his AP art history score demonstrated another side of his academic interests and gave some support for his desire to pursue studies involving his creative and analytic sides. He thought his AP English language score might bolster his critical reading score on his SAT, which was lower than he wished.

He also took a little time to find out how his scores stacked up to the national applicant pool and the NYU pool in particular. He discovered that his SAT reasoning test scores put him in the top 2 to 3 percent of the national applicant pool and made him a solid competitor at NYU, given that these scores put him in the upper end of the applicant pool there. (See scenario #6 and chapter 1 for more information about how to calculate where you fall in comparison to others in a college's applicant pool.)

He couldn't find out as much information against which to compare his AP test scores, but he did know that they were among the highest at his high school, and that he was in the top 20 to 33 percent of those taking each of the particular AP tests. (Search for "score distribution AP," and you will find the charts Blaine used to figure out percentiles for the APs.)

At first, he was disappointed by the lower percentiles on the APs but then he reminded himself that only the strongest students take AP courses and AP exams, so the differences between his percentiles on the SAT reasoning test and his APs were to be expected. Bottom line: Blaine decided he should submit his SAT reasoning test scores and his AP scores in art history, calculus AB, and English language. He rightly took a pass on submitting his AP biology score.

Scenario #5: If You Have More Test Scores Than Are Required

Angela could submit a page full of tests if she wanted to. She had not only taken the SAT and ACT but she had also taken three SAT subject tests and three AP tests. Whew.

She had done pretty well on all of the tests except for the SAT subject test in chemistry, which she had bombed even though she had a 5 on her AP chemistry test. Angela researched the colleges on her list and discovered that none required more than two SAT subject tests and none required the AP tests at all. So what test scores should Angela report?

This is a relatively straightforward application of the rule. Angela should first decide which SAT subject tests to report in order to fulfill that requirement. Presumably the chemistry subject test that she bombed goes by the wayside and she reports the other two.

Now she has the three AP tests to consider. Should she report none, one, two, or all three? That decision is strictly determined by whether they *help* her. Do any help her tell her story? Do any help her in some other way? In Angela's case, it was a bit of a toss-up. Her AP scores were good (two 4s and one 5) but two were in the same subjects as some of the SAT subject tests that she was reporting (English language and US history), and the third was chemistry, which was a subject that she really detested and hoped to never study again.

Our advice in this case? Report all of them or none of them. (They are truly optional, so you don't have to submit any at all.) An admissions officer might flag that Angela had taken three AP courses but submitted only two AP scores, and therefore he might assume she had bombed the AP chemistry test—which she had not! Angela thought about it some more and realized that she wanted the credit for having done all the hard work in her AP courses and doing well on the exams, so she submitted all three.

Scenario #6: If You Are Applying to a Test-Optional College

Drew was applying to some test-optional colleges that would consider scores from either the SAT reasoning tests or the ACT if he chose to submit them at all. Drew understood that he was supposed to apply the second half of our one rule and submit only test scores that would help him, but he wasn't sure how to determine if his test scores helped him or not. In order to decide whether to submit his test scores, Drew had to evaluate two things: whether his scores help him tell his story and how his scores compare to the applicant pool.

When Drew evaluated his test scores in light of his story, there was not much to recommend submitting the scores. His story focused on how diligent and hard-working he was as a student, and his good grades and high standing in his class bore that out. But his test scores were only average and much lower than those of others in his class with the same grades. Drew had never been able to do that well on standardized tests and these were no exception. So the test scores did not help Drew tell his story.

You might assume the evaluation would stop there but it shouldn't. As much as we believe in staying focused on your story, the academic evaluation is so critical that you should report everything that helps you on that front, *even if* it doesn't relate to your story. So we advised Drew to do the second part of the evaluation before making his decision.

Where do Drew's test scores put him in comparison to the applicant pool? In order to do that comparison, Drew, like Beth (scenario #1), needed to look to percentiles rather than just his scores. But the percentiles Drew needed were different. He needed the percentiles that compared him to the college's applicant pool, not the test-taking pool. So Drew needed to get information from the colleges about the mid-50 range of test scores for applicants admitted in past years. Remember from chapter 1 that the mid-50 range shows the scores distributed by quartiles and those scores in the mid-50 range are those scores that range from the 25th to 75th percentiles. (Colleges publish these in the "profile of the incoming class," which is almost always a quick link from the admissions page. The information on the colleges' websites is the most helpful because it will be the most recent, but if you can't find it there, you can always find it on the Department of Education's Integrated Postsecondary Educational Data System [IPEDS] website, which is a database repository of all sorts of information about colleges including this information. The IPEDS data simply lags by a year.)

Drew found the information about the mid-50 for his various colleges. We then asked him to do a quick comparison with his scores for each college. Where did his scores fall?

- In the mid-50?
- In the bottom 25 (below the lower score of the mid-50)?
- In the top 25 (above the higher score of the mid-50)?

He discovered that it really depended on the college, and he was pleasantly surprised to see that his scores did compare favorably at a few of the colleges.

Now that Drew had this information, he could use these guidelines about what test scores to report to test-optional colleges—they are offshoots of the larger rule.

- If you have test scores that fall in the top 25, do report them because they help you.
- If you have test scores that fall in the bottom 25, do not report them because they definitely do not help you, and there is a high likelihood that they will hurt you.

- If you have test scores that fall in the mid-50, report them *if and only if* they help your story because then they help you. Otherwise, they do not help and they might actually hurt you.

JUST FOR INTERNATIONAL APPLICANTS

International applicants have some additional supporting materials to pay attention to. Here are our tips specifically for you.

International Tip #1: Submit Your TOEFL (or IELTS, if Accepted) Results Whether or Not You Are Required to Do So

Here's why: they can only help you. Admissions officers often consider the TOEFL (or IELTS) score in conjunction with the critical reading score on the SAT or the reading score on the ACT, and they give you a bit of a bump if your TOEFL (or IELTS) scores demonstrate that you have better proficiency in English than these other scores would suggest.

International Tip #2: Read the Fine Print When It Comes to How Predictors Are Used by the Colleges

Many of you will receive predictors (predicted scores) for national examinations or the IB. US colleges do not have a uniform policy about how they treat predictors. A few accept them as test scores but then condition their admissions decision on your actual scores being as high or higher than your predictors. Others accept them but treat them as interim grades rather than test scores and evaluate them along with your transcript. Still others will not consider your predictors at all. You absolutely must sweat the details (Ivey Strategy #5) and find out the policy for each college on your list.

JUST FOR HOMESCHOOLED APPLICANTS

Homeschooled applicants also have some different things to consider when it comes to test score reports. Here are tips specifically for homeschoolers.

Homeschool Tip #1: Use Scores from SAT Subject Tests or AP Tests to Demonstrate Your Mastery of the Core College Preparatory Curriculum

One of the primary challenges for homeschooled students is demonstrating mastery of the traditional college preparatory curriculum. Not only is your homeschool curriculum likely to diverge from the traditional curriculum but whatever grades you receive will not have been calibrated or compared against other students. Having good scores from the SAT subject tests and AP tests addresses this challenge. Those scores can show mastery of the subject content and compare you against a national pool of college-bound students. So these scores can be of great help to you, and we recommend that you report them even if they are not required.

Homeschool Tip #2: Read the Fine Print about What Tests Are Required

Many colleges require more tests or different tests from homeschooled students. For example, many times there is no test-optional choice for homeschooled students. So always check to see if the college has a different policy for homeschooled students when doing your research.

LOGISTICS OF REQUESTING TEST SCORE REPORTS

You will be required to request reports from the testing agency that administered the tests. You can make your requests to the testing agencies on their websites. Here are few tips about how to do that.

Logistics Tip #1: Request Your Test Score Reports at Least Two Weeks before the Submission Deadline

If you are following our recommended timeline, you will be submitting your parts of the application right about this same time. Having your application arrive a bit earlier than the test score reports will streamline the processing of your application at the admissions office, so that is the better way to go. But even if you are not ready to submit your parts of the application, you should request your test score reports at least two weeks before the submission deadline so that the college receives them in plenty of time, and you do not have to pay for priority or rush processing.

Logistics Tip #2: Batch Process Your Requests

Batch processing is a work smarter, not harder way of getting your requests handled. Rather than making a request for each college separately, you can make a single request for all of the colleges that are getting the same set of test scores. So before you hop online to order test score reports, make sure to sort through which test scores are going to which colleges, and then put the colleges that get the same test scores into a single group or batch. You should end up with batches that look something like this:

- Batch 1: Colleges that get *all* of your scores
- Batch 2: Colleges that get *only* these scores: X, Y, Z
- Batch 3: Colleges that get *none* of your scores

Now that you have your groups and batches, make a single request for each group or batch. Not only will this save you time, it will also minimize the likelihood of mistakes (the fewer times you have to check the boxes, the better).

Logistics Tip #3: Keep Documentation of Your Requests

It is your responsibility to get your test score reports delivered to the colleges by the deadline. If anything goes wrong, you want to be able to show the college that the problem was with the testing agency, not you. Furthermore, documentation will help you sort it all out with the testing agency and save you from having to pay twice!

Parent Tip: Bring Yourself Up-to-Date on Testing Policies

When we talk to applicants and parents, we almost always have to drop this line at some point in the conversation: "It ain't your momma's admissions process." Nowhere is this phrase truer than when it comes to standardized testing. We want to highlight a couple of realities of standardized testing today that are particularly important that parents understand as their children decide which test scores to present as part of their applications.

- **The SAT reasoning test and ACT with writing are treated as interchangeable.** Back in the day, the SAT and ACT were not interchangeable. There were colleges that took only one or the other, and even if colleges took both, they had a preference for one or the other. The SAT was the preferred test for colleges on both coasts, and the ACT was the preferred test for the Midwestern and Southern colleges. The two tests also used to be fairly different in their construction and what they purported to measure. But that was then. Today, the SAT reasoning test and ACT with writing are treated as interchangeable by almost every college in the United States. Applying Ivey Strategy #2 and thinking like an admissions officer means that applicants are free to submit test scores from either the SAT reasoning test or ACT to any college on their lists, and they should be using whichever one is the stronger score.

- **Choices abound.** What all these test scores actually measure and how effectively they measure it has been the subject of a lot of research and heated debate. One result is the huge variety of testing policies that colleges now have. What this means for your child is that choosing which test scores to report is much more complicated than it used to be. It also requires that he or she employ Ivey Strategy #5 and sweat the details when it comes to what tests are required and what tests are in his or her best interest to report. (And if you have multiple children, assume that by the time your next child is applying to college, the college's policies will have changed!)

CHAPTER 18

School Reports

H ere's a question for you. Do two applicants who have *identical* GPAs and who are both applying to the same college and being evaluated by the same admissions officer get the same academic rating?

Answer: Not necessarily.

Why not? Because not all 3.99 GPAs are created equal. Some applicants with a 3.99 GPA have gotten top grades in the hardest classes at the most competitive schools. Other applicants with a 3.99 GPA have gotten top grades in the easiest classes at the least competitive schools. You know it; the admissions officer knows it; everyone knows it. But how does the admissions officer actually figure out what your 3.99 GPA means?

That's where the school report comes in. It has all the information that the admissions officer needs to interpret your 3.99 GPA, and what the admissions officer learns from the school report will have a direct bearing on your academic rating. In other words, the information there matters a lot. And yet the school report is perhaps the least understood of all of the various forms and documents that an applicant must ask others to submit.

A SCHOOL REPORT BY ANY OTHER NAME

We call this document a *school report* because that's what the Common Application currently calls it. But if you are applying to a college that does not use the Common Application, you may discover that the college calls this report something else or uses a set of forms instead of just one form to collect all this information. For example, Tulane calls this form a *secondary school report* (which is what the Common Application used to call it). We've also seen it called the *counselor recommendation*. Regardless of what it is called, you will find that almost all colleges ask for the information that the school report contains in one way or another. So don't be distracted by what the form is called. Focus your attention on finding out where and from whom the admissions officer gets the information that is contained in that form. Your academic rating depends on it!

YOUR SCHOOL COUNSELOR IS YOUR CONTACT FOR THE SCHOOL REPORT

The school report is the domain of your school counselor. He or she will be responsible for preparing your school reports and submitting them on your behalf. That's why it is essential that you build a good relationship with your school counselor. Before we delve into the various components of the school report, we want to give you some tips for working with your school counselor.

Counselor Tip #1: Respect the Role Your School Counselor Plays in the Process

Most applicants do not appreciate how much influence a school counselor can have on the admissions officer's evaluation. Admissions officers place a good deal of weight on what school counselors have to say about an applicant, and a negative report from a school counselor can be the kiss of death. That is why you should do everything in your power to work well with your school counselor.

Counselor Tip #2: Follow the Rules and Work within the Established System

If you think managing your applications to ten colleges requires a lot of work, think about the challenge of managing applications for fifty to four hundred students! Fifty students is a common load for a counselor at a private school, and four hundred is a common load for a counselor at a public school. Any way you calculate it, it is a huge number of applicants and applications to manage, and the only way that can work is for there to be a system that everyone within the school follows. So follow the rules and work within the established system.

Counselor Tip #3: Give Your School Counselor as Much Lead Time as Possible

Your school counselor is a very, very busy person. Extra time is a gift that you can give the school counselor that will pay off in multiple ways, including making it more likely that your special request will be granted, that the college deadlines will be met, and that whatever he or she submits on your behalf is well done, accurate, and on time. So don't just meet deadlines but beat them. And if you have a special request, ask as soon as you know what you need.

Counselor Tip #4: Take Advantage of Every Opportunity You Have to Let the School Counselor Get to Know You

School counselors generally structure opportunities to get to know their students, but students don't always take advantage of those opportunities, leaving the school counselor with precious little information to include in his or her school report and no guidance from the student about what might be particularly helpful. If your school counselor offers individual appointments, schedule an appointment and talk with him or her face-to-face. If your school counselor distributes questionnaires, fill them out completely and thoroughly. If your school counselor holds group sessions, attend them and participate.

Counselor Tip #5: Recognize That Your School Counselor Is Bound by School Policies and the Law

Your school counselor is a licensed professional who works for your school. He or she must follow the school policies and the law. For example, a school counselor is not going to submit your school report until you have formally authorized him or her to do so (that's a legal requirement, because the school report contains private and confidential information about you). Any special request you make should be framed in such a way that acknowledges your school counselor is obligated to follow policies and the law. For example, if you ask your school counselor to address a personal circumstance in the school report, you could ask by saying something along the lines of, "I'm sure that there are rules about what you can or cannot report about me but I'm hopeful that with my permission, you can report . . ." If you acknowledge that they too have policies to follow, your request is far more likely to be granted.

Counselor Tip #6: Just for International Applicants

Your school may or may not have a school counselor who is well versed in the US college admissions process. If your school counselor is not particularly expert about the US process, then you should educate him or her. One resource that is quite helpful is the *College Counseling Sourcebook* published by the College Board and available on their website (www.collegeboard.org).

Counselor Tip #7: Just for Homeschooled Applicants

Your school counselor is quite different from the norm. First, he or she is probably someone you know incredibly well (one of your parents), and second, he or she probably has no other interests than yours to serve (other students competing against you, the high school's institutional interests, and so on). Because of those differences, admissions officers will assume a certain bias: it is hard to imagine that your mom or dad would not heartily recommend you for admission. That is why many colleges do not require a counselor recommendation from home-schooled students. Even if they do ask for such a recommendation, we encourage you to bolster what your parent has to say about you with your other recommendations, and we'll give you more specialized advice in chapter 19.

WHAT IS THE SCHOOL REPORT ANYWAY?

The school report is best understood if you ignore what is suggested by its title—it is not one report that is submitted once. Instead, it is a set of reports submitted together, and this set of reports is updated at certain junctures through the application process.

The school report and its subsequent updates (midyear report, final report, optional report) are prepared and submitted by your school counselor or another school official. The set of information that is contained within the school report includes the following:

- Information about the applicant's courses and performance (the transcript)
- Information about how the applicant compares to others in the class (comparative data)
- Information about the applicant's school (the school profile)
- A written evaluation of the applicant (the counselor recommendation)

As you may notice almost immediately, much of the information contained within the school report changes over the course of the year and is not final until an applicant graduates from high school. For example, the applicant's transcript is different at the beginning of the twelfth-grade (senior) year than it is at the end because the applicant does not receive final grades for twelfth-grade courses until they are completed. Likewise, the comparative data may change as time goes by: an applicant may begin the twelfth-grade year ranked #20 in the class and end the twelfth-grade year ranked #5 in the class. That is why colleges require updates of the school report at certain junctures through the process.

To distinguish the additional reports from the original report and from one another, they are titled by when they are due: midyear report, final report, and optional report. But don't be fooled by these titles because they are nothing more than *updated* school reports, and they include all of the same elements as the original school report. For that reason, all of the suggestions we make about the original school report in the following section are relevant to the additional reports as well, and you'll need to stay on top of the additional reports, too. For now, we are giving you a brief overview of all of the versions of the school report so you have a heads up about when they come into play and what you need to be paying attention to.

TYPES OF SCHOOLS REPORTS

School Report

The school report is submitted around the same time as your application. It creates the baseline school report, and the additional reports that follow are intended as updates only.

Midyear Report

The midyear report is submitted once your school has released first term grades midway through your twelfth-grade (senior) year. It generally updates only those parts of the school report relating to grades—the transcript and comparative data—but might also update the school profile or counselor recommendation. The midyear report is typically considered during the Regular Decision cycle because it comes too late for the EA and ED cycles.

If your midyear report contains good news, ask your school counselor to get this report out the door as soon as possible. If it contains bad news, then use the suggestions later in this chapter and follow the suggestions we give in chapter 23 for postsubmission supplements to your application.

Final Report

The final report is submitted once you have been granted your high school diploma and it is sent *only* to the college where you have made an enrollment deposit and any colleges where you are holding a spot on the wait list. The final report verifies that you have in fact graduated, and it updates the parts of the school report related to your graduation (the transcript and comparative data). On rare occasions, it may include other updates, but its primary purpose is to confirm that you have graduated.

You must be on top of receipt of your final report, because it is the final hurdle to clear before you can officially enroll in college. So make sure it gets sent to the college where you are enrolling. You may also want your final report to be sent to a college where you are on the wait list (see chapter 23).

Optional Report

An optional report is submitted at any time there are important updates to any aspect of your application. It can include updates to any part of the original school report, whether it's good news (such as grades from the quarter that show an improvement in your performance) or bad news (such as disciplinary action taken by the school against you). Generally, you initiate the submission of the good news optional reports, and the school initiates the submission of the bad news optional reports.

The critical times for you to consider requesting an optional report to be sent on your behalf are (1) in early November when the EA and ED evaluations are being made and (2) in early May when the first round of wait-list decisions are being made. Ask your school counselor to send the optional report at that time if there is any good news to be shared.

If your school initiates an optional report due to bad news, you are no doubt well aware of what that bad news is. Consult the relevant chapters in the book about what to do to counter the various possibilities. For example, if a disciplinary action is being reported, consult chapter 13.

Before you continue reading the rest of this chapter, either *download and print* out the school report forms for the colleges on your list or bookmark the online forms so that you can reference them as you read through the rest of this chapter. Seeing the actual form that your school counselor completes and the admissions officer reviews will help you make sense of the advice we give you. Unless you are an international applicant or a homeschooled applicant, you can skip the next two sections.

JUST FOR INTERNATIONAL APPLICANTS

If you are an international student, there are a few extra things for you to consider when it comes to the school report and the subsequent updates.

Additional Questions on the School Report or an International School Supplement

If you attend high school outside the United States, then your counselor may be asked to answer additional questions on the school report or complete an international school supplement *in addition* to your school report. The additional information requested will usually address the following:

- Primary language of instruction in your secondary school (high school)
- Whether promotion is based on standard examinations (such as Abitur, GCSE or A-Level, ICSE or ISC, and so on) given by a state or national examinations board
- Results from any lower secondary examinations
- Results or predicted results from any higher secondary examinations

Subsequent Reports

It is sometimes quite confusing to international students (and their school counselors) what subsequent reports are required or should be submitted. In general, here are some tips.

International Tip #1: Send a Midyear Report, Even if There Is No Update

Because many international schools operate on different terms or give performance marks (grades) only at the end of the academic year, there is no real update for the school counselor to provide. However, US colleges are expecting a midyear report and if they do not receive one, it can cause problems for you in the process. So just ask your school counselor to send one—even if it is nothing more than a duplicate of the original school report or if it simply reports that there are no updates.

International Tip #2: Send a Final Report That Validates the Receipt of Your Diploma, Whatever That Entails

The final report is really intended to validate that the applicant successfully completed his or her secondary education. In US secondary schools (high schools), successful completion is signified by the receipt of a high school diploma. But in other countries, successful completion of the secondary education often depends on a certain performance on your standard examinations. If that is your situation, then you need to send a final report that validates receipt of your diploma and your successful completion of your secondary education.

International Tip #3: Send an Optional Report Any Time You Have Good News to Share

If you receive any performance marks that show you are doing well academically, then you should ask your school counselor to send an optional report that shares that good news with the admissions officer.

JUST FOR HOMESCHOOLED APPLICANTS

If you are homeschooled, there are also a few extra things for you to consider when it comes to the school report and the subsequent updates.

Additional Questions on the School Report or a Homeschool Supplement

If you have been homeschooled, your counselor or school supervisor will be required to answer additional questions on the school report or complete a home-school supplement. The topics addressed will include the following:

- "Educational Philosophy of the Homeschool"
- "Motivation and Reasons for Homeschooling"
- "Grading Scale and Whether Outside Evaluators Are Used to Grade"
- "Whether a Member of a Homeschool Association"

Subsequent Reports

Because your homeschooling is tailored to your situation, it may or may not align to the calendar and cycle for the subsequent reports. However, it is important that you attend to the subsequent reports regardless. In general, here is what we recommend.

Homeschool Tip #1: Send a Midyear Report Even if There Is No Update

The colleges are expecting a midyear report and if they do not receive one, it can cause problems for you in the process. So just send one, even if it is nothing more than a duplicate of the original school report or if it simply reports that there are no updates.

Homeschool Tip #2: Send a Final Report That Validates You Have Successfully Completed Your High School Education

That is what the final report is really all about, so send whatever documentation you have that you have graduated and received your high school diploma. This will vary from state to state, but you should send whatever documentation is appropriate to your situation.

Homeschool Tip #3: Send an Optional Report Any Time You Have Good News from an Outside Evaluation

If you complete courses and get grades from any non-homeschool entity, then send those. If you take additional standardized tests and have test scores, send those. All outside evaluations help validate your academic abilities and potential, so you always want those considered.

Parent Tip: Let Your Child Practice Navigating Bureaucracy

Getting the school reports is a great opportunity for your child to develop some skills in navigating bureaucracy. These are skills he or she will need the minute she gets to college, when the first two things your child will have to do are (1) register for class and (2) pay fees and handle financial aid disbursements. Even at the kindest, gentlest colleges, these tasks can be hard to manage without any prior experience navigating a school bureaucracy. So give your child some practice in a context where it is easy for you to provide backup support and rescue assistance when needed.

SCHOOL REPORT COMPONENT #1: TRANSCRIPT

You are required to provide official transcripts from every school you have attended since ninth grade. The transcript, along with a transcript legend, must be attached to the school report and submitted directly by the school.

Admissions officers use your transcript in their evaluation because of the fundamental reality that we talked about at the beginning of the chapter: all 3.99 GPAs are not created equal. The transcript gives the admissions officer a window into what is behind that 3.99 GPA. On the transcript, they can scrutinize your grades, identify trends and patterns, and spot markers of brilliance as well as problems. All of this additional information gives them richer insight into your particular GPA.

What would an admissions officer find out from your transcript? Our guess is that you have no idea because you have never actually seen an official copy of your transcript. You've seen report cards, or you've checked your grades online, but you've likely never actually seen your transcript. Now is the time to take a look.

Get an official copy of your transcript and use this checklist to analyze it.

- *Readable:* Is the transcript readable? In a significant minority of cases, the transcript just isn't readable. For example, the print function is messed up and certain words or lines are cut off. If that's the case, work with your school counselor to fix the problem.

- *Understandable to you:* Do you understand all the information that appears on your transcript? If you see information on your transcript that you do not understand, get it explained. It may be important, and just because you do not understand it does not mean the admissions officer won't, and you want to understand what the admissions officer is going to be looking at.

- *Understandable to an admissions officer:* Will your transcript be understandable to an admissions officer? Make sure that the school has provided a legend that allows the admissions officer to make sense of internal abbreviations or codes for course names. Bring any clarity problems to the attention of your school counselor and work to get the problems solved.

- *Accurate:* Is everything on your transcript accurate? Get any errors corrected promptly and make sure that the colleges receive the corrected version.

- *Trends:* Do your grades trend up or down? If they trend up, then you want to make the most of that positive information. You don't have to simply hope that the admissions officers see it; you can call it to their attention by asking your counselor to mention it in the recommendation. If your grades trend down, then you want to do what you can to minimize the negative impact. The best way to do that is to halt or reverse the trend and then provide information that will convince the admissions officer that the downward trend was not so much a trend as a hiccup. Again, your counselor is the one who can get the information to the admissions officer. Ask for the counselor to send an optional report so that the admissions officer sees evidence that you are indeed performing better.

- *Shining stars and black holes:* GPAs are averages and by definition conceal the extremes. But transcripts reveal the extremes. Sometimes the extremes are great for you—they are your shining stars. For example, maybe you aced every history and social studies class, and those grades align quite nicely with your ambitions to become a diplomat. Other times, the extremes are problematic for you—they are your black holes, such as that D in Physics or that bad semester of all Cs. Do you have any shining stars or black holes on your transcript? If so, then make the most of your stars and minimize the damage of the black holes. In either case, you must work through your counselor or your teachers to do so. Ask the appropriate person to address the extremes in the recommendation. It is always better to have a third party play up your star qualities or explain away your problems than to do it yourself. From the third party, it comes across as helpful, reliable, and credible; from you, it risks coming across as arrogant or defensive.

Note: A few colleges actually require that you explain low grades on your transcript yourself. For example, the University of Delaware now has a question on its application that requires applicants to explain any grade below a B! On these applications, you should provide the required explanation *and* ask your counselor or teacher recommenders to address it as well. In your explanation, be sure to go beyond the explanation and speak to what you have done or are doing to earn better grades going forward. In other words, give the admissions officer reason to write off those low grades as past history that will not repeat itself.

Unusual Circumstances

There are three circumstances that are not the norm but that come up frequently enough, and we offer a tip for each.

Transcript Tip #1: If Your High School Has a Nontraditional or Unusual Grading System, Make Sure That an Explanation Is Included Somewhere in the School Report

It can be attached to the transcript or included in the school profile. We suggest that it be attached to both, just so the admissions officer has the information when he or she needs it.

Transcript Tip #2: Just for International Applicants

If your transcript is not in English, you have the responsibility for getting a certified translation. Contact the colleges on your list to find out what certified translation services they recognize.

Transcript Tip #3: Just for Homeschooled Applicants

A college's school report for the homeschooler may include a preformatted transcript that organizes the course work you have done into categories based on the traditional college preparatory subjects. We suggest that you use it because it offers you a great opportunity to show that you have fulfilled the academic expectations of selective colleges.

SCHOOL REPORT COMPONENT #2: COMPARATIVE DATA

On the school report, there are several questions your school counselor is asked to answer that give the admissions officer information about how you compare to others in your class. Specifically, the school report often asks about the following:

- *Rank in class:* What is the applicant's class rank? What is the class size? What period has been included in calculating the class rank? Is the rank weighted or unweighted? How many students share this rank? How do you report class rank (quartile, quintile, decile)?

- *GPA:* What is the applicant's cumulative GPA? What is the scale used? What time period has been included in calculating the GPA? Is the GPA weighted or unweighted? What is the school's passing mark? What is the highest GPA in the class?

WEIGHTED VERSUS UNWEIGHTED

If your school uses a weighted grading system, you get more points for grades earned in honors or advanced courses (the additional points are the *weight*). So, for example, if your school uses a 4.0 grading scale and has a weighted grading system, you might get an extra point for each grade earned in an AP class (this is a typical formula). An A in the AP class would be worth 5.0 points instead of the typical 4.0 points. A weighted GPA is based on your GPA calculated with the weighting factored in; an unweighted GPA is calculated without the weighting factored in. With a weighted GPA it is possible to have a GPA that is higher than 4.0 on a 4.0 scale. Similarly, a weighted class rank is a class rank based on a weighted GPA, whereas an unweighted class rank is a class rank based on an unweighted GPA.

Selective colleges ask about your school's grading system so that they can understand more about what your GPA and class rank really say about your academic ability and performance.

- *Rigor of your courses:* How does the applicant's course selection compare to that of college preparatory students at your school? Is it most demanding, very demanding, demanding, average, or below average?

The answers to these questions, in combination with the transcript, give admissions officers almost everything they need to make a fairly informed and nuanced evaluation of how your GPA stacks up against others in your class.

Let's see how this information could help distinguish Fred from Will. Both of them have 3.99 GPAs and both attend the same high school.

- *Rank:* Their schools don't rank, so the admissions officer gets no information there.
- *GPA:* The highest GPA in their class is 3.99. That means Fred and Will are at the top of their class, right? Aha! A back door to ranking. Of course, there may be many other classmates tied with Fred and Will but still the admissions officer knows that no one is doing better than Fred or Will.

- *Rigor of course selection:* The school counselor has indicated that Fred has taken the "most demanding" schedule, and Will has only taken a "demanding" schedule. What does that tell the admissions officer? That Fred has maintained a 3.99 in the hardest classes, and Will has maintained a 3.99 in an easier set of classes. Whose 3.99 represents more academic accomplishment? Fred's. Whose 3.99 indicates a higher likelihood of success at a selective college? Fred's.

So whom will the admissions officer rate higher on the academic dimension? Fred.

Find Out Your School Policies about Reporting Comparative Data

Your first step in handling the comparative data is to find out what the school's policies are about reporting the comparative data. If the school does not report it, then there is nothing to handle here. But if the school does report it, then you may have a few things to do. Consult your student handbook, or ask your school counselor for the school's policies with regard to all three categories of comparative data (rank, GPA, rigor of course selection). For example, ask about ranking. Does your school rank? If so, when and how? If ranking is not calculated until graduation, then it can't show up on the school report that is filled out before you graduate, can it? What rank will the report show for you?

Assess How You Will Stack Up

If your school counselor will be reporting comparative data, then you need to determine what the data will say about you. How will you stack up against others from your school? The most straightforward way to know is to ask your school counselor what he or she will be answering. But he or she may not be willing or able to answer all of your questions. For example, the school policy may prohibit sharing the highest GPA in the class with any student. (It does not hurt to ask, provided you follow the advice we give about how to couch requests such as these—see counselor tip #5 on working with your school counselor.) If you cannot find out exactly how you stack up, make your best guess. Most applicants have a pretty good idea.

Now that you know how you stack up, what do you do? It depends on how you compare.

If You Compare Favorably

Yay! Your only challenge is to make sure that this piece of information is communicated to the admissions officer. What could be your obstacle? It might be your school's policies. Some high schools have made an intentional decision not to share any information that would reveal how you stack up against others in your class. Their rationale is that they don't want to sacrifice the good of the many for the good of the one. That may be a good outcome for your friends in the class, but it's not a good outcome for you because, in this case, you are the one!

In that instance, talk with your school counselor about your situation, and see what he or she suggests you do to convey your top-student status to the admissions officer. Your hope is that your school counselor will volunteer to note it in the counselor recommendation. If that is not possible, then have a similar conversation with your teacher recommenders. If no school-affiliated person is willing to mention your top-student status, then you simply cannot do anything more. Declaring it yourself does you no good because you won't be deemed to have the authority or credibility to make that assessment.

If You Do Not Compare Favorably

Your challenge is to find ways to compensate for your less-than-favorable ranking. You need to highlight the aspects of your academic profile that are in fact positive or explain the circumstances that account for your less-than-awesome performance in comparison to others in your class. You have two opportunities in your application to do that:

- *Ask your school counselor to make the case for you in his or her recommendation.* Remember that school counselors are expected to play this role in the process. They are trusted advisors to admissions officers, and what your school counselor says will influence the admissions officer. The most appropriate circumstances under which to ask your school counselor to make the case for you are those when your performance has been diminished by things outside of your control. Perhaps your class is full of Einsteins, and if you had been in any other class, you would have been at the top. Perhaps you have transferred into the school and so you are not ranked. Perhaps you had a serious illness or family problem that fouled up your sophomore year, and your sophomore year killed your GPA. Perhaps you were foreclosed from taking the most demanding curriculum because of scheduling conflicts. That's what we mean by external circumstances.

- *Ask your teacher recommender to make the case for you in his or her recommendation.* Teacher recommenders cannot offer the overall perspective that your school counselor can but they can speak to your outstanding abilities in particular subjects or discuss how you hung in there and mastered math even though it was really hard for you. Teacher recommenders are also trusted by admissions officers, so if one or more of your teacher recommenders has something positive to say or can shed some light on why your standing in your class doesn't accurately reflect your abilities, then you definitely want them to speak to that in their recommendations. The circumstances in which you would ask teacher recommenders to make your case are when your school counselor does not know you well enough to speak to the issues but your teacher recommender does or when your grades in a particular subject are the cause for your unfavorable comparison.

SCHOOL REPORT COMPONENT #3: THE SCHOOL PROFILE

One common question about the admissions process is how an admissions officer can possibly know enough about an applicant's school to make an informed evaluation of an applicant's record from that school. That's a great question. After all, there are more than forty thousand high schools in the United States alone, and thousands on thousands more around the world. Not surprisingly then, admissions officers at top colleges routinely evaluate applicants from high schools that the admissions officer knows little or nothing about. That is, until the admissions officer gets a crash course in everything he needs to know from the school report, provided the school counselor includes the school profile.

What Information Is Found in the School Profile?

There is no prescribed format for a school profile, but there is a common expectation about what information will be shared on the school profile. It is expected that the school profile will educate the admissions officer about these aspects of your school:

- *Basic profile of your school:* What is the nature of the community where your school is located? Inner city? Affluent suburb? Rural town? What is the makeup and size of the student body? Faculty? Staff? Is your school public or private? If private, is it religious? Boarding? Military? What accreditations does the school have?

- *Academic program and curricular offerings:* What is the academic program at your school? How is your school year and school day structured? Does your school offer AP, IB, and honors courses? If so, how many? Does your school limit the number of these advanced courses that a student may take? Does your school offer an IB program? If so, how is entry into the program determined? Are there any other special or advanced offerings at your school (for example, a dual credit program with local colleges)? If so, what are they and how is entry determined?

- *Grading system:* What is the grading system? How are GPAs calculated? What is the passing grade? Are students ranked?

- *Profile of most recent graduating class:* What is the grade distribution for the class? What are the standardized test results for the class? AP tests? IB tests? Other tests? What regional, national, and international academic awards were made to members of the class, for example, the number of National Merit Semi-Finalists? What percentage of the class went on to four-year colleges? Which colleges?

There may be other information included in a school profile, such as information about sports offerings, clubs, or community service if those are particularly important aspects of the school.

Although the school profile is not strictly necessary because some of this information is given in summary form elsewhere on the school report, as former admissions officers, we will tell you that a well-done school profile makes all the difference. It gives a much richer context for evaluating an applicant's academic abilities and achievements. For example, it is one thing to have pursued an IB program at a school where all students do so, and another thing to have pursued an IB program at a school where only 20 percent do so. The admissions officer will be impressed by the rigor of the IB program in either case but which applicant is going to leave the impression of being someone who makes an extra effort to pursue the more challenging program? Only the one who was at a school where there was a choice. The school profile gives admissions officers what they want and need—a crash course in everything they want and need to know about any high school.

What Do You Want the Admissions Officer to Know about Your School?

You want admissions officers to know anything that would help you tell your story (Ivey Strategy #3). Take a moment to review your story and think about what information, if it were in your school profile, would help you. Use the information of the typical school profile just described to stimulate your thinking.

For example, if a part of your story is that you are participating in a school-within-a-school program that is open only to the best science students at the school, it would be helpful if your school profile explained that program and the selection criteria for it. Or perhaps part of your story is that you have an unusually deep experience in the arts thanks to your school's nontraditional curriculum and evaluation system, so it would be helpful if your school profile explained that. Maybe your story is about being one of the few in your public school to be college-bound, so it would be helpful for the school profile to include information about the demographics of the student body and the low percentage of graduates who go on to four-year colleges.

Once you know what you want the admissions officer to know about your school, you are ready to review the school profile for your school. Many high schools post the school profile on the school's website, so start there. If you do not find one on the website, ask your school counselor for a copy.

Review Your School Profile to Make Sure It Meets Your Needs

Review the school profile by checking for two things:

- Is the information in it accurate and current?
- Does it include the information you want it to include?

If your review reveals that the information in the school profile is inaccurate, out-of-date, or lacking from your perspective, talk with your school counselor about addressing these issues. Usually school counselors are more than happy to correct any errors and update the school profile, but you may need to do some persuading if you want them to add information that will help you. Come prepared with your best argument about how adding the information is good for you, good for other applicants, and good for the school. Also come prepared with a draft of the information that you would like added—that can go a long way to dissolving objections from time-pressed school counselors. Here are some tips for particular problems people can encounter with their school profiles.

Profile Tip #1: If You Discover That Your School Does Not Have a School Profile, Volunteer to Help the School Put One Together

Doing so will help you and all other applicants from your school. You can do that by using the outline we've just given, as well as samples on the College Board's website. (Search for "sample high school profile" to get to the College Board's information.)

Profile Tip #2: Just for International Applicants

A school profile can be especially helpful to your supporting materials because it can offer more information than the school report forms alone permit. If a school profile does not exist for your school, you should definitely volunteer to help the school put one together. You can work from the outline that we have given but we suggest you also include some additional information about the overall structure and model of secondary education in your country. For example, if your secondary school is based on the UK model, then give some additional information about the UK model for secondary education. Likewise, if your school is an international school that draws on multiple models, you would give some information about what those are and how they work.

Profile Tip #3: Just for Homeschooled Applicants

Much of the information that would be contained in the school profile is often also requested in the additional questions on the school report or in the homeschool supplement. We suggest that you include a school profile only if it adds something to the information you have already shared. There is no need to duplicate information. You simply want to be sure that the admissions officer gets a complete picture of your schooling.

SCHOOL REPORT COMPONENT #4: COUNSELOR RECOMMENDATION

Although the counselor recommendation is a part of the school report, we are not going to address it in this chapter because it is significantly different than the other elements of the school report. It contains less objective data and more subjective commentary. It is, in fact, a proper recommendation, and therefore we address it in the next chapter (19).

Recommendations

Every admissions officer has a reading order for the application—some start with page one and read straight through, others start with the essays, and yet others start with the academic data (test scores, rank, grades, transcript) and then go on to read the rest of the file.

Yet no admissions officer we've ever met starts with the recommendations. Why not? In our experience, that's largely because admissions officers want to form their own opinions about an applicant before getting someone else's. So by the time an admissions officer gets to your recommendations, he or she usually has formed a preliminary opinion about you and is already leaning toward either admit or deny.

What happens then, once the admissions officer actually gets to the recommendations? In the best case, the admissions officer is already leaning toward admitting you and the fabulous recommendations cement that admissions officer's decision and give him backup to advocate for your admission before the committee if necessary. In the worst case, the admissions officer is leaning toward admitting you but negative or ambivalent recommendations cause her to reconsider and may even convince her to wait-list or deny you. In many cases, she is on the fence and the recommendations will push her either to admit or deny.

Best case, worst case, typical case—recommendations make a difference. It is up to you to make sure that the recommendations you get will make a positive difference for you and influence the admissions officer in your favor.

USING CORE RECOMMENDATIONS TO YOUR ADVANTAGE

Your goal is use your recommendations to validate all of your positives and to overcome all of your negatives. That might seem like a tall order but it can be done. Even more important, it can usually be done by using only the core recommendations—the ones that you will use in some combination with every application. The core recommendations are your counselor recommendation and two teacher recommendations. These are the recommendations that are given most weight by admissions officers and are therefore the most important to your application. They are the ones that you absolutely, positively must use to your best advantage. That's why we encourage you to focus on getting your best core recommendations before you consider any additional recommendations. Use our tips to help you get the recommendations that will work for you (Ivey Strategy #6).

Recommendation Tip #1: Check the Requirements for Each College on Your List

Confirm what recommendations are required for each college on your list. Be on the lookout for specific requirements that may influence whom you ask to be a recommender. For example, some colleges or programs may require that you have teachers in certain subjects. Also be on the lookout for colleges that require recommendations from someone other than a counselor or teacher, such as a peer.

Recommendation Tip #2: Know What Your Recommenders Are Being Asked

Begin by reading the recommendation forms so that you have a sense of what your recommenders are being asked to evaluate and comment on. Generally, the counselor recommendation invites your school counselor to provide an overall assessment of you as well as a comparative assessment of how you compare to others in your class on each of the three dimensions that the admissions officer evaluates—academic, extracurricular, and personal. He or she is also encouraged to provide some examples that highlight what differentiates you from others.

By contrast, the teacher recommendations are more focused on an evaluation of you on the academic dimension, although there is opportunity for your teachers to comment on the other dimensions as well. Again, your teachers are asked to provide specific examples in addition to their ratings.

Recommendation Tip #3: Determine What You Would Like Your Recommenders to Say

Once you know what your recommenders are being asked, you can identify what they might say that would be most helpful to you.

What are the positives that your recommenders could validate? Look back to your story. Let's say that your story is that you are a leader. What might your school counselor say about your leadership? Perhaps that you were president of the junior class, and that it was a pretty difficult year and a big test of your leadership. Could she speak to how you helped keep the class on a positive track after the loss of three classmates in a car accident? That would certainly be a good example. What might your teachers say about your leadership? Obviously, they see you operate in a different context—the classroom. How does your leadership display itself there? Could your teachers say that you help the class move through difficult material by asking probing questions? Or could they say that you help other students who are having a tough time getting it? Take some time and think about what your recommenders could validate. Make a short list for each recommender. Later on we will show you how to incorporate this in the materials you will give your recommenders.

Do you have any negatives that your recommenders could help you overcome? We've suggested a few situations when a recommender can be particularly helpful elsewhere in the book:

- Help you overcome a disciplinary or criminal record
- Help you overcome the black holes on your transcript
- Help you overcome a GPA that doesn't stack up so well

Are there any other negatives that your recommenders might help you overcome? Don't lose your perspective here. Limit yourself to the significant negatives. You should have no more than one or two. Make a note of those, and hold onto these notes until you get to tips #6, 7, and 8, where we will show you how to incorporate this into your request to your recommenders and in the materials you will give your recommenders.

Recommendation Tip #4: Choose the Recommenders Who Can Help You Tell Your Story Best

Although you don't always have a choice when it comes to your recommenders (for example, your counselor is usually assigned to you), when you do have a choice, you want to choose the recommenders who can help you tell your story best. Choose recommenders who know you well, who can speak about your positives and negatives based on direct experience, and who like you. If you have significant negatives to overcome (very low grades, a disciplinary or criminal record), choose at least one recommender who can address these negatives either because of the recommender's position or because of the recommender's knowledge of and experience with you.

When it comes to teachers, admissions officers at top colleges are most interested in hearing from teachers who have taught you in a core academic subject—language and literature (English or other), mathematics, science, or history and social studies—in eleventh grade. So consider those teachers first.

Recommendation Tip #5: Ask Your Recommenders Early in the Fall

Recommenders always appreciate having plenty of time to write the recommendation. That is why we suggest that you ask your recommenders at the beginning of your twelfth-grade (senior) year. However, we do know that some private schools encourage applicants to ask teacher recommenders at the end of eleventh grade. In either case, it is clear that you should ask your recommenders earlier rather than later.

Recommendation Tip #6: Ask Graciously

Ask for your recommendation in a face-to-face meeting rather than by a phone call, e-mail, Facebook post, or text message. A face-to-face meeting signals that you are approaching the college application process with great seriousness, and it allows for some conversation about your request. However, we recognize that face-to-face meetings are not always possible and are not always the best way. For example, you may be requesting a recommendation from a teacher who is no longer at your school and no longer lives in the area. In that case, a phone call or e-mail would be appropriate. In the case of a peer recommender, the best way might very well be a text because that is how you communicate with each other all the time. So we leave it to your best judgment.

Whether you are asking the recommender face-to-face or in some other manner, you must ask in a way that allows for a gracious out should the recommender not be willing or able to write you a positive recommendation. We suggest use phrasing something like this: "Mr. Smith, I am talking with teachers about recommendations for college. I hope you would be one of my recommenders. Are you able to write a positive recommendation for me to college?" If Mr. Smith says "no," don't plead your case. Accept the "no," and thank him for considering your request. Trust us, you do not want to be talking someone into writing you a good recommendation; the ambivalence will always come through.

Most of you will not have to ask your school counselor to provide a recommendation for you; he or she will do it as a matter of course. That being said, you will have to initiate the process in some official way. Often, you initiate the process by attending an orientation session about the college application process or by having a first meeting with your school counselor. This initiating action is the equivalent of the ask, and the way to exhibit respect and courtesy with this kind of ask is to do exactly what is required of you on or before the due date.

Recommendation Tip #7: If You Are Going to Ask a Recommender to Help You Overcome a Negative Aspect of Your Record, Discuss It with Your Recommender

For the teacher recommendations, you should bring this up when you ask them to be recommenders. Use language something like this:

> Mr. Smith, one of the reasons that I was particularly hopeful that
> you would be willing to write my recommendation is because you

know how I have worked to make up for my poor performance in ninth and tenth grades and really turned things around in eleventh grade. Could you write a positive recommendation for me that would address that?

For the counselor recommendation, you will need to schedule a meeting to talk with your counselor. Again, you should be direct in your request. For example, you might say, "Ms. Martinez, I was hopeful that in your recommendation you might address how I have turned things around since my disciplinary problem in ninth grade. Would that be possible?"

Broach the subject tactfully and give them a gracious out. You cannot and should not dictate what either your school counselor or teacher says in the recommendation. You can use language along these lines:

Ms. Martinez, I would like to talk with you about the possibility of your including some information about _____ in your recommendation. I have explained the situation in my application but I know it would really help my application if you could address it as well. Would that be possible?

By using the question, "Would that be possible?" you have left the recommender with a way to say "no." Also make sure to provide additional authorizations and information as needed for them to address the topic in their recommendations. You should provide whatever is needed as swiftly as possible so that your recommenders are not delayed or inconvenienced in any way.

Recommendation Tip #8: Provide Your Recommender with a Package of Materials That Contains Everything the Recommender Needs

Great recommendations are detailed and specific. They offer stories and examples. They bring out subtleties and nuances. They validate and support the positives, and they explain and neutralize the negatives. In order to write a great recommendation like this, your recommender needs information to add to the recommendation. Who is the best source for that information and material? You. You need to give your recommenders the information they need to craft a great recommendation. It is relatively easy to assemble a package for your recommenders that will ensure they have absolutely everything they need. Your package should include the following:

- A cover letter. Your cover letter is the place you will mention the positives that you hope the recommender will address as well as confirm what, if any, negatives that the recommender can help you overcome. (We have provided a sample of this cover letter at the end of the chapter.)
- A chart of colleges where you are applying with deadlines and instructions for how to submit the recommendation
- Recommendation forms: paper forms or URLs for downloading the forms
- Postage paid and preaddressed envelopes (as needed)
- Your résumé

The one recommender who may not need your package is your school counselor. Many times school counselors collect all of this information from you in a format that makes it easier for them to process. As long as you have already provided your school counselor with all the information that is in the recommender package, then you are good to go for the counselor recommendation.

Recommendation Tip #9: Check in Politely

Recommenders get busy and they aren't necessarily paying attention to deadlines the way you are. It is actually helpful to them if you check in and follow up just so that the recommendation gets submitted in time and without problem. In this case, a short e-mail is perfectly appropriate.

Recommendation Tip #10: Thank the Recommender

Once you have received word that the recommendation has been submitted, you *must* thank your recommenders promptly and genuinely. When it comes to a proper thank-you, we are fans of a written note. E-mail has probably eclipsed regular mail as a mode of delivery, but either way, put your thanks in writing. You may think that this thank-you note is the only thank-you that is needed but you owe the recommender one last thank-you note. That one should come at the end of this entire process and should let your recommenders know where you will be going to college. (They are invested in the outcome and in your success, after all.) In that note, thank them again. Now you have made your proper thank-yous.

Recommendation Tip #11: Waive Access to Your Recommendations

Under the law, you have the right to see your recommendations (and all other application materials that remain in your student record) after you have been admitted and enroll in a college, unless you waive that right. Typically, the only reason applicants decline to waive access is when applicants are concerned about what the recommender might say and wants to discourage the recommender from saying anything negative. Although this may solve the immediate problem of getting a positive recommendation, it creates a new and equally serious problem: a recommendation that will not have much heft. When you do not waive access, you are not only sending a signal to the recommender, but you are also sending a signal to the admissions officer, who might conclude that this recommendation cannot be fully trusted because the recommender could not be completely frank. That is why we have a different suggestion for how to handle it when you do not trust your recommender: choose a different recommender.

USING OTHER RECOMMENDATIONS TO YOUR ADVANTAGE

In addition to your core recommendations from your counselor and two teachers, you may have additional required recommendations, or you might be considering whether extra recommendations would be beneficial to you. We've assembled our tips for these other recommendations here, but don't lose track of the preceding tips about recommendations in general—they apply, too!

Additional Recommendation Tip #1: If a Peer Recommendation Is Required, Choose an Actual Peer

A peer is someone who is basically your age and someone whom you regard as an equal. Best friends, classmates, and teammates are peers; hero-worshipping younger students or siblings and doting adults are not.

Additional Recommendation Tip #2: If You Have Done Scientific Research or Undertaken a Substantial Academic Project, Submit an Extra Recommendation from Your Supervisor or Instructor

Because admissions officers look to your recommendations for information about your academic achievements, these particular extra recommendations are usually welcome and add something meaningful to your application. The recommendation should come from your research supervisor or the instructor who oversaw your project. If you cannot figure out a way to submit it as an extra recommendation, list your research supervisor as a reference, along with his or her name and contact information and a brief description of the research or project, adding the abstract or paper as additional information (see chapter 15).

Additional Recommendation Tip #3: Think Twice before Obtaining Extra Teacher Recommendations or Recommendations from Coaches, Employers, and Others

Although many applicants have the impulse to provide extra recommendations to colleges, we tell them to think twice before even obtaining those extra recommendations. What we know from our experience and what every admissions officer will tell you is that extra recommendations rarely add anything meaningful to your application. Colleges do their best to communicate this reality to you. Read any college's policies on additional recommendations and you will see that they are full of language like *discourage* or *rarely necessary* or *not accepted* when it comes to extra recommendations. If the college does allow extra recommendations, consider whether that extra recommendation can add anything that would be meaningful to your application. Unless it would provide support and validation for some part of your story (Ivey Strategy #3) and includes information that is not found anywhere else in your application, then the extra recommendation would not add anything meaningful and is, frankly, a waste of time for everyone involved.

Additional Recommendation Tip #4: Do Not Submit Parent Recommendations (Unless You Are Homeschooled, in Which Case It's Actually a Counselor or Teacher Recommendation)

We've encountered thousands of applicants and we've never, ever seen a situation in which a parent recommendation would have been helpful or was in fact helpful. You might be that one in a million we haven't come across, but it's highly unlikely that the admissions officer will be swayed in your favor because of something your mom or dad says. Sorry! Yes, we know that some colleges have now made a parent recommendation optional. But frankly, we see that as a maneuver designed more to curry favor with (and appease) your parents than any real indication that these recommendations can make a positive difference for your application.

Parent Tip: Identify VIPs Who Can Help Your Child

You no doubt have a fairly extensive professional and social network. Now is the time to put it to work on behalf of your child. Identify people you know who are graduates of or who might have connections to the colleges where your child is applying. They are potential VIPs who could be of great assistance to your child. Initiate a conversation with them to see what the nature of their connections are and whether they are willing to do something in support of your child's application. If they are true VIPs and willing to help, then you can ask on your child's behalf. It is usually a good idea to arrange for your child to meet them or at the very least share your child's résumé with them so that they can speak knowledgably about your child when they make contact with the college on your child's behalf. Even if they are not true VIPs (perhaps they are just enthusiastic graduates of the college who really haven't been involved alums), your conversation with them can yield good information about the college and its programs to share with your child. So work your networks and see what turns up. At the very least, you will have some good conversations with people you know!

Additional Recommendation Tip #5: When It Comes to VIPs, You Want a Flag on Your File Rather Than a Recommendation in Your File

Many applicants (and their parents) are quite eager to obtain recommendations from people whom they perceive to be very important or very influential, the people we call VIPs. Although there is no doubt that a good word from a VIP can make a positive difference to your application, it has to come from the *right*

VIP and get noted in your application file in the right way; otherwise, a VIP recommendation is a waste of time.

The right VIP is someone *who knows you and who can influence people at the highest level of the college*—the president, the provost, the head of admissions or development, or members of the board.

The right way for the VIP's good word to be noted in your application is as a flag on the file rather than a recommendation in the file because a flag will not be overlooked and will generally carry more weight than an extra recommendation would. As you know, a flag on the file is a factor in the admissions officers' evaluation of your application (see chapter 5), and it signals to the admissions officer that there is special interest in your application by someone at a very high level at the college or university. It does not depend on the admissions officer recognizing who the VIP is, as a recommendation would.

So what does the VIP do to get a flag on your file? A few different possibilities. The VIP can forego writing a recommendation altogether and simply make a phone call or send an e-mail to the high-level person at the college and ask that the VIP's interest be noted. Another way is for the VIP to write the recommendation and send it directly to the high-level person at the college and ask that it be passed along. A third way is for the VIP to send a copy of the recommendation to the high-level person at the college in addition to sending it directly to the admissions office. Any of these methods is fine; leave it to the VIP recommender to do it whatever way is best for the VIP. You simply must make sure that the VIP knows to do it in a way that gets the flag on your file.

JUST FOR INTERNATIONAL APPLICANTS

International applicants confront some special challenges when it comes to the recommendations, but you can still get the recommendations that will make a positive difference. Just observe these modifications to the general advice we have given others in the chapter.

- If you do not have a school counselor, ask a school official to complete your counselor recommendation. This is completely allowed; in fact, if you read the fine print on most counselor recommendation forms, it explicitly notes that the form may be completed by *any* school official. Because the counselor recommendation asks for an overall assessment of you, the best person to complete it is someone who can make such an assessment. Oftentimes, it is the head of your school or some other school administrator, but it could be a teacher. Ask the person who you believe would be best for that role.

- Include additional information in your recommender package if your recommenders are unfamiliar with what is expected in a recommendation. Many of the people you might ask to be recommenders have never encountered a US-style recommendation and therefore are not really sure what is expected. Part of showing respect and courtesy to these recommenders is to educate them about what is expected in these kinds of recommendations, and you'll need to add some additional information to the package you give your recommender. (See the sample cover letter for international applicants at the end of the chapter.) If you attend school outside the United States, and have teachers who are not fluent in English, your recommender may submit the letter in his or her native language, as long as it is accompanied by a valid translation. It may be translated by the English teacher at your school or by a recognized translation service.

JUST FOR HOMESCHOOLED APPLICANTS

Homeschooled applicants confront some unique challenges when it comes to recommendations, but you can still get the recommendations that will make a difference. Just observe these modifications to the more general advice we have given in this chapter:

- Find out what each college requires and recommends for the homeschooled applicant. Usually the college will spell out a different set of requirements to meet your particular circumstances.

- Extra recommendations can be more helpful to you than they are to other applicants. If there is any non-family-member adult who has observed you in an environment outside your home, particularly if that environment is a group or community setting, then we encourage you to obtain a recommendation from that adult. Adults to consider: advisors to youth groups, coaches, volunteer supervisors, pastors, rabbis, or other leaders of your faith community.

- Ignore our prohibition on recommendations from parents. When we tell applicants more generally not to submit recommendations from parents, that advice does not apply to you. If your parent is the homeschool supervisor, then he or she is writing this recommendation from a different vantage point, and it will be given due consideration.

- Obtain recommendations from people other than your parents whenever possible. Even though your parent recommendation will be considered, you will benefit from having recommendations from others. The best people are those who have observed you in an academic context, such as instructors, tutors, or academic mentors. If you do not have anyone who has observed you in the academic context other than your parent, talk with the college about who might submit recommendations in addition to your parent's recommendation.

SAMPLE COVER LETTERS FOR RECOMMENDER PACKAGES

Sample Cover Letter to Your Recommenders

Dear [Name of Recommender]:

Thank you so much for agreeing to write a recommendation for me. I really appreciate it.

I intend to apply to the colleges listed on the enclosed chart. The chart also shows deadlines for receipt and instructions for submission. I would ask that you submit recommendations to each of these colleges. Please note I am applying to [College X] early and that the deadline for receipt of the recommendation by that college is [Date Y].

I have enclosed the forms your need [or provided you with the URLs for downloading the forms], as well as postage paid, preaddressed envelopes for the recommendations that must be mailed.

In writing your recommendation, I thought you might be interested in knowing a little bit more about what will be in my application. I intend to highlight: [discuss the positives that you hope the recommender will validate—see recommendation tip #3]. Anything you might say that would validate these attributes would be most helpful.

I also thought you might be interested in having information about my activities and accomplishments overall, so I have enclosed a résumé.

[Only if you have negatives to be addressed] As we discussed in our meeting, I am hopeful that in your recommendation, you will address [the negative]. I really appreciate your willingness to help me with this, and if you need anything else from me in order to discuss it in your recommendation, do not hesitate to ask.

I will check in with you in a few days to make sure you have everything you need, and I will also check in closer to the deadlines just to make sure you haven't encountered any difficulties in completing or submitting the recommendations.

I know that your recommendation will be an important part of my application and ultimate success, so again my profound thanks!

[Applicant Name]

Sample Cover Letter to Your Recommenders (for International Applicants)

Dear [Name of Recommender]:

Thank you so much for agreeing to write a recommendation for me. I really appreciate it.

I intend to apply to the colleges listed on the enclosed chart. The chart also shows deadlines for receipt and instructions for submission. I would ask that you submit recommendations to each of these colleges. Please note I am applying to [College X] early and that the deadline for receipt of the recommendation by that college is [Date Y].

I have enclosed the forms you need [or provided you with the URLs for downloading the forms], as well as postage paid, preaddressed envelopes for the recommendations that must be mailed.

I also thought it might be helpful to share what I have learned about what is expected in your recommendation:

- That you will complete the form and include a 1- to 2-page letter with the form.

- That your letter will provide examples and observations from your direct experience of me.

- [For the counselor recommendation] That your assessment will focus on an overall assessment of me as a member of the school community and will include evaluations of my academic and intellectual abilities, my accomplishments and contributions outside the classroom, and my personal character.

- [For the teacher recommendation] That your assessment will focus on an assessment of me as a student and scholar with particular attention paid to my curiosity and interest in academics, my particular interest in specific subjects, my participation in classroom discussions, my ability to work well with my classmates on team projects, my work ethic, and my performance on written assignments and tests.

- [For all other recommendations] That your assessment will focus on anything about me that you believe makes me a strong candidate for admission to the college with particular attention paid to my academic and intellectual abilities, my accomplishments and contributions to my school and larger community, and my personal character.

In writing your recommendation, I thought you might be interested in knowing a little bit more about what will be in my application. I intend to highlight: [discuss the positives that you hope the recommender will validate—see recommendation tip #3]. Anything you might say that would validate these attributes would be most helpful.

I also thought you might be interested in having information about my activities and accomplishments overall, so I have enclosed a résumé.

[Only if you have negatives to be addressed] As we discussed in our meeting, I am hopeful that in your recommendation, you will address [the negative]. I really appreciate your willingness to help me with this, and if you need anything else from me in order to discuss it in your recommendation, do not hesitate to ask.

I will check in with you in a few days to make sure you have everything you need, and I will also check in closer to the deadlines just to make sure you haven't encountered any difficulties in completing or submitting the recommendations.

I know that your recommendation will be an important part of my application and ultimate success, so again my profound thanks!

[Applicant Name]

SAMPLE RECOMMENDATION LETTERS

Many applicants have very little experience with recommendation letters and don't really know what one looks like, so we wanted to provide you with some samples that would give you an idea of what you are asking recommenders to provide.

We've included samples of letters written for three of the applicants you met in the résumés and activities lists chapters (chapters 4 and 8, respectively)—one is a counselor's recommendation and the other two are teacher recommendations. Although these recommendations are quite different from each other (as you would expect given different authors and different applicants), they all are excellent examples of recommendation letters that would influence an admissions officer in the applicant's favor.

Sample Counselor Recommendation—Gabriella

Gabriella Delgado is a truly remarkable young person. An outstanding student who has made contributions to our school and our city, she is someone who has succeeded in spite of difficult family circumstances.

As the record testifies, Gabriella is an outstanding student. She was one of only 35 students in her class of 1,100 to be chosen for participation in the Honors Alpha Program, which is an integrated science, mathematics, technology, and engineering curriculum reserved for our most talented students.

Gabriella's career goal is to become an environmental scientist. Her work in this direction includes an impressive array of course work and hands-on experiences for someone of her age. By the end of this year, she will have completed our entire AP science sequence and as her transcript and recommendations show, she has been in the top of every one of those classes. She has also conducted independent scientific research of the highest caliber as evidenced by her performance at competitive science fairs and her invitation to present her most recent research to the Mayor of Chicago's senior cabinet and other city leaders. During the summers, Gabriella has worked in internships that have allowed her to engage in hands-on work that has benefitted the people and environment of Chicago. Over 500 people have attended her program, "Green Cleaning 101"; and I've had the pleasure of seeing how the clean-up she and others did on the northern fork of the Chicago River transformed it from a fairly disgusting and smelly blight to a pleasant place to picnic and ride your bike. And perhaps most impressive of all, I am typing this letter using energy provided by the solar panels that Gabriella's club Project Sunshine acquired through sweat equity, but no cash, for our school!

Gabriella's accomplishments and achievements would be remarkable for anyone, but I consider them more remarkable because of the additional responsibilities that Gabriella has at home. With her permission, I am sharing her family circumstances with you so that you too can appreciate just how remarkable Gabriella is.

Gabriella is the youngest of five children in her family. Her parents immigrated to the United States from Mexico before Gabriella was born in hopes of giving their children a better life and future. Although both of Gabriella's parents were trained health care professionals in Mexico, they have been unable to obtain the same type of work in the U.S. and the family has struggled economically. Therefore everyone in the family works very hard. Both her mother and her father are often working two jobs in order to pay for the basic necessities of life, and all of the children have been expected to contribute in some way. Even as the youngest, Gabriella had responsibilities.

By the age of 9, Gabriella was the person in the family who did all the grocery shopping and meal preparation for the family of seven. She was also given responsibility for cleaning the house. As far as I can tell, Gabriella's chores equate to at least 30 hours of work per week. Yet even though she had the equivalent of almost a full-time job, Gabriella was determined to succeed in her schoolwork and achieve the better life and future that her parents wanted for her. Furthermore, she has been creative and resourceful in integrating her two lives. For example, she told me she learned fractions by reading recipes. And she found her passion for environmental science when her mother helped her create a container garden to grow tomatoes, peppers, and herbs and showed her how to mix up common household items to create household cleaning products that were cheaper and better for the environment.

Gabriella was directed to Lane Tech, one of Chicago's magnet schools, by her middle school science teacher. The teacher saw Gabriella's potential and talked with her family about how to apply. It is a testament to both Gabriella and her family that they have worked it out so Gabriella could apply and then accept our offer of admission. Gabriella still does all the grocery shopping, meal preparation, and housekeeping for her family, which now numbers 9 with the addition of a husband and child for her oldest sister. But all of the members of Gabriella's family are committed to her success, so they have pitched in and helped Gabriella as they can. For example, the family agreed that Gabriella would not have to find paying employment during the summers, so that she could pursue internships.

The love and support within Gabriella's family is admirable, and Gabriella's own sunny disposition and pride in contributing to the family are reflections of how well this family has managed despite their economic challenges. Nonetheless, in my twenty years as a counselor, I have learned that it is rare for a student, no matter how talented or well-loved, to succeed at the level Gabriella has, when the student also has a high level of responsibility at home. As I said, Gabriella is a truly remarkable young person.

I give her my highest recommendation for admission.

Sample Teacher Recommendation—Andrew

I am delighted to write this recommendation in support of Andrew Smithson's application for admission. He is an exemplary student and an avid athlete who enjoys a trained body every bit as much as a trained mind. I have known Andrew since his arrival at Deerfield because I coach lacrosse and he has been on the varsity team since his 9th grade year. But during the last year I also had the pleasure of teaching Andrew in AP English.

Andrew is someone of great natural ability who combines that with a fierce discipline. The result: huge success in all of his endeavors. For example, Andrew is smart enough that he could slide by in his classes without much work. But that is not how Andrew does it. Instead, he has a policy of going to the school library daily because he says it puts him in "study mode" the same way that coming to lacrosse practice puts him in "sports mode." I have never known Andrew to turn in anything but his best work, whether it was in the classroom or on the field.

In my experience, the Andrews of the world are either leaders or jerks. I am happy to report that Andrew is 100% leader, 0% jerk. I believe that is why he is so admired by both students and faculty alike. In classroom discussions, Andrew could have easily dominated the conversation but he didn't. He listened as much as he spoke, and often his comments built on other comments in a way that both enriched the discussion and brought others along for an intellectual ride they wouldn't have had but for Andrew. On the lacrosse team, Andrew is an offensive star, but he understands that it is a team sport and knows that sometimes it is better for others to "shine." He works as hard to make his teammates successful as he does himself. I suspect that is why there was no question that Andrew would be the team captain this year. I will also note that Andrew has the singular distinction of being the only student in Deerfield history allowed to be captain of two varsity teams in one year. Even though it is a strict rule that a student can only be the captain of one team, the administration and faculty agreed to waive that rule for Andrew without hesitation because we are so confident in his abilities to manage it all well.

In short, Andrew is the best of the best. A young man of tremendous natural ability honed by discipline and a natural leader, Andrew has made Deerfield proud as I'm sure he will the college he attends. I recommend him to you without hesitation.

Sample Teacher Recommendation—Jacqueline

Jacqueline Magaud is a true scholar and an outstanding student.

As a scholar, what impresses me most about Jacqueline is her intellect. Jacqueline "sees" things that other students just don't comprehend yet. Her topic for her extended essay reveals the sophisticated nature of her thinking. Most students would not be able to distinguish the significant, but subtle, differences between being a "destination country" and a "transit country" for human trafficking. Jacqueline not only understands these differences, she also was more intrigued by the more challenging question relating to Switzerland's role as a transit country. There is less scholarship available on this question, yet Jacqueline believed it to be the better topic for just that reason. She wanted to do her own research and formulate her own thesis, rather than borrow from pre-existing scholarship. As she has begun work on the essay, I can see that Jacqueline leaves no stone unturned, a skill I'm sure she acquired through her debate research and the actual discipline of debating. (As you are no doubt aware, Jacqueline is a top debater and has achieved notable recognition for her debating skills at tournaments involving students from all over the world.)

Jacqueline's writing and speaking abilities are equal to her intellect. Her writing is witty and masterful, but equally important, logical and scholarly. Jacqueline has words at her command and manipulates them with an ease that many would envy. Her speaking is seemingly effortless, and she is able to present a complex idea in such a way that even those without her intellect or knowledge can grasp it.

As a student, Jacqueline is diligent and productive. She displays a seriousness of purpose that is welcome. In our class last year, she was a pivotal contributor to the class discussions because she raised both interesting questions and made insightful comments. If she was not in class, the quality of the discussions declined markedly.

I recommend Jacqueline Magaud's admission without reservation.

CHAPTER 20

Interviews

Interviews are wildly different from every other part of your application. Whether you're being interviewed by a student on campus, by an alum at a local Starbucks, or by an admissions officer via Skype, it is a direct exchange between you and another person, and that dynamic changes everything. There is information that gets shared in conversations that would never come out otherwise, and there are observations about behavior and demeanor that make lasting impressions. What happens in an interview is so distinctive that it always either helps or hurts; it is never neutral.

Every seasoned admissions officer has an arsenal of stories about interviews—the good, the bad, and the oh so very ugly. No wonder many applicants worry so much about interviews that they are virtually paralyzed with fear. Rather than seize the opportunity presented by interviews, they do everything in their power to avoid them.

We want interviews to be different for you. We want you to know when it makes sense for you to interview, and—just as important—when not to. And we want you to know what you can do before, during, and after the interview to ensure that you have a good, and even great, interview.

SHOULD YOU INTERVIEW?

Interviews are rarely a required component of the college application process, simply because most colleges do not have the wherewithal to manage the thousands of interviews that would be necessary in any given year. But there are exceptions. For example, Georgetown requires all applicants to interview with an alum unless it is geographically impossible. Other colleges stop just short of requiring interviews and instead *strongly encourage* them. Those that strongly encourage them often offer a variety of options for the interviews, including telephone and Skype interviews. However, there are also colleges that do not offer interviews at all, as well as colleges with interview policies for every variation in between.

Your decision about whether to interview obviously depends on the policies of the colleges where you are applying. Research their policies not only to see whether an interview is required, optional, or not available at all but also to understand what the college is signaling about the optional interview (*strongly encouraged* versus *offered* versus *limited availability*) and whether the optional interview is evaluative or not.

WHAT WE MEAN BY *INTERVIEW*

In this chapter, when we use the word *interview*, we are talking about an evaluative interview, not an informational interview or any other kind of interview an applicant might have during the college admissions process.

A college's admissions policies determine whether an interview is evaluative or not. An interview is evaluative *only* if the interview results in an interview report, which becomes a part of the application and is considered by the admissions officer when making her decision. Who conducts the interview, where the interview takes place, or how the interview is conducted does not determine whether the interview is evaluative or not. An evaluative interview could be conducted by an admissions officer, an alum, or a student. An evaluative interview can take place on or off campus, in person, by telephone, or over the Internet. The only way to know whether an interview is evaluative or not is to consult the college's admissions policies.

Obviously, there are no decisions for you to make with colleges that either require an interview or don't offer an interview at all. But for colleges where interviews are optional, we encourage you to interview for three reasons.

First, you get a second chance to make your case for admitting you—this time through conversation rather than in writing—and two bites at the apple are better than one. Second, an interview is a great way to show, not tell (Ivey Strategy #7) that you have the demonstrated interest that some colleges consider in making decisions (see chapter 5). Third, you can get valuable information that will help you when it comes down to choosing where to enroll. Just as the admissions officer gets a different perspective on you through a direct exchange, you, too, can get a different perspective on the college and whether it really is the right fit for you. You want to know everything you can about the place that will shape your destiny. So seize the opportunity and interview.

Even though we encourage interviews, there are two circumstances when it is appropriate not to do an optional interview:

- *It is cost prohibitive.* Be sure you have considered all the available options before you assume that it is cost prohibitive for you to interview. Your school counselor can probably help you line up a phone interview even if that option isn't expressly mentioned on the college's website.

- *Your ability to perform well in an interview setting is severely compromised due to a disability or a serious medical problem.* For example, you have a neurological syndrome and stress sets off symptoms that would interfere with an interview or perhaps you suffer from debilitating anxiety. In these circumstances, we do suggest you take a pass on the interview unless a central element of your story is how you have overcome your disability or medical problem. In that case, the interview is exactly what you need to make your case and it will be great validation of your story. Consider all the options available and what would be necessary to make an interview work for you. Perhaps you will need to ask for some accommodations. That's fine. Most admissions offices would be quite open to that kind of request.

Assuming that you have decided that you will be interviewing at one or more of your colleges, then you need to do what it takes to conquer the interview. In the rest of this chapter, we will walk you through all the things you need to do before, during, and after the interview.

PREPARE

What you do before the interview is, in many ways, the secret sauce when it comes to the success of the interview. If you prepare well for the interview, it is virtually assured that you will perform well in the interview. Preparation also helps to avert the vast majority of interview disasters.

There are several things you need to know or have thought about before you are ready for an interview, so set aside time to do the necessary research and reflection.

Preparation Tip #1: Know What to Expect in the Interview

This might go without saying, but the interview will go much better if you have some basic information about the who, what, when, and where. Most colleges describe what to expect in their materials for applicants. Find out who will be conducting the interview: an admissions officer, an alum, a student? Find out where the interview will be held: on campus, at your school, at the alum's office place, at an agreed-on location, over the phone? Find out how long the interview generally lasts and what is usually covered in the interview. This information will help you with all of the rest of your preparation.

Preparation Tip #2: Know What You Want to Say in Your Interview

Even though you cannot know what questions you will be asked in your interview in advance, you can prepare yourself for whatever question comes your way by thinking through your answers to the kinds of questions that are most commonly asked in a college admissions interview. The questions will center on four topics, all of which you have already thought about quite extensively: your academic and intellectual abilities and interests, your accomplishments in activities outside the classroom, your personal background and character, and your demonstrated interest in the college. You have answers to questions on these topics in your story, your résumé, and your "Why College X?" essays. Now all you need to do is translate what you have there into answers suitable for an interview. You can practice with the sample interview questions we list at the end of the chapter.

Preparation Tip #3: Think through Your Answers

Work at striking a balance between overselling and underselling yourself. The best way to do this is to claim your successes proudly but without any exaggeration or arrogance. If you are the fastest runner on the track team and close to breaking a school record, then say exactly that. Don't say, "I'm a lightning fast, record-breaking runner on our track team" (oversell) or "I'm a pretty fast runner" (undersell). Don't bother trying to script out an answer for every question because that is not your goal. Your goal is to practice formulating an answer that contains what you want to say and that you could offer in the course of an interview.

Preparation Tip #4: Have Questions Ready

In most interviews, you will be invited to ask whatever questions you would like to ask about the college. Asking the right type of questions takes some thought, so think about them in advance. The interview is not the time to ask questions about the admissions process or to ask the most basic questions about the college. It is expected that you already know these things and that you know how to go to the website and find basic information on your own. Instead, you want to ask questions that actually get to the deeper, more interesting information about the college, the information that you can get only from a person who knows the college well. If you ask those kinds of questions, you will not only impress the interviewer with the quality of your thinking and interest in the college, you are also likely to get answers that will be helpful to you. Here are some of our favorite questions. We like them because they are open-ended and often elicit helpful insights from your interviewers:

- If the interviewer is an alum: why did you choose to attend College X? (Note that many admissions officer are also alums, and that's something you should be able to find out in advance.)

- What is the most popular major? Least popular? Why?

- Can you describe a typical weekday in the life of a student at College X? What about a typical weekend?

- What is one can't-be-missed tradition, event, or opportunity that I should take advantage of if I were a student at College X?

- I am really interested in ABC major, activity, program at College X. Can you tell me more about it?

LOGISTICS

Interviews do not just magically happen. They involve a surprisingly complex set of tasks that must be planned and executed. You can handle most of these tasks without much guidance, but we have assembled a list of things to do that will make your life easier and should keep you from missing anything big.

Logistics Tip #1: Request and Schedule Your Interview Early

Many colleges have a first-come, first-served policy when it comes to interviews, so get your interviews scheduled as soon as you have decided that you will be doing an interview.

Logistics Tip #2: Think through Your Availability before You Schedule Your Interview

It is not always easy to reschedule an interview, so before you schedule one, think through your availability on certain days and at certain times. Make sure you factor in things such as travel time and your ability to be excused from school.

Logistics Tip #3: Plan Your Outfit Well in Advance

Make sure it is clean and ready to go at least two days before the interview. See the following section for the dress code for college interviews.

Logistics Tip #4: Do Whatever You Need to Do to Make Sure You Get to the Interview on the Right Day at the Right Time

Need reminders? Set them up. Need to put it on your mom's calendar as well as yours? Give her the information. Do whatever is necessary to make sure you don't miss your interview or double-book yourself.

Logistics Tip #5: Get Emergency Contact Information for the Interviewer

Just in case something completely unforeseeable happens that will make you late or unable to get to your interview, you need to be able to reach your interviewer. Go ahead and ask for the interviewer's mobile telephone number and e-mail when you are confirming your interview appointment.

Logistics Tip #6: Know Where You're Going

Make sure you know *exactly* how to get where you need to go for your interview. If you are going somewhere you have never been before, get maps and directions. If your interview is going to be in your town or city, do a dry run just to be safe. Leave plenty of time for traffic and travel snafus.

Logistics Tip #7: Assemble a File with All the Information You Need

Your file should include the interviewer's name and contact information, the interview location and directions for getting there, your story, your résumé, notes from your research about the college, your list of questions for the interviewer, and any reminders to yourself.

Logistics Tip #8: For Phone or Internet Interviews Only, Test Your Reception

If you are going to have the interview by phone or online, make sure you have good reception or a good connection and that you can be easily heard and understood on whatever phone or device you will be using. Also make certain that you can take the call in a location that is quiet.

Logistics Tip #9: For Video Internet Interviews Only, Locate the Best Place to Be Interviewed

If you are having a video interview online, for example on Skype, you need to give some careful thought about where to be interviewed, because the setting for your interview will leave an impression on the interviewer. In deciding where to be interviewed, consider the following:

- Is the location well lit? Test what your image looks like on screen and make sure there is enough light and that there are no weird shadows.

- Is the location quiet? Ambient noise is distracting.

- Does the location allow you to be seated in front of the webcam in such a way that you can make direct eye contact? If not, put some books under your monitor or laptop (or switch chairs) so that you are at eye level with the camera.

- Is the background appropriately neutral? Check to see what shows up in the webcam frame. The best backgrounds are solid colors that flatter you. You don't want the interviewer to be focused on anything but you!

DRESS CODE

The dress code for a college admissions interview is midway between casual attire and professional attire. You should not dress in the hoodie, jeans, and flip flops (unless you end up interviewing with Mark Zuckerberg), but you do not need to wear a suit either, let alone dress for a royal wedding. Think instead of a stylish school uniform (if that is possible).

Style Tip #1: What to Wear

Men should wear khakis or other nonjeans trousers, a polo or button-down shirt, a belt, and respectable shoes. A jacket or sweater is optional. Women should wear either nice pants or a skirt (no leggings or minis) with a nice shirt, or a dress, and wear respectable shoes. Jackets and sweaters are optional.

Style Tip #2: What Not to Wear

Here are some dress choices that are *never* appropriate:

- Anything that smacks of a costume or sports attire—this includes all things Goth, anything bling-bling, anything Kim Kardashian or a hip-hop mogul would wear, and any sports uniforms or fan wear.

- Anything with a slogan, joke, or call to arms. Save your "I'm with Stupid" shirt for another day.

- Anything that is supposed to signal what a "fun" person you are, such as a loud tie or a flashing pin. Also avoid holiday-themed and school-spirit clothing.

- Anything that was originally intended as underwear, sleepwear, or workout wear. No boxers, no flannel PJ bottoms, no sweats (not even pretty velour ones). Same goes for shoes: no running shoes, for example.

- Anything that you just bought at the college bookstore that has the name of the college on it, because that's just a little too obvious. It would most likely be a sweatshirt or T-shirt, anyway, and both of those are verboten.

Style Tip #3: Miscellaneous No-Nos

- No hats, whether baseball, knitted, woven, or suitable for church. None.

- No sunglasses on your face, on a cord around your neck, or on the top of your head.

- Only conservative and understated jewelry.

- Subdued makeup only.

- No fragrances—too many people are sensitive to them, plus they're highly subjective. You don't want your interviewer to be allergic to you.

PRACTICE

Interviewing is a learned skill and, like most learned skills, you'll get better with practice. It is actually fairly easy to practice interviewing. Recruit a parent or a teacher or some other adult to serve as your interviewer. Give them sample interview questions and a sample evaluation form (found at the end of the chapter) and go for it!

For the best practice, conduct the interview in a setting as close to the actual setting for the interview as you can manage. If you are going for an interview with someone in an office, practice in an office. If you are going to do an interview over the phone or Skype, practice over the phone or Skype. If you're going to do the interview at a coffee shop, go practice in that coffee shop. Practice every moment of the interview from start to finish—from arrival to departure, from the first word to the last.

After you have completed your practice interview, give your interviewer time to complete a rough draft of the evaluation (found at the end at the chapter). While he is doing that, you do a self-evaluation using the same form. Then talk about the two evaluations. Where is there agreement? Where is there disagreement? What is found on the interviewer's evaluation but not yours and vice versa? After you have finished your discussion, take time to summarize a few key takeaways for yourself by filling in the following blanks:

- Takeaway #1: I did the following things exactly right and should keep doing them: _____.

- Takeaway #2: I need to work just a bit on these things:_____.
  I intend to do the following: _____.

- Takeaway #3: I really need to rethink my approach or develop my skills with regard to these things: _____. I will do that by _____.

Your takeaways will dictate the work that remains to be done before your interview.

AT THE INTERVIEW

There is no way you can predict everything that will happen in your interviews but there are things you can do to be at your best no matter how the interview unfolds and to make the best impression during the interview itself.

Interview Tip #1: Arrive Early

Early is best. Here's why. Although you may be forgiven if something completely unforeseen happens (the car in front of you on the freeway exploded) *and* you get word to the interviewer as soon as possible, you still want to go to great lengths to avoid being late. Arriving on time is fine but that doesn't leave you any time to take a moment and collect yourself. You cannot take three deep breaths and reduce your anxiety. And, if anything small goes wrong in transit, you go from being on time to being late. So plan ahead to arrive early. That gives you time to put your game face on and calm your nerves. Even better, it gives you recovery time should something go wrong in transit or even just as you arrive. A little unanticipated traffic? No problem. Windblown and wet from the short and unexpected rain storm? You have time to go to the bathroom and comb your hair, dry off, and look cool as a cucumber before the interviewer even arrives.

Interview Tip #2: Introduce Yourself Properly

Interviews that start smoothly have a certain positive momentum and it all begins with the greeting and introduction. Greet your interviewer by shaking his or her hand and introducing yourself. (Practice this with an adult in advance. You want to sound and look confident.) Be sure to say your name clearly and slowly enough that the interviewer will have no trouble understanding it or pronouncing it throughout the course of the interview.

Interview Tip #3: Offer Your Résumé

Just as you and the interviewer get settled, offer your résumé. You can say, "I wasn't sure what information you would have about me, so I brought you a copy of my résumé." This extra effort on your part is sure to impress any interviewer. Besides, it shows that you are aware that the interviewer may or may not know anything about you. Alums almost never get anything beyond your name, high school, and some contact information before the interview. Student interviewers, who usually work for the admissions office, may get a little more than that. Even admissions officers may not know much, because even though they have access to your application materials, you may not have submitted anything yet, or whatever you have submitted may not have been processed yet.

Interview Tip #4: Engage in Conversation

Let go of the idea that the interview is an oral examination in which the interviewer asks questions and the interviewee answers them. Instead, an interview is a structured conversation in which the interviewer leads the conversation with the interviewee. So your job is to be a good conversation partner.

- *A good conversation partner talks rather than recites.* So talk rather than recite. Don't try and retrieve answers that you have prepared. Instead, listen to the question that the interviewer asks. Then respond with the answer that comes to you in that moment. If you've practiced sufficiently, your previously prepared answers will be incorporated in a spontaneous and authentic way if you just answer the question asked.

- *A good conversation partner has personality.* Don't be afraid to let your personality shine. If you try to be someone you are not, then you will not be able to keep up your end of the conversation. You will be too busy maintaining the pretense. Relax and focus on demonstrating the qualities that your close friends and family say you have. Remember those? They are the ones found in sentence #4 of your story. Those qualities are authentically yours and are worth putting on display. But what if those qualities include something like introverted, shy, reserved, or quiet? No worries. None of these qualities render you incapable of conversation with one other person. Concentrate on answering the questions and you will be fine.

- *A good conversation partner is relaxed enough to participate.* It is completely natural to be a little anxious in an interview. In fact, being a little nervous can be helpful because it gives you a little adrenaline kick. But you do have to manage your anxiety so that it does not get out of control. You do not want to shut down or babble uncontrollably.

- *A good conversation partner responds with more than a one-word answer.* "Yes" or "no" is a perfectly legitimate answer to a question, but it is an absolute conversation killer, as are almost all one-word answers. There is no place for the interviewer to go from there, unless he shifts to interrogation mode. If you give answers that take it beyond the one-word answer and give a few details, you invite follow-on questions. That sustains the conversation and reduces the possibility of awkward silences.

INTERROGATION VERSUS CONVERSATION

Exchange #1

Interviewer: Do you have a favorite subject in school?
Applicant: Yes.
Interviewer: What is it?
Applicant: English.
Interviewer: Why?
Applicant: Because I love stories and I have a really great teacher.
Interviewer: That's interesting. What makes the teacher so great?

Exchange #2

Interviewer: Do you have a favorite subject in school?
Applicant: Yes, English is my favorite because I have a really great teacher.
Interviewer: That's interesting. What makes the teacher so great?

Exchange #1 sounds tortured. Exchange #2 sounds pleasant. The only real difference? The applicant in the first exchange gave one-word answers; the applicant in the second exchange did not.

Interview Tip #5: Don't Bluff

You should not bluff or lie about *anything*. If you speak all of three words of French, don't suggest that you are conversational in it. You are likely to suddenly find yourself scrambling to understand the interviewer's next question because she will ask it in French. If you are asked about your favorite novel, don't offer up the one you only know through CliffsNotes. It will be really hard to keep the conversation going when the interviewer starts probing about a particular scene or character because the interviewer happened to have written his master's thesis on that novel. Not only is it embarrassing to get caught in even the smallest bluffs by the interviewer, but there is no faster or surer way to get denied than a breach of integrity.

Interview Tip #6: End in Style

When the interviewer brings the interview to a conclusion, you need to do three things in order to end the interview in style:

- Ask the interviewer for a business card or contact information (including the interviewer's full name spelled correctly)—you will need it for your follow-up.
- Thank the interviewer for taking the time to interview you.
- Shake the interviewer's hand and be on your way.

AFTER THE INTERVIEW

Once your interview is over, you have very little to do in the way of follow-up. However, you will not get the full benefit from your interview if you skip the follow-up. You can get it all done in an hour or less and you should do it as soon after the interview as possible.

Follow-up Tip #1: Write Down Your Impressions

Take ten to fifteen minutes and write down your thoughts about the college based on what you learned in the interview. For example, did you learn something that made this college more attractive to you or less attractive to you? Did you learn anything new or change your mind about something? Is there anything you need to investigate further? Add those notes to the file you keep for that college.

Follow-up Tip #2: Send a Thank-You Note to the Interviewer

You may send that note by e-mail if, and only if, your e-mail follows the conventions of professional correspondence. That means no emoticons, no abbreviations, no sentence fragments, no slang, and no "hey." You may also send it as a handwritten note if your writing is legible. Ask your parents or another trusted adult to check for professionalism and tone before you send it.

Follow-up Tip #3: Let the College Admissions Office Know That You Had Your Interview

If you did not have your interview on campus or with an admissions officer, let them know that it took place. Thank the office for their help in setting up the interview and tell them how much you enjoyed it. (This little bit of follow-through will ensure that the interviewer's evaluation becomes a part of your file.)

ETIQUETTE

There are certain behaviors that you should exhibit with every person and at every juncture when you interact with the admissions office or anyone else at the college and during your interviews.

Etiquette Tip #1: Be Polite

Rudeness is a huge negative. Your politeness should extend to everyone you encounter. Flippant comments to the administrative assistant at the front desk often find their way up the chain of command.

Etiquette Tip #2: Be Respectful of People's Time and Effort

Interviews are big investments for everyone involved. Under no circumstances should you fail to keep an interview appointment or fail to respond to an invitation to interview. In our experience as former admissions officers, we'd say that about 10 percent pull a no-show or simply fail to respond. And guess what, they don't get in . . . even with perfect scores. No lie.

Etiquette Tip #3: Be a Grown Up

This is not the time for your fun-loving kid side to assert itself. Even with student interviewers, be a grown up. What do we mean? Don't answer a question by talking about the time you got wasted or played a wicked practical joke or ask a question about the party atmosphere of the school. That too works its way up the chain of command. Maturity counts.

Parent Tip: Interviews

Parents can be of great help to their children with interviews, as long as they observe appropriate boundaries along the way.

- Help your child develop interview skills and boost confidence. Be a practice interviewer or recruit friends to do it. Volunteer to make a video of the practice interview so your child can review it. Remind your child of how he or she has mastered new skills in the past.
- Do not schedule the interview for your child. Do drive your child to the interview but *do not go into the interview* with your child. If possible, stay completely clear of the building where the interview is being conducted. If you overstep these bounds, the admissions officer will assume that your child is irresponsible, immature, and cannot handle basic tasks on his or her own.
- Help your child with composing a thank-you note, if help is needed.

TWENTY SAMPLE INTERVIEW QUESTIONS

Questions about Your Academic Profile

- Tell me something about your courses.
- Is your record an accurate gauge of your abilities and potential?
- What might your teachers say are your greatest strength and your greatest weakness as a student?
- Would you rather write a report or give an oral report? Why?
- What is the most important thing you've learned in high school?

Questions about Your Extracurricular and Activity Profile

- Tell me about your involvement in extracurricular activities, hobbies, and interests outside of school.

- How did you spend last summer?

- Which of your activities is most rewarding and why? Most enjoyable and why?

- Would you make different choices of activities if you were to do it all over again?

- In what ways have you been a leader?

Questions about Your Personal Profile

- Tell me about yourself.

- What has been your biggest achievement? Biggest challenge?

- What do you want to do after you graduate from college? What do you expect to be doing five years from now? Ten years?

- What are your strengths and weaknesses as a person? What would you like to change about yourself? What makes you special? What three adjectives best describe you? What are some of your unique qualities?

- What is your favorite book, movie, song, TV show, website, newspaper, piece of art, and so on? Who is your favorite author, actor, musician, comedian, and so on?

Questions about College and this College in Particular

- Why do you want to go to college? Have you ever thought about not going to college and what you might choose to do instead?

- Why do you want to attend our college? What other colleges are you considering? What can our college offer you that these other colleges can't?

- What do you want or expect to get out of your college experience?

- What do you want to major in? What activities do you want to pursue outside the classroom? What personal traits would you like to see yourself build in the next four years?

- What will you contribute to our college community as a student? As an alum?

SAMPLE INTERVIEW EVALUATION FORM

Academic Abilities and Intellectual Engagement

Please comment on the candidate's demonstrated academic abilities and intellectual engagement: e.g., in-depth pursuit of particular study, extra study in summers, academic projects or research, intellectual curiosity, academic experiences that have impacted his/her thinking, love of learning, creativity or originality in thinking, depth of thought, breadth of awareness, and articulateness in idea expression. Also, please cite specific examples from your conversation (other than rank-in-class, grade-point-average, SAT/ACT scores, etc.) to support your observations.

Please rate the candidate on this dimension using the scale below:

_____

1   Exceptional
2   Above Average
3   Solid/Average
4   Below Average
5   DO NOT ADMIT
9   No basis for evaluation

Accomplishments Outside the Classroom

Please comment on the candidate's demonstrated accomplishments outside the classroom, paying particular attention to the candidate's ability/potential to make a positive, significant contribution to the college community and go on to make positive, significant contributions to the world. Note special talents, depth of commitment, initiative required, and/or leadership. Also note the level of the candidate's impact or accomplishment—family, school, local community, state, regional, national, international. Please cite specific examples from your conversation to support your observations.

Please rate the candidate on this dimension using the scale below:

_____

1 Exceptional
2 Above Average
3 Solid/Average
4 Below Average
5 DO NOT ADMIT
9 No basis for evaluation

Character and Personality:

Please provide your impressions of the candidate in relation to qualities that speak to the candidate's character or personality: e.g., energy, enthusiasm, tolerance, resilience, sense of humor, integrity, independence, compassion, and maturity. Please cite specific examples from your conversation to support your observations, including any specific events, unusual circumstances, or life experiences shared by the candidate, which provide insight into his/her character.

Please rate the candidate on this dimension using the scale below:

_____

1 Exceptional
2 Above Average
3 Solid/Average
4 Below Average
5 DO NOT ADMIT
9 No basis for evaluation

Interest in the College:

Please comment on the candidate's level of interest in the college as demonstrated in the interview. Note whether the candidate impressed you with informed and interesting questions about the college, what might convince the candidate to choose the college, and any obstacles identified to accepting admission. Please cite specific examples from your conversation to support your observations.

Please rate the candidate's interest using the scale below: _____

1 High
2 Moderate
3 Low
9 No basis for evaluation

Anything Else?

Please comment on anything else you think is important to a full evaluation of candidate. Note anything you discovered about the candidate that might not appear elsewhere on the application and that has not been reported above. Please cite specific examples from your conversation to support your observations.

CHAPTER 21

The Application as a Whole Redux

Now that you have completed all of the various components for your first application, it is time to take one more look at that application as a whole. You need to make sure that your entire application comes together into a coherent and compelling story about you (Ivey Strategy #3). If it does, then you have produced a standout application, an application that presents you at your very best and maximizes your chances for admission.

READ YOUR APPLICATION FILE

The easiest and best way to review your application as a whole is to assemble your own application file and then read it from start to finish just as an admissions officer would.

You don't need to take a huge amount of time to assemble your application file. Make it paper or electronic, whichever is easier, and put only the substantive materials in it—the materials that the admissions officer will consider as he or she reads and evaluates your application. Here is a short checklist for what your application file should contain:

☐ Your application (with all questions answered)

☐ Your supplementary materials (if any are being submitted)

☐ Your test score report (if you have a copy, otherwise, just a piece of paper or file that says *test score report* to remind you)

☐ Your school report (a blank form with a couple of notes about what you hope your counselor said and a copy of your transcript)

☐ Your recommendations (a blank form for each recommendation with a couple of notes about what you hope each recommender said)

☐ Your interview report (if you had an interview, use our sample evaluation form and just make a couple of notes about what you hope the interviewer said)

☐ A list of any flags that you hope will be on your file (see chapter 5)

Once you have your application file assembled, sit down with it and read it from start to finish just as an admissions officer would. Apply everything you have learned about how to think like an admissions officer (Ivey Strategy #2). Read it through once and then consider these questions:

- Are all of the elements of your story coming through? If not, which elements are missing or getting lost? Where could you incorporate them into the application materials?

- Have you presented your academic achievements in the best way possible? Have you highlighted your strengths? Have you done what you can to neutralize any weaknesses?

- Have you presented your extracurricular accomplishments in the best way possible? Have you focused on the core four and demonstrated passion, talent, initiative, and impact (Ivey Strategy #4)?

- Have you presented your personal qualities and character in the best way possible? Have you shown, rather than told (Ivey Strategy #7)? Have you revealed who you are as a person through what you have shared? Is everything on the application the truth and nothing but the truth?

- Have you brought forward any other factors that might weigh in your favor? Any demographics? Your demonstrated interest in the college? Your ability to pay? Obtained all possible flags on your file?

What you should notice about this list of questions is that they track what the admissions officer will consider when he or she reads and evaluates your application file. They are focused on what matters to the admissions officer. No surprise, right? It is the admissions officer you must persuade to admit you, and so, of course, you are focused on what matters to him or her.

Once you have reviewed your application as a whole and are satisfied that it is your best effort, then you are ready to turn your attention to crossing the finish line! That's what the next section covers.

A FEW TIPS FOR THE SECOND THROUGH LAST APPLICATIONS

If you have been following our suggestion to work your way through the process application by application, then when you come to the end of this section, you will have completed only your first application, and you will have several more to go. We want to give you a few tips about how to make your life easier each time around—that's right, more ways to work smarter, not harder (Ivey Strategy #1).

Next Application Tip #1: Sustain Your Momentum

Some applicants complete and submit their first application and then poop out. Hear us clearly on this point: pooping out is a *very bad idea*. You have built a certain amount of momentum by completing your first application, and your momentum will grow if you keep at it. But if you poop out, you lose all the momentum you have built and each application will be as hard as the first. Once you are in the application groove, it is good to stay there until all of your applications are complete. You have probably applied early to a top-choice college, and you're really hoping that you don't have to submit any other applications at all. If it all works out as you hope and you get in early to your top-choice college, then your plan will seem brilliant. But if it doesn't work out as you hope (and there is always some chance it won't), then you will have to produce a lot of applications in a very short time (usually two weeks), and you won't be in any mood to do it. You'll be disappointed and upset, and the likelihood is that the additional applications you produce will be less than standout. Then you'll feel the opposite of brilliant.

Next Application Tip #2: Pick Up Speed as You Go by Reusing Answers

Many of the really short answer, short answer, and essay questions on college applications are similar to each other. As you work through your applications, you should find that you will have opportunities to reuse answers. Some you will be able to reuse as is. For example, if you are applying to both Columbia and Stanford and each asks for a list of favorite books, then you only have to create one list. Or if you are applying to Yale and realize that you can use any essay for the second essay to Yale, you could borrow a topical essay from another application to use. Other answers you may have to tweak a bit. But revising beats starting from scratch! For example, you have already learned how to use a template format for your "Why College X?" answers, so those will be fairly quick to produce after you have come up with your template. All of these tricks will help you pick up speed as you go. One important caveat: don't reuse answers unless they actually respond to the question being asked. Doing that is *not* working smarter. It saves you time at the expense of getting in.

Next Application Tip #3: Make Use of Alternate Versions of the Common Application When That Serves You

The time-saving feature of the Common Application is that you complete it once and submit it to multiple colleges. We love that feature and encourage applicants to do that in most cases. However, there are times when you may want to submit one version of the Common Application to one college and another to another college. For example, let's say that you are applying to some colleges where your deep involvement in your faith community would be a positive and you're applying to others where your artistic endeavors would be a bigger positive. Therefore, you want to write your personal essay focused on your faith for some and focused on your art for others. Or let's say that you have written a great personal essay about a person who influenced you and then you discover that the college-specific writing supplement asks for an essay on that very same topic. In that case, you would want to be able to use your personal essay for the supplement and use another personal essay on the Common Application. In these kinds of cases, it's worth your time to create alternate versions of your Common App.

Alternate versions of the Common Application are possible, even though most applicants do not realize it. Common App 4.0 will permit applicants to have three versions of their essays. In previous incarnations of the Common App, the method for creating alternate versions was a bit clunky and hard to find (we hope it will be improved in Common App 4.0), but regardless, the important point you should take away is that *it is possible and worth doing in certain circumstances.*

PART 3

Crossing the Finish Line

CHAPTER 22 The Logistics of Submitting and Following Up

CHAPTER 23 Application Updates (Including Deferrals, Wait Lists, and Correcting Mistakes)

The Logistics of Submitting and Following Up

Last essay finished. Jennifer clicked "save" and sank back into her chair. Hooray! College applications done! Now she could kick back and start enjoying her senior year without any worries for a while. She didn't have to think about college at all until decision time.

Well, okay, so there were a few little things she still had to do. Her applications were pretty much finished, but she hadn't exactly entered everything into the online forms. But how much time could some quick copy and paste take? Then a few clicks and everything would be submitted in no time. She'd do it all in the next thirty minutes, and then she would absolutely be done! Or would she?

We know how tempting it is for Jennifer to think that she is only thirty minutes or so from crossing the finish line. But, unfortunately, that is not the case. First, Jennifer has several things she needs to do before she is ready to submit, and she is overly optimistic in her estimate of how much time those few little things will take. Second, submitting her application will not get her across the finish line. She has to follow up and make certain her application file is complete before she can consider it really, truly done.

You probably find yourself in much the same place as Jennifer. You are so ready to be done. You have worked hard and you are eager to take a break from all things college.

We understand.

But we also know that you need to hang in and do the work it takes to make it across the finish line if you are going to be successful. A standout application requires this last stretch. So hang in there. You *are* almost done and you don't want to blow it now. That finish line is in sight, and you can finish strong!

NO EXCEPTIONS IS THE RULE

The horror stories you have heard are not urban legends. They are not cautionary tales invented to scare you into good behavior. They are just run-of-the mill, real-life examples of what happens in the ordinary course of a college admissions cycle.

The Common Application or some other online system will crash at the eleventh hour and that will be too bad for those applicants who have not yet submitted their applications because a good number of selective colleges will reject their applications because they arrive after the deadline. No exception will be made for them.

World events (such as the Egyptian revolution) or a natural disaster (such as a record-breaking snow storm) will disrupt school operations, and applicants who had delayed their requests for the necessary supporting materials will not be able to get them in before the deadline. Without those supporting materials, their applications will not be complete by the deadline, and a good number of selective colleges will not evaluate their incomplete applications. Again, no exception will be made for them.

Applicants will discover after all decisions have already been made that their applications were not evaluated because they were incomplete. These applicants will be shocked and angry, because they did not receive any word from the college that there was anything missing. The college will point out that it was the applicant's responsibility to ensure that their applications were complete. Again, no exceptions will be made for them.

Are you shocked by how harsh and unforgiving the system is? Most applicants are. They really cannot believe that their applications will not be accepted or evaluated in circumstances such as the ones we have just described. But that's really how it works.

To understand why, you simply must think like an admissions officer (Ivey Strategy #2) and understand a bit of the back-office work that must happen in order to prepare your application for evaluation by the admissions officer. All of the various documents that make up your application have to get into your application file. Whether your file is electronic or paper or both, processing all of these application documents is a mammoth task that requires both accuracy and speed by the admissions staff.

Think about it. If you assume a minimum of five documents per applicant (an application, a school report, a test score report, and two recommendations), and multiply by the number of applicants, you have a pretty good estimate of how many documents must be processed. For most selective colleges, which attract twenty thousand applicants or more in a typical year, that means one hundred thousand or more documents. That mountain of documents arrives over a very short period of time and must be processed in an equally short period of time. Many, perhaps most, application documents arrive in the two weeks before the deadline, and application files must be ready for evaluation by admissions officers as soon as possible after the deadline but no later than two weeks after the deadline.

One hundred thousand or more documents received, logged, sorted, and filed within a four-week time frame: that's the back-office work that has to happen. The only way admissions offices can get that back-office work done is to use highly efficient processing systems. Highly efficient systems are harsh and unforgiving. Deadlines will not be negotiated; exceptions will not be made. That's just the way it is.

But you can do a few simple things to keep yourself from being the subject of a horror story. It is all about working smarter, not harder, and sweating the details (Ivey Strategies #1 and #5) to the very end. It is all about crossing the finish line.

STICK TO YOUR MASTER PLAN

Pull out your master plan. If you followed the format we set out for you in chapter 2, you will see that your master plan shows the following:

- You are scheduled to submit your applications at least two weeks before the submission deadline.
- You are scheduled to do some follow-up to ensure that your application is complete in the four weeks following the application's submission.

In other words, your master plan calls for you to do two things: submit before the deadlines and follow up at the right times. If you stick to your master plan and do these two things, you will cross the finish line strong.

SUBMIT BEFORE THE DEADLINE

Your master plan calls for you to submit your applications two weeks before the application deadline. The primary reason we suggest this is that it averts countless disasters. It prevents the mistakes that come from the last-minute scramble to get your application finished and it gives you time to resolve any unexpected problems that arise. It gets your application into the admissions office before the rush, and that usually means fewer processing problems on their end.

Submitting your application is actually a bit of a chore in itself, so you will need to set aside a chunk of time to do it. We advise that you give yourself a couple of hours just to complete the submission logistics. It may take more or less time depending on your particular circumstances.

CHECK IN WITH THOSE PROVIDING SUPPORTING MATERIALS

Your master plan calls for you to check in with those providing supporting materials two or three weeks before the deadline, which is about the same time as you are submitting your application. Here is a quick checklist for you to use:

- School report or its equivalent has been sent.
- Test score reports have been sent.
- Recommendations have been sent.

SUBMISSION LOGISTICS

Staying on top of submission logistics will be much easier if you follow these tips.

Submission Tip #1: Submit Application by Application

You will make fewer errors and be less likely to overlook special items for particular colleges if you proceed application by application. So even if you are going to submit more than one application in a single session, you should work through your submissions application by application.

Submission Tip #2: Read and Follow *All* of the Instructions for Submission

You will discover that there are lots of instructions about submission. Frequently, you have to consult multiple sources in order to find all of the instructions. Start with the college's instructions because you always have to follow those. Then move on to the instructions from your high school, the testing agencies, and the Common Application or other online application systems as relevant. Pay particularly close attention to the sequence of submission that you must follow. Do you pay first, then submit the application or vice versa? If the application consists of multiple parts, which must be submitted first? When do you submit supplementary materials?

Submission Tip #3: Do One Final Proofread

Before you mail it away or click "submit," you should do one final proofread. Pay particular attention to making sure that you have not made any errors with your identifying and contact information. Once you are in the system with the wrong identifying or contact information, those mistakes will haunt you forever.

Submission Tip #4: Even if You Are Submitting Online, Print and Review Your Application on Paper before Submission if That Option Is Available

Just because you are submitting your application online does not mean that the admissions officer will read your application on a computer. Some online applications are designed to allow admissions offices to print the applications and review them in that format. If the admissions officer is going to read a paper version of your application, then you should review a paper version of your application to ensure that what you are uploading is what actually appears in the paper version. Text you have entered online has a nasty habit of getting cut off when printed out, and uploaded documents have a nasty habit of showing up as gibberish when printed. If you spot problems when you print preview, then consult the technical people who support the online application system for guidance about how best to resolve them. Furthermore, reading your application on paper is another great technique for proofreading it. Errors that you haven't spotted on the computer screen sometimes just leap off the printed page.

Submission Tip #5: Get All the Necessary Signatures, Including Your Own

Your application must be signed by you (either electronically or in ink on a paper copy). Other components of your application may need to be signed by you *and* by others. For example, most ED agreements now require the signature of you, your parent, and your school counselor. So be sure to get all the necessary signatures.

Submission Tip #6: If You Are Submitting Online, Verify That You Have Actually Completed the Submission Process before You Log Out

If you do not get a confirmation screen telling you that your application has been submitted, then return to the status screen to confirm it for yourself before you log out.

Submission Tip #7: Keep a Copy of Your Completed Application (the One You Submit)

You'll need a copy just in case yours does not arrive at its intended destination. You can save it in electronic or paper form. Keep your copies until you have completed your first year of college, because if you decide to transfer, you will want all that information. After your first year of college, you can ditch them or keep them as you please.

Note that you should save both your Common Application and your college-specific writing supplements that you submit through the Common Application *separately* from your Common Application account because the Common Application wipes the system clean each year in mid-July (about a year before you will have completed your first year of college).

Submission Tip #8: Keep Documentation of Submission

You should have proof that you have submitted your application. If you submit your application via mail, then you should use a mailing option that provides you with documentation that it was mailed on this date and documentation that it was received on that date. The US Postal Service, UPS, Federal Express, and DHL all offer these options. If you submit your application online, then the online system will provide you with some documentation. Save that documentation. You can print it, take a screen shot, or use any other method that works for you, as long as you can pull it up again.

Submission Tip #9: Make Sure You Pay or Get a Fee Waiver

The college will not accept your application if you have not paid or gotten a fee waiver. Many colleges (and the Common Application) will wait until your payment has cleared before accepting your application. Payments can sometimes take several days to clear. If you have waited until the deadline—or even the day before the deadline—to pay, your application might not be considered submitted or complete by the deadline. Don't run the risk!

FOLLOW-UP LOGISTICS

Submitting your application brings you one giant step closer to the finish line but it does not get you across it. Your next step is to follow up and make sure your application is *complete,* because until it is, no admissions officer is even going to see it.

Your application will be complete once the college has received and processed *all* of the required components of your application. That means your application, your school reports, your test score reports, your recommendations, and your payment have all arrived and have all made it into your application file.

Confirm That Your Application Is Complete

The only way that you will know that your application is complete is for you to have confirmation from the college. No other confirmation will do. Just because the Common Application says "downloaded by the college," or your counselor has confirmed to you that something was sent, doesn't mean that the college has received that item and put it in your application file. Until you have confirmation from the college, you don't have confirmation. Period.

Many colleges make it relatively easy for you to get confirmation. They either notify you or they have established an online system that allows you to check the status of your application at any time. But there are some colleges that leave it up to you to make contact with the admissions office and obtain confirmation yourself.

Whether getting confirmation is easy or hard, you must do it. If you have not received confirmation that your application is complete within two weeks of having submitted your application or the deadline (whichever comes first), then you should initiate contact with the admissions office and check the status of your application.

If Something Is Missing, Handle It Promptly

If your follow-up reveals that something is missing from your application file, then it is up to you to address the situation. Here is how we suggest you handle any problems you discover.

Follow-up Tip #1: Don't Delay in Your Follow-up Assuming That if Everything Has Been Submitted and Received, It Will All Eventually Work Itself Out

That is a faulty assumption. Things get misfiled and lost. Computer glitches happen. Admissions staff, your school counselor, the testing agencies, and your recommenders are all busy and may or may not have the time to sort it all out or make it right in time. You must take the initiative and ensure that your application file is complete.

Follow-up Tip #2: Clarify Exactly What Is Missing or What Is Keeping Your Application from Being Complete

You need to get precise information so that you can take the appropriate action. What exactly is missing from your file? If it is a teacher recommendation, which recommendation is it? If test score reports are missing, which test scores? Make sure you know exactly what you must submit in order for your application to be complete.

Follow-up Tip #3: Identify the Fastest Way to Get the Missing Item to the College and into Your Application File

Your primary concern is completing your application quickly. Colleges have a short window of time to evaluate and decide on the applications. If you hang out in incomplete land too long, your application cannot be evaluated within the college's time constraint, so the timeline for resolving the problem really matters. Often the fastest solution is just to resubmit the missing item rather than letting time go by while some computer glitch is ironed out or a misfiled document is located.

Follow-up Tip #4: Take Action

Once you have identified the fastest way to get the item to the college and into your application, take action and get it done. Be as proactive as necessary. For example, volunteer to mail the recommendation yourself rather than wait for the recommender to find the time to get it mailed.

Follow-up Tip #5: Communicate with the College Along the Way

When you discover that something is missing, let the college know that you are aware of the problem and are working to get the missing item there as soon as possible. If the submission deadline has passed, include documentation that shows that the missing items were submitted before the deadline so that you preempt any problems related to late submission. Notify the college of how you intend to resolve the problem. If you are going to resubmit any item, then alert the college when that item has been submitted. Thank them for their assistance once your application is complete.

Follow-up Tip #6: Persist until You Get Confirmation That Your Application Is Complete

Stay on it like a pit bull because letting the problem drag on is to your detriment. Remember, you do not want to linger in incomplete land.

Follow-up Tip #7: Stay on Top of Snail-Mail and E-mail

Check both at least daily. Very few colleges still use snail-mail but some do. So check yours. As you scan your e-mail, make sure to actually open, read, and save any communication from the colleges where you are applying.

Follow-up Tip #8: Call, Don't E-mail

Once reading season starts in admissions offices, e-mail responses are slow in coming, and you don't have time to wait. Furthermore, you can often get the whole thing resolved in one call, whereas e-mail often requires a long chain of back-and-forth correspondence.

Follow-up Tip #9: Know When to Do It Yourself and When to Enlist the Help of Others

Generally speaking you should do the follow-up yourself. It is *your* application, and admissions offices are paying attention to both privacy laws and what you reveal about your maturity in this phase of things. What does it say to admissions if Dad handles everything for you? Nothing good. After all, Dad won't be attending college for you, and that's what this whole ordeal is about—an evaluation of *your* ability to perform at a selective college. So buck up, grow up, and take care of your business. You can do it. However, there are times when you need help to take care of your business. You may need Mom to fax the information because she has a fax machine at her office, or you may need your school counselor to resolve the hiccup with the school's online transcript submission service, because you don't have any way to contact the service directly.

Follow-up Tip #10: Be Polite and Respectful

Of course it is frustrating to encounter administrative snafus and have to clean up other people's mistakes but taking your frustration out on others does not help. Being angry or high-handed in your dealings with others usually makes it harder to solve the problem, not easier. Furthermore, such behavior reflects badly on you. A report of your rudeness on the phone or your disrespectful e-mail will be considered by the admissions officer evaluating you. He or she might even dock your personal rating as a result, potentially costing you admission.

WHO STAFFS YOUR HELP DESK?

As you near the finish line, expect that you will need help to resolve some of the problems that will inevitably come your way. Whom are you going to rely on for help? In other words, who will staff your help desk? How and when can you call on them? It is wise to think about these things now when you are relatively cool, calm, and collected rather than try to think of whom you can call at midnight when you are on the verge of a total meltdown. Make a little directory for yourself and keep it at hand for when the time comes. Here are a few entries that should be in every applicant's directory:

Parents

- Contact any way that works. Available 24/7.
- Can help me get a grip, stay motivated, and resolve problems.

Admissions Office at College X (for Every College on Your List)

- Contact by phone [phone number] or e-mail [e-mail address]. Available [days, hours].
- Can help me address problems with all components of my application.

School Counselor

- Contact by phone [phone number] or e-mail [e-mail address]. Available [days, hours].
- Can help me address problems with school reports, recommenders, and school systems such as Naviance. Might also be able to help me resolve problems with applications at colleges.

Common Application Technical Team

- Contact by e-mail [e-mail address]. Available [days, hours].
- Expect that it will take 24–48 hours for response.
- Can help me address problems with the Common Application.

Testing Agencies (College Board or SAT, ACT, TOEFL, and so on)

- Contact via my online account: [username, password]. Available [days, hours].
- Expect that it may take some time for response and may require phone calls.
- Can help me address problems with my test score reports.

(continued)

Recommenders (list each one)

- Contact by phone [phone number] or e-mail [e-mail address]. Available [days, hours].
- Can help me address problems with my recommendations.

We have not listed friends or classmates among these entries, because calling on them for help on your college applications is a tricky business. On the one hand, they know you and they understand what you are going through better than almost anyone else. They also may have some very good information about how to handle particular problems because they may be dealing with similar problems themselves. On the other hand, they are likely to be just as freaked out as you and may not be available when you need them or in a position to offer the kind of measured and reasonable advice that will help you the most.

Parent Tip: Minimize Meltdowns

We call this phase of the process *meltdown season* because the stress and pressure on your child peaks right now and meltdowns are frequent. The bad news is that we know of nothing you can do to prevent your child from having meltdowns. The good news is that we can give you a few tried-and-true suggestions for how to minimize the number and severity of the meltdowns so that the whole family can survive meltdown season with no lasting damage.

Dial Down the Family Obligations and Expectations as Much as Possible during Meltdown Season

There are a huge number of competing demands on your child during this time. If you can grant your child a bit of a reprieve when it comes to family obligations and expectations during this time period, you can reduce the stress your child feels considerably.

Manage Your Own Stress

All too often, parents are just as stressed as their children during meltdown season. Life is going at full tilt, the holidays are looming, and a major family transition is under way. You will be stressed, no doubt about it. But here's the thing. You are the parent and the real grown-up here, so you have to manage your own stress. You have to keep it from spilling over and feeding your child's stress.

Intervene as Little as Possible and as Much as Necessary to Resolve What Triggered the Meltdown or Any Consequences That Come from the Meltdown

Most of the time, meltdowns are triggered by nothing more than emotional overload. If that is the case, you don't need to do anything beyond offering your sympathy and encouragement. If, however, your child's meltdown was triggered by a serious underlying problem with his or her college application, then you need to do more than just offer sympathy and encouragement. Likewise, if the meltdown itself comes at an inopportune time and results in serious consequences for your child's college application, then you will need to intervene at some level. Your goal when intervening is to find that sweet spot and intervene just enough and no more. In other words, intervene as little as possible and as much as necessary. A good guideline to follow in this regard is to limit your intervention to providing help and assistance to your child rather than doing it for your child. For example, if your child needs to get another copy of his transcript from the school office, arrange to take your child to school early so he can go to the school office before school starts rather than simply dropping by the office yourself.

CHAPTER 23

Application Updates (Including Deferrals, Wait Lists, and Correcting Mistakes)

Your application file is complete. You are queued up for evaluation by the admissions officer. Surely, now you are done, right? Yes, you are! You are now officially an applicant, and you will receive a decision on your application in due course. Take a bow. You have earned it.

There is only one last thing for you to consider—whether or not an application postscript is warranted. The application postscript is a set of materials that you submit after your application file is complete but before the final decision is made.

But wait, if you have already submitted your best and most compelling application, your standout application, why would an application postscript ever be warranted?

Good question. In our experience, an application postscript is warranted only in three cases:

- When you have significant updates to your application
- When you have been deferred
- When you have been wait-listed

WHEN YOU HAVE SIGNIFICANT UPDATES

Life continues between the day your application file is complete and the day you receive your decision. Much of what happens during this period is not particularly significant to your application. It is simply more of the same. However, some of what happens may be significant to your application, and it is not more of the same if it is something that improves your credentials substantially. Likewise, it is not more of the same if it compromises your credentials substantially. In either case, you have significant updates to your application.

If Your Updates Improve Your Credentials

Geoffrey had great grades for the first quarter of senior year—better grades than he had ever had—and he was taking some really tough courses. Caroline was named an all-star field hockey player by a regional sports association after a fabulous fall season. Melanie headed up a big community project that mobilized one hundred teens to do home improvement projects for twenty-five low-income homeowners. Should they update their applications? Absolutely. These are perfect examples of significant updates that justify adding something to your application.

If you find yourself with a similarly significant update to make to your application, you want to communicate it to the college as quickly as possible and in a way that gets the information into your application file so the admissions officer can consider it when making his or her decision. The format for your communication should be a short letter that briefly describes what has happened and requests that the information be added to your application file. Make sure your letter includes key identifying information so it can be easily matched with your application file. We generally suggest that you include your full legal name, your birth date, your school, and what you are applying for. Here's an example:

Shannon Leigh Cartwright

10/27/1994

Heritage Hills High School, Kansas City, MO

Applicant for Harvard College, Class of 2017

Practically speaking, there are three ways to deliver your letter to the admissions office: (1) by an expedited mailing service, such as overnight FedEx or DHL, (2) by fax; or (3) by e-mail. Identify each college's preferred method of delivery from information on their website or by calling.

In addition to the update you provide, consider whether you should arrange for supporting materials to be submitted. For example, if you are updating your grades, you should definitely consider asking your school counselor to send an optional school report with your better grades showing on your transcript (see chapter 18 for more information about optional reports).

If Your Updates Compromise Your Credentials

Lionel hit a rough patch during the fall term, and his first quarter grades showed it. He was hoping to improve by the end of the term but only time would tell. Emily got in the first real trouble of her life when she was caught with alcohol at the school homecoming dance and received a one-day in-school suspension. Lionel and Emily are in a tough spot. It is really hard when things go wrong in your senior year. That is why we always caution applicants that they must stay focused on school and avoid trouble even after applications have gone in. But stuff happens. It happened for Lionel and Emily. It might happen for you.

If it does, we suggest that you move forward on two fronts at the same time. First, you have to do what is necessary to halt whatever is going wrong and come out of your senior year "death spiral." Second, you have to do what you can in terms of damage control for your applications.

Part of your damage control is how you handle updates to colleges about bad news. You are not under an obligation to give day-to-day updates to your application, and not every piece of bad news must be reported. But if it must be reported, you want to deal with it. Hiding and avoiding the problem will not help you at all.

Colleges set their own policies about when an applicant must update. The requirements set out by the Common Application colleges are fairly typical. Applicants must update in two circumstances: first, the applicant is expected to provide a midyear school report following the conclusion of the first term and that updates the school report. Second, the applicant is expected to update if the applicant does something that results in a disciplinary or criminal record. Given these policies, both Lionel and Emily will have to provide updates, but Lionel has some time and he may be able to recover substantially before the midyear report goes in. However, Emily needs to update promptly. Check the colleges where you are applying for what updates are required and then update if you must.

In terms of what should be included in the updates, we advise that you follow the suggestions we have given elsewhere about how to neutralize or minimize problematic credentials. Consult chapter 7 for guidance related to bad news about your grades. Consult chapter 13 for guidance related to disciplinary or criminal records.

WHEN YOU HAVE BEEN DEFERRED

If you have applied early to one or more colleges, the decision letter might not actually contain a final decision. Instead of being admitted or denied, you may be notified that you have been deferred. Although this news is no doubt a bit disappointing, you have not been denied. And that is indeed good news.

Parent Tip: Preparing for the Worst Case

If your child applied early, then he or she is likely to get a decision in the first or second week of December; otherwise, decisions will come in late March. At decision time, it is wise for parents to do a bit of worst-case scenario planning.

In the case of college admissions decisions, we have found that the worst case is actually deferral (in the early round) or wait list (in the regular round), not denial. Are you surprised? Many are. But, as it turns out, for most applicants living in the limbo of not admitted, not denied is far more stressful and difficult than handling the disappointment that they feel when they are denied. You know your child best, so you will probably have a good instinct about what his or her worst case really is. Just consider that it may be getting deferred or wait-listed rather than being denied.

Regardless, get ahead of the worst case by doing a bit of planning about how you are going to help your child handle it, when and if the worst case materializes. One thing we know for sure is that you are a seasoned, veteran parent with nearly eighteen years of raising this child under your belt, so you'll know what you should plan to do. We just want to give you the heads up that you'll need to be ready.

Treat a Deferral as a Second Chance

Your deferred application will be reconsidered in the regular round of decision making. Although your odds of being admitted in an early round are higher than in the regular round, you will usually have the same odds of being admitted in the regular round as you would have if you had not applied early. In other words, you get no benefit, but you suffer no penalty for having applied early and been deferred. Think of the deferral as a second chance at being admitted.

We advise applicants to treat their second chances in the same way that they have treated their first chances. You want to do everything you can to produce your best and most compelling application.

Of course, you have already produced your best and most compelling application to the college. But that was then and this is now. Assuming you have continued on a positive course in the first part of your senior year, you have information that can and will make that best and most compelling application even better. You also have a bit of time that you might be able to use to enhance what you have to report.

Update with a Purpose

In order to determine what updates would make your application better, you need to think like an admissions officer (Ivey Strategy #2): what does a deferral signify about how the admissions officer is thinking about your application? A deferral indicates that the admissions officer is on the fence about whether to admit or deny. He or she wants more information before a final decision is made. The admissions officer may want to see how things go for you in senior year, she may want to see how you stack up against the applicants in the larger Regular Decision pool, or both. Because the admissions officer wants more information, your job as a standout applicant is to provide it. That's where updates come in.

You want to provide updates that have a positive influence on the admissions officer. Not all updates accomplish that. That is why we encourage you to update with a purpose. Your purpose is quite straightforward: push the admissions officer to admit.

Here is our checklist for deciding how you might update your application following a deferral. We have ranked them in order of most to least positive influence. But every little bit helps, so if you can add something from each of these categories, by all means do so.

- *New (and good) grades:* If you have good grades to report, do it! Forward a copy of your most recent grade report and get your school counselor to send an optional report (if the grades are midterm) or make sure your school counselor sends that midyear report pronto.

- *New academic honors or awards:* If you were named to National Honor Society or received any other new academic honor or award, share the news!

- *New (and higher) test scores:* Did you take a standardized test in the late fall that could not be considered in the early round? Were your scores better (consult chapter 17 for how to analyze your scores if you aren't sure)? Now is the time to send those scores!

- *Anything that demonstrates more of the core four (passion, talent, initiative, and impact):* Were you elected to a new leadership position? Did you receive a major award for your community service? Did your team win state? If you have had major developments on the activity front, let the admissions office in on them! (If you've forgotten about the core four, refer back to chapters 4 and 8).

- *Anything you have done that demonstrates interest in the college:* Have you visited the campus? Talked with an admissions representative at a college fair? Don't assume that this initiative on your part has made its way to your application file. Let the admissions office know directly!

There are other updates that you could make. For example, you can send additional essays, additional supplementary materials, or more recommendations. But we cannot wholeheartedly endorse any of these because they get mixed reviews from admissions officers. Rarely do these kinds of updates add anything meaningful to an application file; they just make the file fatter and more time-consuming to read. They are, in fact, more of the same. For the harried admissions officer who must read a huge number of applications during the regular season, these extras are irritating and off-putting. Why risk annoying the admissions officer when you should have plenty to add with the updates that they actually welcome and find helpful?

In order for your updates to pack the most positive punch, we suggest you gather your updates into a package of materials and submit them all together with a short cover letter. Updates that dribble in don't come together in a cohesive and persuasive statement, and the more updates you have, the more likely it is that one or more will be misfiled or lost.

Your cover letter should say or contain the following information: (1) you remain interested in the college and it is still your top choice (if it is) or among your top choices (if others now vie for the top choice title); (2) you are enclosing updates that you would like included in your application file; and (3) you provide a summary statement that connects your updates back to your story (Ivey Strategy #3), and thus back to your application.

It is absolutely essential that you link your updates to your application as a whole. If you do not, you undermine your efforts to convey a cohesive and compelling story with your application. That summary statement in your cover letter is the key to making that link. Once you have your updates gathered, look back to your story and your application for the connections. How do these updates continue or add to the story that you have been telling about yourself? Here are some examples of the summary statements that the applicants you have come to know and love in this book could include in their cover letters (you can go back and read their stories in chapter 3):

> *Lucy:* As you will see, my updates focus on what I have been able to accomplish in my two new passions (photography and martial arts) since I retired from gymnastics due to an injury last spring.
>
> *Matthew:* I have been really engaged by my two classes this fall that have allowed me to do some more hands-on learning, and my updates detail the end-of-term projects I did for each one—both got As and very nice comments from my teachers.
>
> *Rania:* Since I applied, I have been quite busy writing, and I am proud to say that I am now a published journalist with an ongoing column in a local newspaper; my updates detail what has been published and also a few of my other writing triumphs.
>
> *Tom:* Once I finished my applications, I was able to turn my attention back to my academics and activities, and as you will see from my updates, there have been big developments in both areas. I have taken my work in physics to a whole new level, and my garage band has debuted on YouTube.

Nancy: The fall has been a busy time for me, and I have enclosed updates for both my academics and my activities, but I am most proud that a play I wrote and directed was staged at a local community theater and was sold out three nights in a row.

To ensure that your updates make it to your application file by the time the admissions officer reconsiders it, we recommend that you get your updates to the admissions office as soon as possible, but no later than two weeks after the regular submission deadline. So if you get news of your deferral in early December, and the regular submission deadline is January 1, then your updates should be submitted no later than January 15.

Do Something Worthy of an Update

You have a very short window of opportunity between the time you get the news of your deferral and the time your updates must be submitted. If you can act quickly, you may be able to do something in that time that would, in and of itself, be worthy of an update.

Ace Your End-of-Term Examinations and Projects

The grades you receive in December and January are the most recent grades you have to report. Doing well gives you updates of the most positive kind!

Consider a Hail Mary Standardized Test

If you believe that your standardized test scores are what stand in your way, you can retest in December, January, or February. We call these Hail Mary tests because like Hail Mary passes in football games, they are a last-ditch effort with a low probability of success. But sometimes they work, so why not? Two notes here: first, confirm that the college will accept a test score from the later test. Second, do not wait on these test scores to send your updates because they might not arrive in time (or you might not like the scores). Send everything else and then send the test scores separately when they come in.

Do a Project or Activity That Demonstrates Initiative and Impact (Two of the Core Four from Ivey Strategy #4)

The winter break is often a perfect time to do something like this. For example, if you are head of the school's community service group, you could organize a

New Year's clean-up of a local park or strip of highway. Or if you are an artist, you could organize a show of your works to hang for three days only.

Activate Your Network

You have already asked people for help and support with your application. At this point, it is wise to check in with all of them and let them know what, if anything, they might do for you now. Here are our suggestions.

Your School Counselor

Promptly notify your school counselor that you have been deferred. Discuss your plans for updates and additional efforts with your school counselor and ask for help in the form of an updated note with the midyear report or an optional report.

Your Recommenders

You do not require help from them, but you should keep them updated. It is simply the courteous thing to do.

Your VIPs (Very Important People)

If you have mobilized any VIPs on your behalf, you should advise them of your deferral, provide them with the updates you are providing to the college, and ask them to do whatever they can to help. If you have not mobilized any VIPs, brainstorm if there are any that you might mobilize. For more information about VIPs, consult chapters 5 and 19.

Your Interviewer

If you had an interview for the college, check in with your interviewer. Advise him or her of your deferral and provide a copy of your cover letter and updates. Do not ask him or her to do anything; your check-in is enough of a nudge. The interviewer will take the initiative if he or she is willing and able to do something on your behalf.

WHEN YOU HAVE BEEN WAIT-LISTED

Being wait-listed may be the cruelest fate of them all. You want a decision. You need a decision. And instead, you get a decision that isn't a decision. What do you do now?

Wait List Tip #1: Accept That Your Chances for Admission Are Somewhere between Zero and Low

Can't you get a better idea than that if you do some research? Unfortunately, no. The empirical and historical data that you would need in order to refine your odds do not exist. Sure, you can get information for some colleges about their past rates of admission from the wait list. But you can't get it for all colleges, because it is not part of the data that colleges are required to release publicly. So you may or may not be able to find data for the college where you were wait-listed. Even if you can find the data, you will discover that it is wildly inconsistent from year to year. That's because a wait list is a safety net for the college. Some years they need that safety net more than others. You can't predict with precision because the college itself can't predict with precision.

What you can know for sure is that your chances are low and perhaps zero. If all goes as predicted for the college, then the college admits *no one* from the wait list. That's right, no one. That's an unusual outcome but it happens. So your chances may be zero. More commonly, there are a small number admitted from the wait list either to fill up or fill out the incoming class. When fewer applicants than predicted accept their offers of admission, applicants will be admitted off the wait list to fill up the incoming class. When the makeup of the incoming class is off from the institutional goals regarding demographics, then applicants will be admitted off the wait list to fill out the incoming class. Based on the data available, the percentage of applicants accepted off the wait list at selective colleges tops out at less than 10 percent. That means, in the best case, your chances are less than one in ten. Like we said: low.

Wait List Tip #2: Decide Whether to Hold a Place on the Wait List

Given that your chances are low, you may decide that you have no interest in holding a spot on a wait list. But if you are considering holding on the wait list, you do have to make a decision and communicate it to the admissions office promptly. We believe that there is only one legitimate reason to hold your place on a wait list, and that is this: you know that if you received an offer from this college, you would accept it immediately, and you would happily turn down all of your other offers of admission. If you would not accept that offer of admission, then there is no reason for you to be on the wait list. Staying in limbo keeps you from moving forward, directing your energies to ending your senior year well, and investing emotionally in the college you will attend. Keeping yourself in the running for a college you will not attend is also unkind to others on the wait list who really do want to attend that college. Be a good applicant citizen and do the right thing.

TAKING THE RIGHT ACTIONS AT THE RIGHT TIMES

The right actions are those that will make the admissions officer more likely to admit you. The right times are the moments when admissions officers will be acting on the wait list. Use the following guide to help you take the right actions at the right times.

The Right Actions

There are really only three actions for you to take. But each is important if you want to maximize your chances of being admitted from the wait list.

Communicate That You Will Say "Yes"

Colleges are not interested in admitting applicants off the wait list who are going to say "no." It decreases their yield (yield is the percentage of applicants who accept offers of admission), and yield is important to rankings. If you have followed our advice about staying on a wait list only if you will say "yes," then you should not be hesitating to communicate that fact. Now is not the time to be coy. If you have never answered the "Why College X?" question (because it was not asked on the application), then include a brief answer to "Why College X?" in this communication. (See chapter 12 for how to answer the "Why College X?" question.)

Update Your Application, as Advisable

There are several kinds of updates you can make if you find yourself wait-listed.

- Any positive report on your grades: If you have good grades to report, do it! Forward a copy of your most recent grade report in April, and ask your school counselor to send an optional report in support. Likewise forward your final grades in June, and ask your school counselor to send a final report as well.

Note: Currently, the Common Application will not allow the school counselor to submit the final report to any college other than the college where you have enrolled, so the school counselor should send this final report directly to the college where you are wait-listed.

- Any new academic honor or award: If you have received any new academic honor or award, share the news! It is common for high schoolers to receive awards at graduation, so be sure those awards get mentioned in your June update.

- Any new and higher test scores: If you take AP examinations, IB examinations, or national standardized examinations at the end of your senior year, then send your scores the minute you have them and request supporting documentation from the testing agency at the same time.

- Anything you have done that demonstrates more of the core four (passion, talent, initiative, and impact): what were you able to accomplish as the president of your class? Did you receive a major award for your community service? Did your team win state? If you have had major developments on the activity front, let the admissions office know! (If you've forgotten about the core four, refer back to chapters 4 and 8.)

Activate Your Influential Advocates

Because the college is focused on serving its institutional goals when admitting from the wait list, admissions officers are very attuned to who is advocating for particular applicants. At this juncture, it is the nature of the advocate's relationship to the college that will determine the amount of influence that the advocate will have. Here is the short list of possible influential advocates:

- Your school counselor, if he or she has a relationship with an admissions officer at the college or your school is a *feeder school* for the college (feeder schools provide a steady stream of students to the college every year)

- Anyone you know who is a graduate of the college, if he or she has been involved with the college since graduation as a volunteer, donor, and so on

- Anyone you know with a high-level contact at the college (a high-level contact would be someone like the president or one of the vice presidents of the college, a board member at the college, or a particularly influential faculty member at the college)

- Anyone you know who is on the board, faculty, or senior staff at the college
- Anyone you know who has been a major donor to the college (a major donor would have been recognized for at least a six-figure gift and might have something at the college named in his or her honor)

Ask them to call, e-mail, or fax the admissions office with a note that advocates for your admission, and to copy that note to whoever their contacts are at the college. The notes can be quite short: they only have to communicate the advocate's relationship to the college and the advocate's desire for you to be admitted. The best time for your advocates to be in touch is April because the first round of admission from the wait list is always the largest. But if you have a willing advocate, and if you persist, then it is not inappropriate for your advocates to chime in again in June and July.

Be mindful, though, that you are asking these contacts to spend their reputational capital on you. They're not going to make hundreds of those phone calls for hundreds of applicants (if they are VIPs at that college or VIPs in general, they get solicited all the time for this kind of intervention), and they're not going to say "yes" to everyone who asks. If they agree to advocate on your behalf, you risk doing serious damage to your relationship with that VIP if he spends his reputational capital on you, you get an offer, and then you say "no." That's another reason not to signal that you'll accept an offer if, in fact, you won't.

The Right Times

Although a college might admit applicants from the wait list at any time, there are three times when admission is most likely. The first time is May. By May 1, the college will have a good sense of the size and composition of its incoming class, and they will begin making offers to applicants on the wait list as soon as they can. This round of offers will be the largest in number.

The second time is July. Actions on the wait lists in May will have a ripple effect through the system. If you get in off the wait list at your dream school, you open up a spot at another college that will likely be filled by an admission off that college's wait list, and so it goes. By late June, the ripples will have subsided and the college will have a good sense if the size or composition of their class has changed as a result. If it has, they may make another small round of admissions from the wait list in July.

The third time is right before the first day of class, usually mid-August. This last round of offers will occur only if the size of the incoming class has dropped below a minimum number (set for financial reasons) due to a phenomenon admissions officers call *summer melt*. Summer melt happens when applicants who have been admitted and have paid enrollment deposits change their minds about starting at that college in the fall. Some summer melt is attributable to ripples from the wait lists, but most is driven by idiosyncratic and individual situations on the part of the applicants.

You should time your actions to be just ahead of when the admissions officers are most likely to act, so that whatever you do will have its intended effect by the time the admissions officers act. Specifically, we suggest you concentrate your actions during these windows of time:

- Second and third week of April
- First two weeks of June
- Last week of July

And if you get to a point when you are done waiting, then remove yourself from the wait list.

CORRECTING MISTAKES

Even with multiple reviews and careful proofreading, you may discover that your application contains mistakes after you have submitted it. If this happens to you, we recommend you do the following.

Submit a Corrected Version

Unless the mistakes are truly inconsequential (one typo in the name of the your swim club), you should submit a corrected version of your application with a brief cover letter asking that your corrected version be substituted for the previous application. However, this is much easier said than done with online applications because once an online application has been submitted, usually you are prohibited from changing it or resubmitting it. Here are the choices you have:

- If the mistake was in a document that you uploaded as an attachment to the application, then submit a corrected version of the attachment only directly to the college.

- If the mistake is on the application form itself, and the completed form can be printed, then print the completed form and make a handwritten correction on it. Submit the hard copy with the handwritten correction directly to the college or scan the hard copy with the handwritten correction and submit it electronically. Make sure that your handwriting is legible.

- If the mistake is on the application form itself and the completed form can be saved as a PDF or other electronic file that you can annotate, then save the completed form and annotate it with your corrections. Submit the annotated form electronically to the college.

- If none of these solutions is possible, contact the college directly and ask how you should submit corrections.

Note that if the college is a Common Application college, you should submit your corrected version and your cover letter *directly to the college*. You cannot submit any updates or corrections to a submitted application through the Common Application.

Correct the Mistake Now for the Applications You Have Not Yet Submitted

If your mistake is on the Common Application or another form that you are submitting to multiple colleges but you have not yet submitted it to all of the colleges, stop now and correct the mistake.

On the Common Application, if your mistakes appear on any component other than the essay, you can correct them without creating a new version of the Common Application. If, however, your mistakes are on the essay, then you will need to create an alternate version. Because this alternate version will use up one of the three alternate versions you are allowed, make sure that you are comfortable using the alternate version for this purpose. If you are not, then check with the college and see if it will accept a corrected version of the essay if you submit it directly. For more information about alternate versions, see chapters 11 and 21.

NO-NOS

There are a few absolute no-nos when it comes to your behavior during the in-between times—the time between when your application file is complete and you get a decision, the time between your deferral and your final decision, the time between being put on the wait list and receiving all your offers of admission.

No-No #1: Don't Be a Pest or a Time Suck

Contact the admissions office when necessary, send in the suggested updates, and then leave them alone. Unnecessary updates and overly frequent contact can get annoying and distracting. Admissions officers need to concentrate on evaluating application files, yours included. They can't do that if they are taking your eleventh phone call, returning your ninety-ninth e-mail, or waiting for your application file while your seventh additional recommendation is processed.

No-No #2: Don't Ask Questions That Admissions Officers Cannot or Will Not Answer

No admissions officer is going to tell you the reasons for a particular decision or provide you with tips for improving your application. The only feedback that the admissions officer will give you is the decision. So don't bother asking why you were deferred instead of admitted or whether it would help your chances if you submitted another recommendation. It is just a waste of your time and the admissions officer's time.

No-No #3: Don't Make Dramatic or Over-the-Top Gestures

Occasionally applicants get it into their heads that the best way to persuade an admissions officer to admit them is to do something outside the box. Bad idea. Do not pitch a tent outside the admissions office until you can speak to the director of admissions personally. Do not send one hundred handmade fortune cookies, each filled with a reason to admit you. As creative and well-meaning as these types of gestures may be, they do not help your cause. The most likely response from the admissions officer? "Uh oh, we have a total whack job on our hands. Call security and deny right away."

You're Done, Now What?

You are *done!* You have prepared and submitted standout applications to every college on your list. You may have even submitted some application postscripts. Now what?

This is an awkward time in the college admissions process. You are left with nothing to do but wait for the decisions to come back. This is what psychologists call a *transition period,* and transition periods are tough. They are marked by a certain amount of ambiguity, anxiety, and uncertainty. In other words, they aren't exactly fun. No wonder most applicants (and their parents) would just as soon skip right over this transition period. Because skipping over it is not an option, most opt to do their best to ignore it. We think there is a better way to pass the time during the transition period—or at least a more fun way.

Celebrate! That's right, celebrate. You have lots to celebrate *even before* you get in.

CELEBRATE THE MILESTONE

Preparing and submitting a standout application is a *major* milestone in the college admissions process. As we are fond of saying, "You cannot be admitted if you do not apply." Don't lose sight of how much work it took or how significant it is in the midst of all the hubbub of life. Take a moment to acknowledge that your standout applications are accomplishments unto themselves.

We also suggest you take the time to read through your applications and take note of all of the accomplishments that underlie those applications. Every grade, every activity, every idea presented in your application represents an accomplishment. There are lots of them! Just because they can be distilled into a few pages does not mean they are not significant. This is your life's work up to now. It is significant. Pat yourself on the back for a life well lived for the last seventeen or eighteen years.

Celebration Tip #1: Do Something to Mark the First and Last Applications You Submit

Submitting your first application is a mini-milestone, and you need a marker of some sort. It can be goofy and small—just make it something that is shared with at least one other person. A happy dance in the kitchen, a whoop shouted aloud in the counseling office, a star sticker posted on your Facebook wall. Something.

The marker for your last application should be a bit more significant and something that you can look forward to doing. That little reward will help keep you motivated. Most of the applicants we work with choose to do something social with friends because that's what they have missing while they have been locked away working on applications!

CELEBRATE THE LIFE SKILLS THAT YOU HAVE ACQUIRED

You may not realize it but preparing and submitting standout applications develops skills that you will serve you for *life*. Take a little inventory of what you have learned how to do:

- You have learned how to present yourself, both in writing and in person.
- You have learned how to advocate for yourself.
- You have learned how to write a personal essay (and probably improved your writing skills overall).
- You have learned how to navigate bureaucracy.
- You have learned how to manage a complex project.

Along the way, you have also mastered the seven Ivey Strategies, each of which will serve you well far beyond your college applications. That means you've mastered an even dozen life skills in the space of less than a year.

You are going to call on each of these skills and strategies again and again. You will use them every time you apply for anything—a scholarship, an internship, a job, graduate or professional school, a promotion. You will also use them as you go about the business of everyday grown-up life. There is no way to go a week without having to present or advocate for yourself, write something, navigate a bureaucracy, or manage a project. Really.

Celebration Tip #2: Celebrate Your Mastery of a Dozen Life Skills

How you choose to celebrate is up to you and your imagination, but our favorite is the un-birthday cake celebration. Gather some friends and family. Bake (or buy) a cake, put a dozen candles on it (one for every skill mastered), light them, and blow them out. You know what to do from there. Will you e-mail us a photo of your un-birthday cake? You can reach us at college@annaivey.com, and we'll start a collection for our website!

Parent Tip: Have Your Own Mini-Celebration

There is so much for you to celebrate at this point in the process as well. Celebrate all that you've done. Pat yourself on the back for every moment you've been patient, every time you've held your tongue, and every little thing you've done to support your child during the last several months. It is a trying time and you've survived! Celebrate who your child is and what your child has accomplished. It is all on paper, ready for you to read and savor. Read your child's applications and then toast to a job well done!

ABOUT THE AUTHORS

Both former admissions officers at top universities, **Alison Cooper Chisolm** and **Anna Ivey** work together at Cambridge, Massachusetts–based Ivey College Consulting, an admissions coaching firm that helps applicants around the world get into top US colleges.

Alison draws on her admissions experience at three of the nation's most selective universities: Southern Methodist University, the University of Chicago, and (most recently) Dartmouth College. At these schools, Alison determined the fate of thousands of hopeful applicants and learned what it took for applicants to get in. She knows what makes a student go from LMO to Admit. She has seen and evaluated every kind of applicant from homeschooler to top-of-the-class prep schooler. She knows how students with disabilities are handled. She knows what flags move students into the center of attention. She knows what will make an applicant a fast-track deny. She even knows why and how applicants with criminal records can gain admission because she has read their files, interviewed them, and made admissions decisions on their applications.

Alison received her undergraduate degree at Yale and her law degree at the University of Virginia.

As the former dean of admissions at the University of Chicago Law School, Anna made final admissions decisions on thousands of applicants. She saw over and over again what people had done right and where they had gone off course. Inspired to help applicants navigate the admissions process more effectively, she founded Ivey Consulting and assembled a first-rate team of experts to coach college, law school, and business school applicants one-on-one. She has been featured as an admissions and career expert in a variety of media, including the *New York Times, Wall Street Journal, Forbes,* CNN, and Fox News.

Anna received her undergraduate degree from Columbia and her law degree from the University of Chicago.

A

Ability to pay, 70

Academic credentials: assessing your, 8; being honest about your, 49; college list factor of, 6; GPA and self-reporting GPA, 7, 40, 49, 87–89; as one admission evaluation dimension rating, 24, 67; required by specific colleges, 7; restraining explanations regarding your, 200; résumé information on your, 39–41, 49; sample interview evaluation form on your, 287; sample interview questions asked about your, 285; school information, 85–87; school profile on recent graduating class, 246; sending postscript on significant updates on your, 310, 311–313; test scores and self-reporting test scores, 7, 40, 87–89, 212–228

Academic honors: application information on, 89–90; résumé information on your, 42–43

Academic interests: telling the story about your, 191; tips on talking about your, 192–193

Academic work samples, 208–209

ACT: being up-to-date on college testing policies, 228; "concordance table SAT ACT" to compare SAT and, 217–218; contact information for, 307; homeschooled applicants and, 225–226; international student applicants and alternatives for the, 225; know when to stop taking the, 215; logistics of requesting reports on, 226–227; requirements for submitting, 214; SAT reasoning test as interchangeable with ACT with writing, 228; scenarios on what scores to submit, 216–225; tips for choosing which scores to submit, 214–216. *See also* Test scores

Activities lists: Common Application instructions on, 91–92; examples of effective, 99–115; five ways to stay within the character limit for, 116; as one admission evaluation dimension rating, 24, 67–68; résumé information on your, 41–42; sample interview evaluation form on your, 287–288; sample interview questions asked about your, 286; think "impact" when describing your, 29–30; tips on how to present your, 93–99; work smarter, not harder (Ivey Strategy #1) by using the, 93

Additional Information: "Do you have anything to add?" opportunity for, 197; optional explanations

or, 198; parent tip on restraining yourself on providing, 200; required explanations, 198; supplemental statements or essays, 198–199; tips for adding helpful, 199–200. *See also* Factual information; Résumé

Admission: disciplinary and criminal background that change your chances of, 179–187; questions that change your chances of, 193–196

Admissions officers: contacting about your résumé, 50; evaluative interviews with, 271–289; "holistic approach" request by, 12; how recommendations may influence the, 250–251; looking for quality and not quantity from applications, 94–95; no-nos for correcting mistakes by contacting, 325; other factors considered by, 27–28, 68–71; scheduling interview to discuss disciplinary/criminal information with, 186; three dimension (3-D) evaluation used by, 24, 67–69; your application as seen through eyes of, 66–71. *See also* Thinking like an admissions officer (Ivey Strategy #2)

Adversity stories, 32–33

Affordability issue, 5

AP (advanced placement) weighted grade, 242

AP test scores, 221–223

Applicants: homeschooled, 26, 39–41, 225–226, 241, 248–249, 258–259, 261–262; international, 76, 78, 225, 241, 248, 260–261; recruited athletes, 207–208; VIP interest in, 71, 259–260

Applicant's directory: admissions office for every college on your list, 307; all testing agencies, 307; Common Application technical team, 307; parents' 24/7 contact information, 307; recommenders' contact information, 308; school counselor's contact information, 307

Application decisions: affordability of college as issue to consider, 5; deferral, 310, 313–318; to have an interview or not, 272, 273; likelihood for admission as issue to consider, 5; to send application postscript, 310–325; wait-list, 310, 313, 318–323; where (if anywhere) to apply early, 8–12; where to apply, 3–8

Application factors: ability to pay, 70; academic achievement dimension, 24, 67; demographics, 27–28, 68–69, 76–81, 193; demonstrated interest, 69, 193–195;

extracurricular accomplishments dimension, 24, 67–68; flags on your file, 70–71, 196; personal qualities and character dimension, 24, 68; 3-D (three dimension) evaluation of the, 24

Application piles: divisions within the college, 189; Early Action, Early Decision, or Regular Decision, 191; entry term, 190; full time, degree seeking, 191; name of correct college, 189; programs and majors, 190. *See also* Flags on your file

Application postscripts: for correcting mistakes, 323–325; significant updates reported through, 310, 311–329; when you have been deferred, 310, 313–318; when you have been wait-listed, 310, 313, 318–323

Application questions: academic and career interests, 191–193; Additional Information, 197–200; disciplinary and criminal background, 179–187; "Do you have anything to add?," 197; essay, 133–166, 294; need-based financial aid, 195–196; really short answer, 117–126; short answer, 127–132; "stump the student," 134–135, 137–138; that change your chances of admission, 193–196; that get your application into the right pile, 188–191; "Why College X?," 69, 167–178

Application review: did you show, not tell?, 291; have you focused on the core four?, 291; to make sure it tells your story, 290; read your application file from start to finish, 290–292; sustain your momentum during second through last applications, 292–293; while thinking like an admissions officer, 291

Application timelines: application deadlines dictated by colleges, 17–18; application planning and consideration of, 17–21; check in with those providing supporting materials, 300; no expectations rule for late submissions, 298–299; Sample Master Plan and tips on planning for, 18–21; submit before the deadline, 300; tips for staying on top of the submission logistics, 300–303

Applications: approaching it as a whole, 63–66; correcting mistakes made on, 323–325; disciplinary and criminal background issues and withdrawal of, 187; Early Action or Early Decision, 8–12, 17, 191; follow-up logistics, 303–309; legacy, 70, 84, 196; LMO ("like many others"), 23, 32, 128; logistics of submitting, 297–303, 307–309; other materials included with your, 66; planning your, 13–21; questions that get it into the right pile, 188–191; recommendations attached to, 249, 250–270; résumé included with your, 35–59; school reports, 229–249; as seen through the eyes of an admissions officer, 66–71; sending a postscript to, 310–325; supplementary materials, 201–211; supporting materials for your, 65–66; sweating the details, personal and family factual information, 72–84; telling your story in, 22–34, 36–37, 43; tips for your second

through last, 292–294. *See also* Common App (Application); Parent tips

Arts Portfolios, 206

Athletic materials, 207–208

Awards. *See* Academic honors

B

Barnard College, 205

Big decisions. *See* Application decisions

Birthdate, 74, 75

C

Capitalization, 74

Career interests: telling the story about your, 191–192; tips on talking about your, 192–193

Celebrating, 327–329

Character. *See* Personal qualities/character

Citizenship status, 78

Class ranking, 241, 242

College Boards: contact information for, 307; GPA and test score statistics information from, 7

College communication: be polite and respectful during all follow-up, 306; follow-up should be by telephone and not e-mail, 305–306; international telephone numbers made available for, 76; provide a professional voicemail greeting for, 50; remember your telephone manners during any, 50; stay on top of any e-mail sent by college, 305

College Counseling Sourcebook (College Board), 232

College lists: admissions office contact information for entire, 307; check the recommendation requirements of your, 251, 258; classic mistakes to avoid, 6; making early applications to schools on your, 8–12; reaches, 6; research interview policies of your, 272; research test policies of each college on your, 212–214; safeties, 6; targets, 6

College visits, 194

Common App (Application): activities lists instructions on the, 91–92; correcting mistakes made in your, 324; creating alternative versions of the essay question of the, 139; family information on the, 81; follow-up from college confirming submission of, 303–304; interrupted education explanation required by, 86–87, 204; keep copy of your submitted, 302; make use of alternate versions that serve you, 293–294; marketing questions prohibited by 4.0, 194, 195; no exceptions for late submissions, 298–299; origins and increased use of the, 201; preview release timeline of, 18; realities about the, 15–16; "recount an incident of failure" question on, 139; *requirements grid* of the, 213; school reports to include with, 229–249; self-reporting GPA and test scores on, 87, 88; short answer questions eliminated in the 4.0, 128; significant update requirements for, 312–313; technical team contact information, 307; three essay versions allowed by

4.0, 294; timeline for, 18; unrealistic assumptions about the, 13–14. *See also* Applications

Communication. *See* College communication

Comparative data: assess how your data stacks up, 243–244; finding ways to best convey your favorable, 244; finding ways to compensate for less favorable, 244–245; information included in, 241–243; your school policies about reporting, 243

Contact information, 75–76

Core four (Ivey Strategy #4): activities list and use of the, 92; passion, talent, initiative, and impact, 37–38; review your application for evidence of the, 291; submit optional arts portfolio only if you have talent, 206; update with information on a project demonstrating, 317–318. *See also specific core*

Correcting application mistakes: corrected for those not yet submitted, 324; no-nos for, 325; submit a corrected version, 323–324

Costs. *See* Financial issues

Course rigor, 243

Criminal background. *See* Disciplinary and criminal background questions

Curriculum vitae (CV), 36

D

Deadlines. *See* Application timelines

Decision making. *See* Application decisions

Deferral decisions: making application postscripts in case of, 310, 313–318; parent tip on preparing for, 313

Demographics: admissions officers' consideration of, 68–69; residency questions that may impact your chances for admission, 193; telling your story by including your, 27–28; tips on answering application questions about your, 76–81

Demonstrated interest: as admission factor, 69, 193–195; example of the fake question on, 195; preparing for interview question on your, 274, 275; sample interview evaluation form on your, 288–289; sample interview questions to assess your, 286. *See also* "Why College X?" question

Development (aka fundraising) flag, 70

Disabilities/medical problems, 273

Disciplinary and criminal background questions: disclose what you are required to disclose, 183–184; need to update application as needed, 187; parent tip on helping your child with issues of, 181–182; providing explanation or recommendation to answer, 179–187, 252; scheduling personal interview with admissions officer to discuss, 186; show, not tell strategy for answering, 184, 185; supplemental essay to explain, 184–185; sweat the details when answering, 179; telling your story approach to, 185; thinking like an admissions officer when

answering, 179–181, 184; tips when providing information on, 181, 183–187; when to consider withdrawing application, 187

"Do you have anything to add?" question, 197

Dress code (interview), 276, 278–279

E

E-mail communication: be polite and respectful during follow-up, 306; Common Application technical team, 307; follow-up should be by telephone instead of, 305–306; stay on top of any received from college, 305

Early admission applications: colleges dictate the timeline for, 17; Early Decision (ED), Early Action (EA), versus Restrictive Early Action (REA), 8–10; getting your application to the right pile for, 191; two rules to follow when making, 11–12; making a decision on, 8–11; Single-Choice Early Action, 8, 10; to your top-choice college, 11

Editors, 147–148. *See also* Proofreading

English proficiency, 78–79

Essay questions: being anxious about the, 133; Common App 4.0 permitting three versions of, 294; five-paragraph structure warning, 141–142; samples of effective, 152–166; sending additional essay as supplementary material, 209; seven deadly sins of personal essays, 151–152; thinking like an admissions officer when writing, 142–143; tips for picking a topic, 133–139; tips on writing the, 140–149; University of Chicago's "stump the student," 134–135; your final draft checklist and tips, 149–151

Ethical issues: don't try to bluff during your interview, 283; honest self-reporting of GPA and test scores, 7, 40, 87, 87–89, 212–228

Ethnic categories, 80–81

Etiquette during interviews, 284–285

Explanations: disciplinary and criminal background issues, 179–187, 252; if your high school uses nontraditional or unusual grading system, 241; interrupted education, 86–87, 204; optional, 198; regarding low grades on your transcript, 240, 252; required, 198; restraining yourself regarding academic record, 200; situations where a recommendation can help with, 252; transcript "black holes" (low grades), 240, 252. *See also* Supplementary materials

Extra-curricular accomplishments. *See* Activities lists

F

Factual information: contact information, 75–76; demographic questions, 27–28, 68–69, 76–81, 193–195; family information, 81–84; identifying personal information, 73–75; importance of, 72; school information, 85–87. *See also* Additional Information

Faculty/staff related applicant, 70

Family information, 81–84
Final school reports, 234, 236, 237
Financial aid: citizenship issue of, 78; need-based financial aid questions on, 195–196; planning tip on, 20
Financial issues: ability to pay, 70; affordability of college, 5; as consideration for not having an interview, 273; make sure you pay submission fee or get fee waiver, 303
First language, 79
Five-paragraph structure, 141–142
Five-sentence story template: examples of written stories using, 25; telling your story using the, 25; ten story tips using the, 27–34
Flags on your file, 70–71, 259–260. *See also* Application piles
Focusing on core four. *See* Core four (Ivey Strategy #4)
Follow-up logistics: be polite and respectful through all, 306; confirm that your application is complete, 303–304; contact information which may be helpful with, 307–308; minimizing meltdowns as part of the, 308–309; tips for handling anything missing from application, 304–306

G

GPA/grades: explanations regarding specific low grades, 240, 252; high schools using nontraditional or unusual grading system, 241; requirements for specific colleges, 7; résumé information on your, 40, 49; school profile on grading system used for, 246; school report on comparative data on, 241–243; school reports used as tool for interpreting, 229; self-reporting your, 87–89; weighted versus unweighted grading system, 242. *See also* Transcripts
Grammatical rules: US (English) versus UK (English), 150–151; when to break, 151
Guardian information, 82–83

H

Hail Mary standardized test, 317
Half-siblings, 83
Hamilton College, 204–205
Homeschooled applicants: educational credentials of, 39–41; example of application story by a, 26; recommendations for, 258–259, 261–262; reporting test scores by, 225–226; school counselors of, 232; school profiles for, 248–249; school reports for, 237–238; tip on transcripts for, 241
Honors. *See* Academic honors
Household information, 81–82

I

Identifying information, 73–75
Impact: activities that make an, 93–94; describing your activities for, 29–30; Ivey Strategy on focusing on your, 37–38, 92; using language to express your, 45; résumé to express your, 37–38, 47; review your application for evidence of, 291; update with information on a project demonstrating, 317–318
Information. *See* Factual information
Initiative: activities that reflect your, 93–94; Ivey Strategy on focusing on your, 37–38, 92; using language to express your, 45; résumé to express your, 37, 38, 47; review your application for evidence of, 291; update with information on a project demonstrating, 317–318
Integrated Postsecondary Educational Data System [IPEDS] website, 224
International applicants: financial aid and citizenship issue of, 78; international telephone numbers included on applications by, 76; recommendations from, 260–261, 263–265; school counselors of, 232; school profiles for, 248; school reports for, 235–236; tip on reporting test scores for, 225; tip on transcripts for, 241; TOEFL (IELTS) scores by, 225
International recommenders: providing them with adequate information, 260–261; sample cover letter with recommendation package to, 263–265
Internet interviews, 277–278
Interrupted education explanation, 86–87, 204
Interviewers: inform them of your deferral, 318; send thank-you note to, 284
Interviews: clothing preparation and dress code for, 276, 278–279; decision to have an, 272, 273; don't try to bluff during your, 283; emergency contact information for interviewer, 276; engage in conversation instead of an interrogation, 281–282; etiquette to use during your, 284–285; evaluative nature of your, 272; follow-up to your, 283–284; Internet or video Internet (Skype), 277–278; logistics of, 276–278; making best impression during your, 280–283; offer your résumé during your, 281; parent tip on helping your child prepare for, 285; practicing your, 279–280; preparing for, 274–275; research college policies on, 272; sample evaluation form used for, 287–289; sample questions asked during, 285–286; telephone, 277–278; two circumstances to forget optional, 273; as way to show, not tell, 273; "Why College X?" question asked during, 274, 275, 286, 288–289
Ivey Strategies: introduction to #1: work smarter, not harder, 14; introduction to #2: think like an admissions officer, 24; introduction to #3: tell your story, 24; introduction to #4: focus on the core four, passion, talent, initiative, and impact, 37–38; introduction to #5: sweat the details, 72; introduction to #6: make the form work for you, 73; introduction to #7: show, don't tell, 30. *See also specific strategy for more information*

L

Language: essays with the right tone and, 146–147; essays with vivid, 145–146
Language proficiencies, 79–80
Late submissions, 298–299
Legacy applications, 70, 84, 196
Legal name, 73, 75
Life skills celebration, 328–329
LMO ("like many others") applications: how short answer questions can separate the, 128; scenario on being relegated to the, 23; telling your story refinement as separating from, 32
Low-likelihood colleges, 6

M

Making the form work for you (Ivey Strategy #6): "Do you have anything to add?" question for, 197; family information and, 82; special circumstances on siblings for, 83; tips to help recommendations in, 251–257
Master Plans: putting together your, 13–18; sample, 18–21; submit application on time by following the, 299–300
Medical problems/disabilities, 273
Midyear school reports, 234, 236, 237
Minimizing meltdowns, 308–309

N

Naviance, 307
Need-based financial aid questions, 195–196
Nicknames, 73–74
No-likelihood colleges, 6

O

Online application submissions: keep a copy of your completed, 302; keep documentation of, 302–303; print out and review, 301–302; verify completed submission, 302
Optional school reports, 234–235, 236, 238
Over-the-top gestures, 325
Overcoming adversity, 32–33

P

Parent information, 82–83
Parent tips: adjusting family schedule to accommodate time to apply, 17; be a conversation partner and not a coauthor, 34; on being up-to-date on testing policies, 228; collaborating on the résumé, 45; on college visits, 194; on disciplinary and criminal background issues, 181–182; encouraging ethical behavior during application process, 87; have fun conversations with your child on really short answer questions, 122; have your own mini-celebration, 329; help your child be realistic about talents, 206–207; helping to finalize college application list, 4–5; helping your child on "Why College X?" question, 170; helping your child prepare for an interview, 285; identify VIPs who can help your child, 259; investigating possible legacy status, 84, 196; let your child navigate the bureaucracy of school reports, 238; on minimizing meltdowns, 308–309; on not being your child's administrative assistant, 93; preparing for deferral or wait-list decisions, 313; on restraining yourself on going overboard with explanations, 200; try out some short answer questions yourself, 129. *See also* Applications
Passion: activities that reflect your, 93–94; Ivey Strategy on focusing on your, 37–38, 92; using language to express your, 45; résumé to express your, 37, 38, 47; review your application for evidence of, 291
Peer recommendations, 257
Personal essays. *See* Essay questions
Personal qualities/character: as one admission evaluation rating, 24, 68; sample interview evaluation form on your, 288; sample interview questions asked about your, 286. *See also* Telling your story
Planning: disciplinary and criminal background issues for, 186–187; get your application submitted on time by following the, 299–300; realities of, 14–18; Sample Master Plan and tips on, 18–21; scenario on poor, 13–14; work smarter, not harder applied to, 14
Planning realities: applying to college takes time, 16–17; colleges dictate the timeline, 17–18; each college has its own application, 15–16
Procrastination: essay question and, 147; MIT application scenario on dangers of, 13–14
Proofreading: don't just rely on spellcheck, 150–151; one final time before submitting your application, 301; "Why College X?" question, 174; your contact information, 76; your essay question, 150; your personal information on every document, 75; your résumé, 49. *See also* Editors

Q

Questions. *See* Application questions

R

Racial categories, 80–81
Reaches college list, 6
Really short answer questions: examples of effective, 123–126; parent tip on having fun conversations with your child on, 122; the purpose of the, 117; ten standards of most frequently asked, 118; thinking like an admissions officer when answering, 118–120; tips on answering, 120–123
Recognitions. *See* Academic honors
Recommendations: check requirements for specific colleges, 251, 258; homeschooled applicants and, 258–259, 261–262; how the admissions

officer may be influenced by, 250–251; international applicants and, 260–261, 263–264; peer, 257; from research supervisor or instructor, 258; sample letters of, 265–270; specific situations where they are a help, 252; think twice about adding extra, 258; tips on making them work for you, 251–257; unfavorable comparative data compensated with good, 244–245; waive access to your, 257

Recommender packages: information to provide international recommenders, 261–262; sample cover letter for international recommenders with, 263–265; sample cover letter for your recommenders with, 262–263

Recommenders: ask them early in the fall and ask graciously, 253–254; be polite when checking on deadlines, 256; choose those who can best help tell your story, 253; choosing peer, 257; contact information on each, 308; determine what you'd like them to say, 252–253; discuss any negative issues they should know about, 254–255; inform them of your deferral, 318; international, 260–261, 261–262; know what they are being asked, 251–252; provide them with all the materials they will need, 255–256; recommender packages sent to, 262–265; sample letters from, 265–270; school counselor role as, 249; send thank-you note to, 256–257; submitting logistic of checking in with, 300; VIP (very important people), 259

Recruited athletes, 207–208

Residency questions, 193

Résumé: examples of a, 51–59; final check on honesty, proofreading, and converting to PDF, 49–50; first, second, and final drafts and formatting of your, 38–48; offer a printed copy during your interview, 281; as opportunity to add information, 199; parent tip on collaborating on the, 45; passion, talent, initiative, and impact focus of your, 37–38, 45, 47; prepare to be contacted about your, 50; submitted as supplementary material, 205–206; ways to use it for your application, 35; what it is and what it isn't, 36–38. *See also* Additional Information; Supplementary materials

Résumé information: any other relevant information, 43; educational credentials, 39–41; extracurricular activities, hobbies, and work experience, 41–42; honors, awards, and other recognitions, 42–43; name and contact, 39

S

Safeties college list, 6

Sample Master Plan: planning tips to use with, 20–21; timelines for, 18–20

SAT: ACT with writing as interchangeable with SAT reasoning test, 228; being up-to-date on college testing policies, 228; "concordance table SAT

ACT" to compare ACT and, 217–218; contact information for, 307; homeschooled applicants and, 225–226; international student applicants and alternatives for the, 225; know when to stop taking the, 215; logistics of requesting reports on, 226–227; requirements for submitting SAT subject tests, 213–214; scenarios on what scores to submit, 216–225; tips for choosing which scores to submit, 214–216. *See also* Test scores

Scholarship planning, 20

School counselors: *College Counseling Sourcebook* reference for, 232; contact information of your, 307; discuss your deferral with, 318; of homeschooled applicants, 232; of international applicants, 232; recommendation by, 249; tips on the school report, role of your, 230–232

School information, 85–87

School profiles: homeschooled applicants and, 248–249; how to review your, 247–248; information included in, 245–247; international applicants and, 248; what do you want the admissions officer to know about your, 247; what to do when your school doesn't have a, 248

School report components: comparative data, 241–245; counselor recommendation, 249; the school profile, 245–249; transcript, 238–241

School report types: final report, 234, 236, 237–238; midyear report, 234, 236, 237; optional report, 234–235, 236, 238; subsequent reports, 237

School reports: components of the, 238–249; description and information included in, 232–233; for homeschooled applicants, 237–238; for international applicants, 235–236; official transcripts attached to, 238–240; other names that may be used for the, 230; parent tip on letting your child navigate the bureaucracy of, 238; as tool for interpreting GPA, 229; types of, 234–235; your school counselor as contact for the, 230–232

Scientific research abstracts, 208

Short answer questions: description of, 127; think like an admissions officer when answering, 127–128

Show, don't tell (Ivey Strategy #7): for disciplinary and criminal background information, 184, 185; essay question and, 141; evaluative interviews as way of, 273; provide proof of your story by, 30, 141; review your application for, 291; using vivid language to, 145–146; when submitting supplementary materials, 203

Siblings, 83, 84

Significant updates: correcting mistakes, 323–325; when they improve or compromise your credentials, 311–313; when you have been deferred or wait-listed, 310, 313–323

Skype interviews, 277–278, 279
Snail-mail address, 75–76
Social security numbers, 74–75
Spellcheck, 150–151
Standardized tests: considering a Hail Mary,
   317; know when to stop taking, 215; parent
   tip on being up-to-date on college policies
   on, 228; planning tip on, 20; requirements
   for specific colleges, 7; research the test
   policies of specific colleges, 212–214. *See also*
   Test scores
Stepparent information, 82–83
Stress management, 308–309
"Stump the student" questions: choose best essay
   topics versus the, 137–139; University of
   Chicago's famous, 134–135
Submitting logistics: check in with those providing
   supporting materials, 300; contact information
   which may be helpful with, 307–308; don't relax
   until the finish line, 297–298; minimizing
   meltdowns as part of the, 308–309; no exceptions
   for late submissions, 298–299; stick to your
   master plan, 299–300; submit before the
   deadline, 300; tips to help stay on top
   of, 300–303
Submitting logistics tips: do one final
   proofread, 301; get all necessary signatures, 302;
   keep copy and documentation of submitted
   application, 302–303; make sure you pay or get
   fee waiver, 303; print and review application even
   for online applications, 301–302; read and follow
   all of the instructions, 301; submit application by
   application, 300–301; verify completed
   submission of online submissions, 302
Subsequent school reports, 237
Supplementary materials: caution regarding use
   of, 201–202; how to get them done right,
   202–203; seven basic types of, 203; tips on
   preparing and sending, 203–211. *See also*
   Explanations; Résumé
Sweat the details (Ivey Strategy #5): for disciplinary
   and criminal background questions, 179;
   get your application submitted on time by
   following, 299; importance of, 72; when it
   comes to how predictors are used by
   colleges, 225; when submitting your test
   scores, 225, 228

T
Talent: activities that reflect your, 93–94; Ivey
   Strategy on focusing on your, 37–38, 92; using
   language to express your, 45; parent tip on
   helping your child be realistic about, 206–207;
   résumé to express your, 37, 38, 47; review your
   application for evidence of, 291; special talent
   recruit flag, 70; submit optional arts portfolio
   only if you have, 206
Target colleges list, 6

Telephone communication: always be polite and
   respectful during follow-up, 306; follow-up any
   application issues using, 305–306; international
   telephone numbers, 76; professional voicemail
   greeting for, 50; remember your manners for, 50
Telephone interviews, 277
Telling your story: choose recommenders who can
   best help with, 253, 262–263; demographics as
   part of, 27–28, 68–69, 76–81, 193; excellent
   examples of, 26–27; five-sentence story template
   for, 25–34; résumé as means of, 36–37, 43;
   sample interview questions related to, 286;
   scenario on importance of, 22–23; tips on
   effectively, 27–34. *See also* Personal qualities/
   character
Telling your story (Ivey Strategy #3): activities list
   used for, 97; application as opportunity for, 24;
   consider how test scores play into, 219, 220;
   creating alternative essay versions of, 139; use
   demographics as part of, 77; on disciplinary and
   criminal background, 185; for guiding your essay
   question, 135; recommendations that best
   help, 253, 262–263; review your entire application
   presentation of, 290; supplementary materials
   used for, 202–203; think twice about extra
   recommendations for, 258; thinking like an
   admission officer when, 92; when writing your
   essay question, 143; on your academic and career
   interests, 191–193
Test scores: AP (advanced placement), 221–223;
   batch processing and documenting your requests
   for, 227; Common Application requirements grid
   on, 213; contact information for testing
   agencies, 307; homeschooled applicants
   and, 225–226; international applicants and, 225;
   logistics of requesting reports on, 226–227;
   parent tip on being up-to-date on testing
   policies, 228; requirements for specific
   colleges, 7; research the test policies of specific
   colleges, 212–214; résumé information on
   your, 40; self-reporting, 87–89; tips on choosing
   which scores to list on application, 214–225. *See
   also* ACT; SAT; Standardized tests
Testing agency contact information, 307
Thank-you notes: to the interviewer, 284; to your
   recommenders, 265–270
Thinking like an admissions officer (Ivey Strategy
   #2): activities list and, 92; deferral decisions and
   updating by, 314–317; disciplinary and criminal
   background questions and need for, 179–181,
   184; personal information filled out by, 74; really
   short answer questions and, 118; review your
   application while, 291; short answer questions
   and, 127; submit your test score by, 220, 228;
   understanding that nothing is trivial, 188;
   understanding the "no exceptions rule for late
   submissions" by, 298–299; when considering
   supplementary materials to submit, 209; when

filling out your application, 24; when submitting supplementary materials, 203; when writing your essay question, 142–143; "Why College X?" question answered by, 168–169. *See also* Admissions officers

3-D (three dimension) evaluation: academic achievement, 24, 67; extracurricular accomplishments, 24, 67–68; personal qualities and character, 24, 68

Timelines. *See* Application timelines

TOEFL (IELTS): contact information for, 307; submitting test scores, 225

Transcripts: explanations regarding low grades ("black holes") on your, 240, 252; high schools using nontraditional or unusual grading system, 241; homeschooled applicants and, 241; international applicants and, 241; school report and attached official, 238–240; self-reporting by copying from actual, 88–89. *See also* GPA/grades

Transition period: description of, 327; taking the time to celebrate during the, 327–329

Twin or triplet status, 83, 84

U

University of Chicago's "stump the student" questions, 134–135

U.S. Department of Education: College Navigator on website of, 7; ethnic and racial category definitions by the, 80; Integrated Postsecondary Educational Data System (IPEDS) website of the, 224

V

Video Internet interview (Skype), 277–278, 279

VIPs (very important people): flagged application due to interest from, 71; inform them of your deferral, 318; recommendations from, 259–260

Voicemail greeting, 50

W

Wait-list decisions: application postscripts due to, 310, 318–323; most likely admissions from, 322–323; parent tip on preparing for, 313; taking the right actions at the right times response to, 320–323

Websites: College Boards, 7; Department of Education's College Navigator, 7

West, Cornel, 144

"Why College X?" question: check your facts and proofread, 174; develop the right content for answering, 169–171; different forms of the, 167–168; example of poorly done, 168–169; parent tip on helping your child take long view when answering, 170; preparing for interview on the, 274, 275; rewording poorly done, 175–178; sample interview evaluation form on your, 288–289; sample interview questions related to the, 286; use a template for answering, 172–174, 293; thinking like an admissions officer when answering, 168–169. *See also* Demonstrated interest

Work experience: recommendations from research supervisor, 258; résumé information on your, 41–42

Work smarter, not harder (Ivey Strategy #1): batch processing your test score requests, 227; get your application submitted on time by following, 299; a good plan required for, 14; how the activities list allows you to, 93; how your résumé allows you to, 35; really short answer questions used to, 119; submit supplementary materials only if welcomed, 204–205; when writing your essay, 140; "Why College X?" question answer by, 169, 172

Writer's block, 148

Writing voice, 144

Y

Your story. *See* Telling your story